Analyzing Business Data with Excel

Gerald Knight

O'REILLY®

Beijing · Cambridge · Farnham · Köln · Paris · Sebastopol · Taipei · Tokyo

Analyzing Business Data with Excel
by Gerald Knight

Copyright © 2006 O'Reilly Media, Inc. All rights reserved.
Printed in the United States of America.

Published by O'Reilly Media, Inc., 1005 Gravenstein Highway North, Sebastopol, CA 95472.

O'Reilly books may be purchased for educational, business, or sales promotional use. Online editions are also available for most titles (*safari.oreilly.com*). For more information, contact our corporate/institutional sales department: (800) 998-9938 or *corporate@oreilly.com*.

Editor: Simon St.Laurent	**Indexer:** Lucie Haskins
Production Editor: Darren Kelly	**Cover Designer:** Karen Montgomery
Copyeditor: Derek Di Matteo	**Interior Designer:** David Futato
Proofreader: Carol Marti	**Illustrators:** Robert Romano, Jessamyn Read, and Lesley Borash

Printing History:

January 2006:   First Edition.

RepKover™   This book uses RepKover™, a durable and flexible lay-flat binding.

ISBN: 0-596-10073-6
[M]

Table of Contents

Preface

Excel is everywhere, one of the most widely used desktop applications ever created. Over the years its power and versatility have grown, and so has its complexity. Today, most Excel users do not know all the things that it can do. There are plenty of good books that explain functions and features, but making Excel solve problems is not just a matter of learning new workbook functions or mastering Visual Basic. The real challenge is to understand what Excel's many features can accomplish, and especially how you can combine them to make your job easier.

Most of the chapters in this book start with a business problem or question, and then show how Excel can be used in that situation. Several of the chapters include complete applications that you can use and modify as you like. Each solution basically shows the reader how I would handle the problem. In nearly every case, Excel offers many ways to do things so the solutions presented are not the only option. You could produce solutions that do the same thing as the ones in this book using a different approach. This is not a manual and it doesn't include every workbook function. The object is to show the reader what can be done and to explain at least one way to do it.

Who Should Read This Book

This book is written for experienced Excel users. It doesn't spend much time on basics and assumes the reader already knows how Excel works. If you are starting from scratch or need a comprehensive manual, you might consider *Excel: The Missing Manual*, also from O'Reilly.

If you are already comfortable with Excel and would like to see how some of the more advanced features are used, this is the book for you.

What's in This Book

This book starts with some necessary general tools and then moves into more specific problem areas.

Chapter 1, *Excel and Statistics*
> Covers averages, trends, correlation, distributions, and array formulas.

Chapter 2, *Pivot Tables and Problem Solving*
> Examines pivot table basics and ways to modify data to make it work better with pivot tables.

Chapter 3, *Workload Forecasting*
> Covers the application development process, worksheet organization, and forecasting techniques. This chapter includes an application that forecasts a typical workload.

Chapter 4, *Modeling*
> Explores regression, problem definition, analysis, model construction, and interpretation of results.

Chapter 5, *Measuring Quality*
> Works with statistical process control, X and Y charts, and application design. This chapter includes an application that uses statistical process control to measure quality in an operation.

Chapter 6, *Monitoring Complex Systems*
> Examines data requirements, statistical techniques and logic, application design, and organization. This chapter includes an application that uses regression to monitor the relationship between metrics in a complex business process.

Chapter 7, *Queuing*
> Applies formatting, VBA, and logic in an application that measures worker performance in a queuing operation.

Chapter 8, *Custom Queuing Presentation*
> Continues the discussion of queuing with another application focusing on the status of the queue.

Chapter 9, *Optimizing*
> Explains how to use Goal Seek and Solver for various kinds of problems.

Chapter 10, *Importing Data*
> Covers importing from text files, databases, and XML.

Chapter 11, *The Trouble with Data*
> Examines common problems with dates, numeric information, dealing with data in report form, and equivalence problems.

Chapter 12, *Effective Display Techniques*
> Covers display design, color combination, dealing with complexity, and visual considerations.

How to Use This Book Effectively

This book covers most of Excel's advanced features. If you are interested in specific features, this section will guide you to the information you are looking for:

Feature	Chapter
VBA in code modules	3
VBA in a sheet	8
Build a custom function	11
Building an add-on	1
Code to work with text	11
Regression in analysis	4
Regression in an application	6
Using pivot tables	2
Design conventions	3
Goal Seek and Solver	9

Typographical Conventions

The following typographical conventions are used in this book:

Italic
> Introduces new terms and indicates URLs, commands, file extensions, filenames, directory or folder names, and UNC pathnames.

`Constant width`
> Indicates command-line elements, computer output, code examples, methods, variables, functions, properties, objects, events, statements, procedures, values, loops, and formulas formatted as equations.

`Constant width italic`
> Indicates placeholders (for which you substitute an actual name) in examples and in registry keys.

`Constant width bold`
> Indicates user input.

 Indicates a tip, suggestion, or general note.

 Indicates a warning or caution.

Sample Code

All of the applications for this book are available at *http://www.oreilly.com/catalog/analyzingbdwe*. You'll probably want to download them and follow along with the chapters. You can also customize them to analyze your own business data.

Using Code Examples

This book is here to help you get your job done. In general, you may use the code in this book in your programs and documentation. You do not need to contact O'Reilly for permission unless you're reproducing a significant portion of the code. For example, writing a program that uses several chunks of code from this book does not require permission. Selling or distributing a CD-ROM of examples from O'Reilly books *does* require permission. Answering a question by citing this book and quoting example code does not require permission. Incorporating a significant amount of example code from this book into your product's documentation *does* require permission.

We appreciate, but do not require, attribution. An attribution usually includes the title, author, publisher, and ISBN. For example: *Analyzing Business Data with Excel,* by Gerald Knight. Copyright 2006 O'Reilly Media, Inc., 0-596-10073-6.

If you feel your use of code examples falls outside fair use or the permission given above, feel free to contact us at *permissions@oreilly.com*.

We'd Like Your Feedback!

The information in this book has been tested and verified to the best of our ability, but mistakes and oversights do occur. Please let us know about errors you may find, as well as your suggestions for future editions, by writing to:

> O'Reilly Media, Inc.
> 1005 Gravenstein Highway North
> Sebastopol, CA 95472
> 800-998-9938 (in the U.S. or Canada)
> 707-829-0515 (international or local)
> 707-829-0104 (fax)

You also can send us messages using email. To be put on our mailing list or to request a catalog, send email to:

> *info@oreilly.com*

To ask technical questions or comment on the book, send email to:

> *bookquestions@oreilly.com*

For corrections and amplifications to this book, check out O'Reilly Media's online catalog at:

http://www.oreilly.com/catalog/analyzingbdwe

Safari® Enabled

 When you see a Safari® Enabled icon on the cover of your favorite technology book, it means the book is available online through the O'Reilly Network Safari Bookshelf.

Safari offers a solution that's better than e-books. It's a virtual library that lets you easily search thousands of top technology books, cut and paste code samples, download chapters, and find quick answers when you need the most accurate, current information. Try it for free at *http://safari.oreilly.com*.

Acknowledgments

Thanks to O'Reilly for the opportunity to write the book and to my editor Simon St.Laurent for guidance and encouragement along the way.

Thanks to Michael Schmalz for suggestions (all good) and for keeping me out of trouble.

And finally to my wife Betty and daughter Helen: thanks for putting up with me during the last few months. It's safe to come back into the computer room now.

CHAPTER 1

Excel and Statistics

Several chapters of this book solve common business problems by creating complete applications using Excel features like VBA, forms, and array formulas. Before we start building applications, we need to cover some key basics. In this first chapter we look at array formulas and indexed addresses, two key Excel features used throughout the book. Next we will look at Excel's ability to handle common statistical calculations. These features will be the building blocks for the later applications. This is not a statistics textbook and we will not examine all of Excel's 50+ statistical functions; instead, we will look at the most commonly used functions with particular attention to those used in other parts of the book.

Array Formulas

Excel array formulas give you the ability to work on ranges of cells all at once. Suppose we have a list of numbers, and we want to know the average amount of change from one number to the next. This situation is illustrated in Figure 1-1.

The normal way to approach a problem like this is to add a new column with an intermediate calculation. In cell B2 we calculate the difference between A2 and A1. Then we fill this formula down to cell B10. In cell B12 we simply take the average.

With an array formula we can get the same answer using only one cell. The formula in B15 is:

```
=AVERAGE(A2:A10-A1:A9)
```

This makes sense. We want the average of the differences, and that is what the formula is asking for. However, this returns a value error! The error appears because we need to enter the formula in a special way that tells Excel the formula applies to the ranges and not to individual cells.

This is done by pressing Ctrl-Shift-Enter, all at the same time while entering the formula. Excel then displays the formula in brackets, as shown in cell B17:

```
{=AVERAGE(A2:A10-A1:A9)}
```

	A	B	C	D	E	
1	17,240					
2	12,445	-4,795	◄───────	=A2-A1		
3	18,639	6,194				
4	17,065	-1,574				
5	13,760	-3,305				
6	13,671	-89				
7	12,437	-1,234				
8	15,379	2,942				
9	14,876	-503				
10	17,923	3,047				
11						
12		76	◄───────	=AVERAGE(B2:B10)		
13						
14						
15		#VALUE!	◄───────	=AVERAGE(A2:A10-A1:A9)		
16						
17		76	◄───────	{=AVERAGE(A2:A10-A1:A9)}		
18						
19						
20						

Figure 1-1. Using an array formula

The values returned in cells B12 and B17 are the same. Excel does all of the intermediate calculations and returns the result.

Array formulas save space on the worksheet; often whole columns of formulas can be eliminated. By reducing visual complexity, they make things easier to understand, and can speed up sheet recalculation.

 Array formulas can also contain truth values. Excel considers true to be a binary 1 and false to be a binary 0, and sometimes this can be helpful.

In Figure 1-2 we need to find the average of the odd numbers in the list.

In the non-array approach, we would start by identifying the odd values. If a number divided by two is not equal to the integer value of itself divided by two, it is odd. The formula in cell B1 is:

```
=A1/2<>INT(A1/2)
```

This fills down to B10 and returns a value of true (binary 1) if the number is odd and false (binary 0) if it is even.

In cell C1, this is the formula:

```
=B1*A1
```

If B1 is false, it equals zero and the returned value will be zero. But if the value is true, as it will be if A1 is odd, it is a one and the returned value will be equal to A1.

	A	B	C	D	E	F
1	17,240	FALSE	0	0		
2	12,445	TRUE	12445	1		
3	18,639	TRUE	18639	1		
4	17,065	TRUE	17065	1		
5	13,760	FALSE	0	0		
6	13,671	TRUE	13671	1		
7	12,437	TRUE	12437	1		
8	15,379	TRUE	15379	1		
9	14,876	FALSE	0	0		
10	17,923	TRUE	17923	1		
11						
12			107559	7	15365.57	
13						
14					15365.57	
15						
16						

Figure 1-2. Averaging the odd numbers

In column D we do the same thing, but this time we multiply by one using this formula:

```
=B1*1
```

This is useful because many Excel functions do not recognize binary TRUE and FALSE values. This simple formula converts the binary value into a number that can be used in other calculations.

 We could avoid this issue, and the need for the formulas in the D column in Figure 1-2, by using the COUNTIF function. But it is still important to know how to get truth values into other calculations.

The formulas in C12 and D12 take the sum of the cells above, and in cell E12 we divide C12 by D12. Since C12 has the sum of the odd values and D12 has the count, this gives the average.

We can get the same result with this array formula:

```
{=(SUM((A1:A10/2<>INT(A1:A10/2))*A1:A10))/(SUM((A1:A10/2<>INT(A1:A10/2))*1))}
```

It does the work of two columns, two sums, and a division function. And, it does it exactly the same way. The difference is that the formula is built on ranges, not individual cells. All of the same logical steps are in the array formula.

Addressing Cells Indirectly

The INDEX, INDIRECT, ADDRESS, and OFFSET functions are used extensively in this book, providing formulas with much greater flexibility than cell references can provide.

All cells on a worksheet have a unique address (e.g, A1) and Excel lets you refer to any cell by its address. But what if you don't know what cell you are going to want? This can happen if the address of the required piece of information changes based on other values on the worksheet.

If there is a list of items you need to be able to select from, the INDEX function will do the job. The list can be in a column or a row. An example is shown in Figure 1-3.

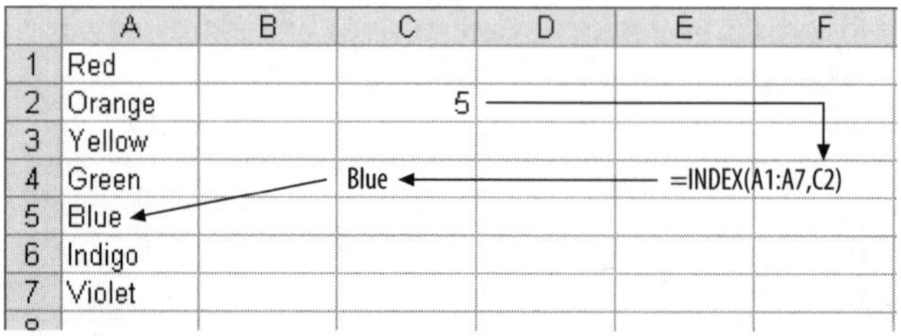

Figure 1-3. Using the index function

We have a list of seven colors. In cell C4, the formula is:

```
=INDEX(A1:A7,C2)
```

The first entry in the formula is the range where the names of the colors are. The number in cell C2 tells the formula which color is required. In this case it is color number five. The fifth color, the one in cell A5, is Blue. The formula in cell C4 returns a value of Blue as text.

The INDEX function works in most cases but sometimes you may not know the row or column of the required value. It could be anywhere on the worksheet, or even on another worksheet. Figure 1-4 contains just such an example.

This time the data extends over several columns. The value in cell D3 is 373. D3 is the fourth column and the third row. The row and column numbers are in cells D12 and D11. The ADDRESS function in cell D14 uses them to build the address.

If you need an address to include the sheet name, and you will if you are referencing data on a different sheet, use the version in cell D17. It lets you include the sheet name and builds it into the returned value.

The address alone does not help much, but the INDIRECT function returns the value corresponding to an address. In cell D20 the INDIRECT function uses the address built in cell D14 to retrieve the value in cell D3.

The formula in cell D20 could thus also be written as:

```
=INDIRECT(ADDRESS(D12,D11))
```

Although this may seem a little complex, these functions are very useful when referencing data using both row and column values. It takes a little practice to become

	A	B	C	D	E	F	G	H	I
1	Region	Week 1	Week 2	Week 3	Week 4				
2	North	309	212	216	201				
3	South	159	411	373	175				
4	East	262	385	8	215				
5	West	53	412	19	6				
6									
7									
8									
9									
10									
11			Column	4					
12			Row	3					
13									
14			Address	$D$3		=ADDRESS(D12,D11)			
15									
16			With sheet						
17			name	MyDataSheet!$D$3		=ADDRESS(D12,D11..."MyDataSheet")			
18									
19									
20			The value	373		=INDIRECT(D14)			
21									

Figure 1-4. Working with INDIRECT and ADDRESS

proficient with ADDRESS and INDIRECT, but it's worth it because they provide great flexibility in referencing data in Excel.

Excel, as usual, offers more than one way to do things. The OFFSET function does the same thing that the INDIRECT and ADDRESS functions do, using a different approach. The example in Figure 1-5 shows how the OFFSET function handles the same situation.

	A	B	C	D	E	F	G
1	Region	Week 1	Week 2	Week 3	Week 4		
2	North	309	212	216	201		
3	South	159	411	373	175		
4	East	262	385	8	215		
5	West	53	412	19	6		
6							
7							
8							
9			373		=OFFSET(A1,2,3)		
10							
11							
12							
13							

Figure 1-5. Using the OFFSET function

INDIRECT uses a text string containing the address of the required cell. OFFSET uses row and column numbers from a given starting point to locate the cell. In this case the starting point is cell A1 and the offset is two rows down and three columns to the right. This is the same cell we referenced in Figure 1-4.

In most cases the choice between OFFSET and INDIRECT is a matter of personal preference. INDIRECT lets you reference a different sheet, making it better for applications that have several worksheets. The advantage of OFFSET is that it works with numbers rather than a text string. This means it does not need the ADDRESS function and can be easier to use.

Statistical Functions

Statistical functions are used to describe data. When working with a list of numbers, we need to be able to find the average, to understand any trends, and to describe the distribution. In this section we look at Excel's most commonly used statistical functions.

The Average

The average is the most common measure of the center of a group of numbers, and Excel makes taking an average easy. The basic approach is shown in Figure 1-6.

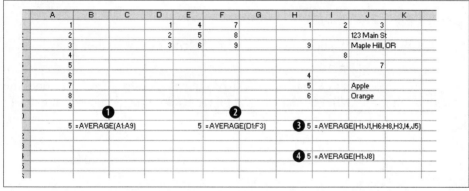

Figure 1-6. Taking an average

Five is the average of the numbers from one to nine (in column A, rows 1 through 9). Usually numbers will be in a column, as in item 1, but it really doesn't make any difference as long as you know where the numbers are. In item 2 the average formula is looking at a three by three range, and in item 3 the numbers are mixed with non-numeric information.

Excel ignores cells that do not contain valid numbers, and item 4 uses this behavior to simplify taking the average of scattered numbers. The AVERAGE function finds the numbers in the range. I don't have to tell Excel where they are.

AVERAGEA

The AVERAGE function is usually convenient, but fails in Figure 1-7.

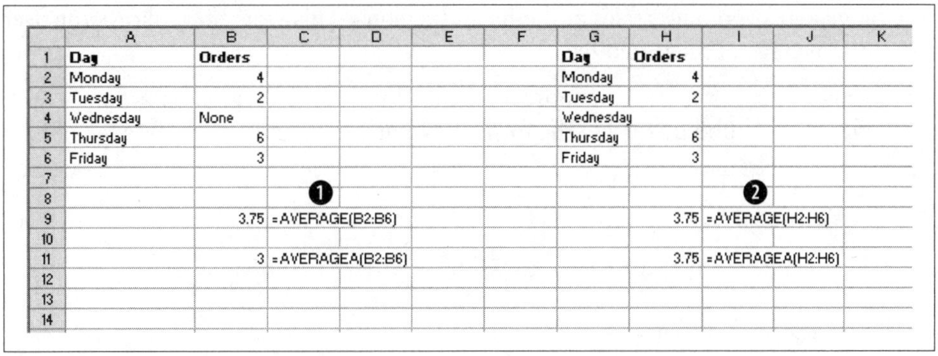

	A	B	C	D	E	F	G	H	I	J	K
1	**Day**	**Orders**					**Day**	**Orders**			
2	Monday	4					Monday	4			
3	Tuesday	2					Tuesday	2			
4	Wednesday	None					Wednesday				
5	Thursday	6					Thursday	6			
6	Friday	3					Friday	3			
7											
8			❶						❷		
9		3.75	=AVERAGE(B2:B6)					3.75	=AVERAGE(H2:H6)		
10											
11		3	=AVERAGEA(B2:B6)					3.75	=AVERAGEA(H2:H6)		
12											
13											
14											

Figure 1-7. Averaging text as a number

On Wednesday we did not get any orders. The data contains the word "None," but the value is really zero. In item 1, the AVERAGE function gets the wrong answer because it ignores the cell with "None" in it. The AVERAGEA function is made for this situation. AVERAGEA works just like AVERAGE, except it considers non-numeric cells to have a value of zero. In item 1 formula 2, the AVERAGEA function calculates the average correctly.

AVERAGEA ignores cells that are not used. In item 2, the Orders cell for Wednesday is empty and the AVERAGEA function does not consider the cell to have a value of zero.

DAVERAGE

Excel can also calculate the average of selected items in a list using the DAVERAGE function. Figure 1-8 shows how this function is used.

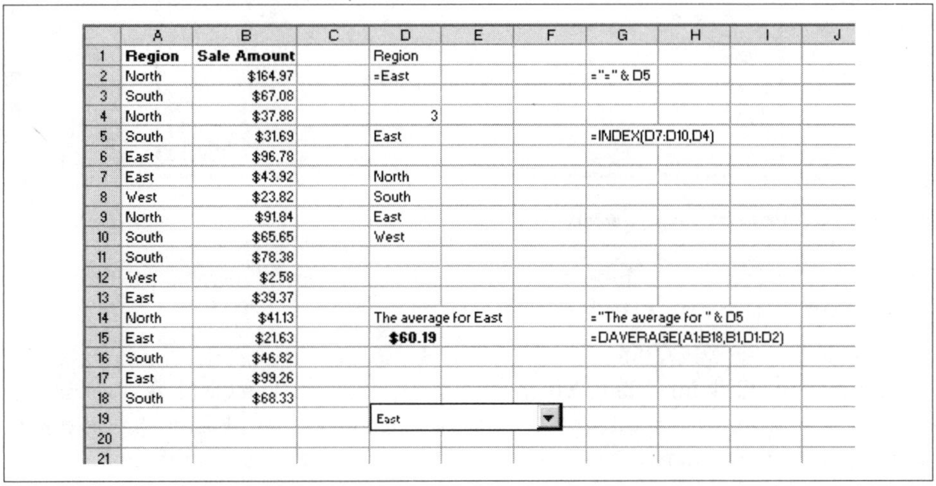

	A	B	C	D	E	F	G	H	I	J
1	**Region**	**Sale Amount**		Region						
2	North	$164.97		=East			="=" & D5			
3	South	$67.08								
4	North	$37.88			3					
5	South	$31.69		East			=INDEX(D7:D10,D4)			
6	East	$96.78								
7	East	$43.92		North						
8	West	$23.82		South						
9	North	$91.84		East						
10	South	$65.65		West						
11	South	$78.38								
12	West	$2.58								
13	East	$39.37								
14	North	$41.13		The average for East			="The average for " & D5			
15	East	$21.63		**$60.19**			=DAVERAGE(A1:B18,B1,D1:D2)			
16	South	$46.82								
17	East	$99.26								
18	South	$68.33								
19				East						
20										
21										

Figure 1-8. Using DAVERAGE

The range A1:B18 contains sales amounts and regions. This worksheet allows the user to get the average of a selected region.

First we give the user a way to choose a region. We enter the region names in D7:D10. Then we add a combo box using the forms tool bar shown in Figure 1-9.

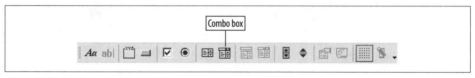

Figure 1-9. Adding a combo box

If the forms tool bar is not visible, go to the View → Toolbars menu and check Forms.

We click on the combo box icon and drag it to the sheet. Then we right click on it and select Format Control. This displays the dialog in Figure 1-10.

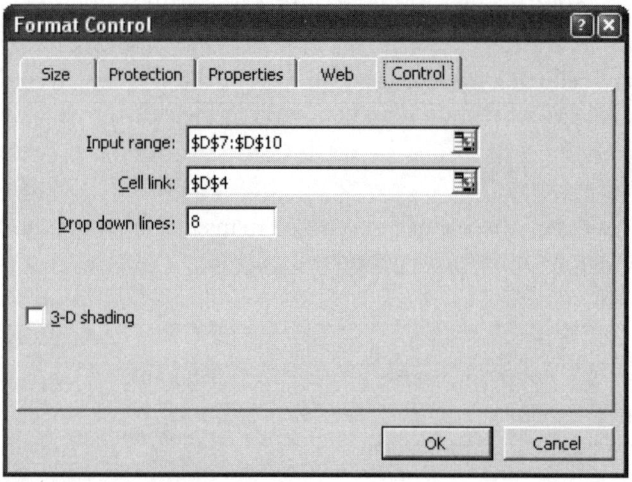

Figure 1-10. Formatting the combo box

The Input range tells the combo box what values to display. The region names are in the range D7:D10, so that is the Input range.

The Cell link is D4. When the user selects one of the four regions, the combo box puts a number in the Cell link telling which region was selected. The Cell link does not get the region name, only a number. In Figure 1-8, East is selected. East is the third item in the list of regions, therefore the Cell link (D4) contains the number three.

We need the name of the selected region, and to get it we use the formula in cell D5 in Figure 1-8:

```
=INDEX(D7:D10,D4)
```

The INDEX function returns an item from a range. The range D7:D10 contains our region names. Cell D4 has the number three. The INDEX function returns the third item in the range, the name "East".

The DAVERAGE function is in cell D15 and has this formula:

```
=DAVERAGE(A1:B18,B1,D1:D2)
```

There are three parameters. The first is the range A1:B18, containing all of the data including column headings. Next is B1. This is the heading of the column we want to average. The formula could have been entered as:

```
=DAVERAGE(A1:B18,"Sales Amount",D1:D2)
```

The third parameter is the criteria range. It consists of a heading and a logical test. The heading tells the function what column to apply the test to. DAVERAGE takes the average of the rows where the test is true.

We are only averaging sales amounts for East. The criteria range is D1:D2. The formula in D2 is:

```
="=" & D5
```

This uses the result of the combo box selection in cell D5 and builds the text string "=East".

This makes the sheet interactive without using a macro. The DAVERAGE function in cell D15 calculates the average for the selected region as soon as the user changes the selection.

DAVERAGE is a database function. Database functions allow you to perform common calculations on worksheet data. But the data has to be set up correctly for them to work. They require headings and a criteria range. This is fine if you are designing an Excel solution from scratch, but can lead to complications if you are adding calculations to an existing sheet.

Excel has a wide range of functions, and in most situations there is more than one way to get the desired result. In this case, I could replace the DAVERAGE function in cell D15 with this formula:

```
=SUMIF(A2:A18,D2,B2:B18)/COUNTIF(A2:A18,D2)
```

It uses the SUMIF and COUNTIF functions to get the same answer, avoiding the formatting requirements of database functions. There is no best way to do this. It depends on how the sheet is designed and what you are trying to accomplish.

Trimmed average

All numbers are not created equal. In examples, like the ones in this chapter, the numbers are made up. They can't be wrong because they don't mean anything. In the real world things are different.

Numbers can be recorded incorrectly, unusual events can produce odd values that confuse our view of the past and make the average inaccurate. These troublesome values are called outliers or anomalies.

When we use data that might have outliers we can increase the accuracy of calculations by ignoring the highest and lowest values. This is also sometimes called a filtered average. Excel does this with the TRIMMEAN function.

In Figure 1-11 you can see how this works.

	A	B	C	D	E	F	G	H	I	J	K	L
1	Calls											
2	17,240		Trimmed Average	14937.57		=TRIMMEAN(A2:A26,2/COUNT(A2:A26))						
3	12,445											
4	18,639		Average	16,265		=AVERAGE(A2:A100)						
5	17,065		Filtered Average	14,938		=(SUM(A2:A100)-(MAX(A2:A100)+MIN(A2:A100)))/(COUNT(A2:A100)-2)						
6	13,760											
7	13,671											
8	12,437											
9	15,379											
10	14,876											
11	17,923											
12	16,044											
13	11,182											
14	13,049											
15	12,711											
16	13,830											
17	18,930											
18	19,475											
19	14,433											
20	11,006											
21	52,055											
22	14,356											
23	14,876											
24	12,405											
25	16,628											
26	12,210											
27												

Figure 1-11. A trimmed average

We want the average number of calls per day handled by a call center. Figure 1-11 has the call count for the 25 most recent days. But in cell A21 something is wrong. A network problem on that day incorrectly routed tens of thousands of calls to our call center.

If we just take the average we get 16,265. But that is not good estimate of the real average, since it includes the problem data. We can get a better estimate by using this formula:

```
=TRIMMEAN(A2:A26,2/COUNT(A2:A26))
```

The first entry in the TRIMMEAN function is the range of cells to be averaged. The second entry is the percentage of cells to ignore. In this case I want to eliminate the maximum and the minimum values. Therefore, I need to set the value to trim only one item at the top and bottom of the distribution. That is equal to two divided by the number of items.

This is equivalent to this formula:

```
=(SUM(A2:A100)-(MAX(A2:A100)+MIN(A2:A100)))/(COUNT(A2:A100)-2)
```

This takes the sum of all the numbers, subtracts the maximum and minimum, and then divides by two less than the item count.

It would be nice to have a function that just removes the maximum and minimum, and a custom function can do just that.

First we go to the Tools → Macros menu and select Visual Basic Editor. The editor can also be started by pressing Alt-F11. This code is then entered:

```
Public Function FAverage(MyRange As Excel.Range) As Double

'Find the sum of the range
FAverage = Application.WorksheetFunction.Sum(MyRange)

'Subtract the maximum value
FAverage = FAverage - Application.WorksheetFunction.Max(MyRange)

'Subtract the minimum value
FAverage = FAverage - Application.WorksheetFunction.Min(MyRange)

'Divide by two less than the count of values in the range
FAverage = FAverage / (Application.WorksheetFunction.Count(MyRange) - 2)

End Function
```

We do not have to actually code the logic to calculate the sum, maximum, or minimum, because the application object already knows how to do these things. In effect, we are using normal Excel functions inside our code. With this code in place, our sheet has a new function called FAverage. Its only parameter is the range of cells we are working with, and it returns the filtered average.

A custom function is fine for a one-off problem, but you may want to reuse your solution later, or there may be other Excel users doing a similar job who could use the same function. If this is the case, an Excel Add-In is an easy way to publish one or more custom functions.

We start with a new blank workbook. We bring up the Visual Basic Editor as before and add the same code. We save the workbook with the name *StatHelper* as an Excel Add-In. It will be saved with an extension of *.xla* in your *Application Data/Microsoft/AddIns* folder.

Then exit and restart Excel, and bring up another blank workbook. Go to the Tools → Add-Ins menu and you will see *StatHelper* on the list of available Add-Ins. Make sure it is checked, and your new workbook will have the FAverage function.

You can distribute the *StatHelp.xla* file to others. It needs to be placed in their *Application Data/Microsoft/AddIns* folder. You can add additional functions to your XLA file, or even make it a group project with functions added by other users.

Moving average

Tracking changes in the average is an easy way to find trends in data. A moving average is shown in Figure 1-12.

	A	B	C	D	E
1	Closing Price				
2	45.57				
3	45.74				
4	46.28				
5	45.56				
6	45.96				
7	45.72				
8	45.59				
9	45.75				
10	45.53				
11	45.06				
12	44.98				
13	44.74				
14	44.71				
15	45.16				
16	45.5				
17	45.25				
18	45.5				
19	46.48				
20	46.45				
21	46.87	45.62		=AVERAGE(A2:A21)	
22	47.58	45.7205			
23	47.33	45.8			
24	48.2	45.896			
25	48.87	46.0615			
26	48.26	46.1765			
27	48.94	46.3375			
28	49.18	46.517			
29	48.68	46.6635			

Figure 1-12. The moving average

In this example we have 65 days of closing prices for a stock. The formula in cell B21 takes the average of the preceding 20 days. The formula fills down, creating a moving average.

Moving averages are often used in charts to make trends easy to understand.

Changes in the Average

The simplest change is a linear trend. In business this means the value is going up or down by the same amount each time period (e.g., each month sales are going up by $10,000). The TREND function can identify the points on the trend line or forecast future values. Figure 1-13 shows how the TREND function can build a trend line.

Figure with three spreadsheet views labeled 1, 2, 3. Formula bar in view 2 shows: SUM ▾ ✕ ✓ fx =TREND(A2:A26,,)

1

	A	B
1	Stock Price	Trend
2	44.98	
3	44.74	
4	44.71	
5	45.16	
6	45.5	
7	45.25	
8	45.5	
9	46.48	
10	46.45	
11	46.87	
12	47.58	
13	47.33	
14	48.2	
15	48.87	
16	48.26	
17	48.94	
18	49.18	
19	48.68	
20	48.7	
21	48.52	
22	48.82	
23	48.75	
24	48.85	
25	48.91	
26	48.65	
27		

2

	A	B	C	D
1	Stock Price	Trend		
2	44.98	ND(A2:A26,,)		
3	44.74			
4	44.71			
5	45.16			
6	45.5			
7	45.25			
8	45.5			
9	46.48			
10	46.45			
11	46.87			
12	47.58			
13	47.33			
14	48.2			
15	48.87			
16	48.26			
17	48.94			
18	49.18			
19	48.68			
20	48.7			
21	48.52			
22	48.82			
23	48.75			
24	48.85			
25	48.91			
26	48.65			
27				

3

	A	B
1	Stock Price	Trend
2	44.98	44.9247385
3	44.74	45.1272769
4	44.71	45.3298154
5	45.16	45.5323538
6	45.5	45.7348923
7	45.25	45.9374308
8	45.5	46.1399692
9	46.48	46.3425077
10	46.45	46.5450462
11	46.87	46.7475846
12	47.58	46.9501231
13	47.33	47.1526615
14	48.2	47.3552
15	48.87	47.5577385
16	48.26	47.7602769
17	48.94	47.9628154
18	49.18	48.1653538
19	48.68	48.3678923
20	48.7	48.5704308
21	48.52	48.7729692
22	48.82	48.9755077
23	48.75	49.1780462
24	48.85	49.3805846
25	48.91	49.5831231
26	48.65	49.7856615
27		

Figure 1-13. Finding the trend

In Step 1 are the closing stock prices for 25 days. In column B is a heading for the trend.

In Step 2, we select the range B2:B26 and click on the formula bar. In the formula bar we enter the following:

```
=TREND(A2:A26,,)
```

The TREND function has three parameters. First is the range of the Y values. In this case these are the stock prices. The next parameter is the range of the X values. When we are working with a value that is changing over time, like a stock price, these are just the numbers 1,2,3...to the number of values, 25 in this case. This is the default, so we don't have to enter anything except a comma as a place holder. The third parameter is the X values we want the function to return. Here we also take the default. This is an array formula and must be entered with Ctrl-Shift-Enter. The result is shown in Step 3.

The result is a line. Each value in column B goes up by the same amount, in this case by 0.202538. If we build a chart using the data in columns A and B, it will look like Figure 1-14.

The TREND function can also forecast future values. The next value can be predicted with this formula:

```
=TREND(A2:A26,,COUNT(A2:A26)+1)
```

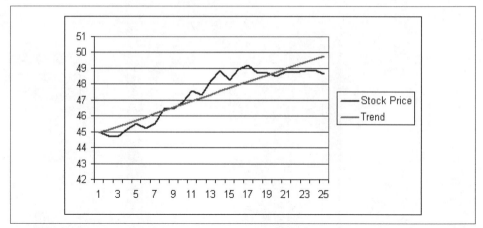

Figure 1-14. Chart with trend line

The COUNT function returns the number of cells in the range. Adding one tells the TREND function that we want the next value.

Forecasting the next value is something that we might want to do from time to time, and it would be convenient if we had a function to do this based only on the range.

We can create a custom function with this code:

```
Public Function TrendNext(MyRange As Excel.Range) As Variant

'Find the next value from a range using the TREND function
TrendNext = Application.WorksheetFunction.Trend(MyRange, , _
Application.WorksheetFunction.Count(MyRange) + 1)

End Function
```

Once again, we use the application object to get to Excel's built-in functions. If this code is added to the *StatHelper.xla*, the TrendNext function will be ready to use. Figure 1-15 shows an example.

	A	B	C	D	E	F	G	H
1	Stock Price							
2	44.98							
3	44.74		46.85067		=TREND(A2:A11,,COUNT(A2:A11)+1)			
4	44.71							
5	45.16		46.85067		=TrendNext(A2:A11)			
6	45.5							
7	45.25							
8	45.5							
9	46.48							
10	46.45							
11	46.87							
12								

Figure 1-15. Using the TrendNext function

Both formulas return the same value, but TrendNext is specialized and easier to use.

Growth

Trends are not always linear. Values can go up or down in ways that cannot be described with a line. Exponential growth is based on multiplication. In a linear trend each item changes by the same amount. In growth each item changes by the same ratio. Excel has a GROWTH function that models exponential growth. It works just like the TREND function but returns different results.

Figure 1-16 demonstrates the difference between the GROWTH and TREND functions.

	A	B	C	D	E	F	G
1	Values	Trend	Growth		Trend Change Amount	Growth Change Ratio	
2	9.67	-162.08	23.06				
3	56.73	-49.62	35.92		112.45	1.557388464	
4	123.40	62.83	55.94		112.45	1.557388464	
5	100.23	175.28	87.12		112.45	1.557388464	
6	82.56	287.73	135.68		112.45	1.557388464	
7	288.45	400.18	211.31		112.45	1.557388464	
8	224.98	512.63	329.09		112.45	1.557388464	
9	522.75	625.08	512.52		112.45	1.557388464	
10	907.64	737.53	798.19		112.45	1.557388464	
11	1,123.14	849.99	1,243.09		112.45	1.557388464	

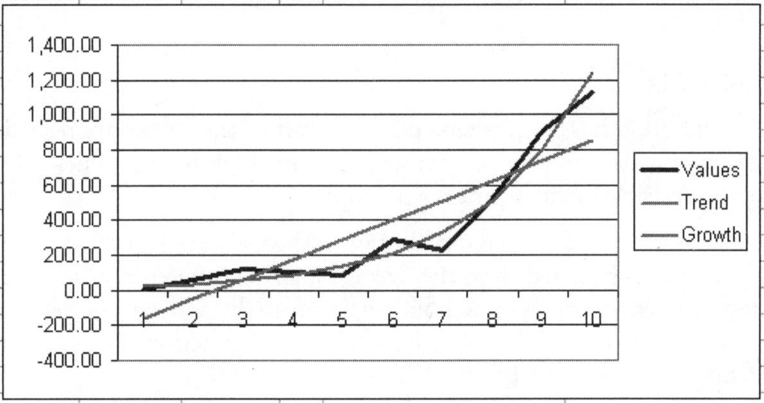

Figure 1-16. GROWTH and TREND measure different things

Here the values in column A are changing exponentially. We use both the GROWTH and TREND functions to try to model the values. In the chart it is clear that the GROWTH function does a better job. The trend line doesn't really explain what the values are doing, and even starts with a negative value.

If we predict the next few values in this series, we will get better results if we use GROWTH.

Column E shows how the TREND function works. It starts with -162.08 and adds 112. 45 each time. This gives the best fitting line possible for the values. In Column F the GROWTH function starts with 23.06 and multiplies by 1.557 each time. This produces the best fitting exponential curve.

In most business situations the TREND function works fine. But GROWTH makes more sense when working with returns on investments, inflation rates, or other values that change by a percentage over time.

It is easy to see how the data is behaving in these examples, but in the real world trends are likely to be subtle and the data less consistent. It is important to under-stand the data before you choose which function to use. It is helpful to look at a chart before deciding between GROWTH and TREND.

Distributions

The average number of calls coming into a call center is 12,534 per day. But a day with exactly 12,534 is rare. If we are going to manage this process, we need to know how spread out the data is and how it is distributed.

Excel offers functions to handle the kinds of distribution most frequently encoun-tered in business.

Normal distributions

A normal distribution has a bell shaped curve. Most of the values are near the mid-dle. The tails of the distribution contain uncommonly high or low values. This is the most common distribution in business situations.

The simplest measure of a normal distribution is the variance. To calculate the vari-ance, each value is subtracted from the average and the difference is squared. Then the squared differences are summed and the sum is divided by one less than the number of values. In Excel all this is done by the VAR function. Figure 1-17 shows how this works.

We will calculate the variance of the 20 numbers in column N. The formula in cell O1 is:

```
=(N1-AVERAGE(N$1:N$20))^2
```

It takes the difference between the value in cell N1 and the average of all 20 cells. This fills down to row 20.

Cell Q6 contains this formula:

```
=SUM(O1:O20)/19
```

	L	M	N	O	P	Q	R	S
1			45.57	0.0025	◄			=(N1-AVERAGE(N$1:N$20))^2
2			45.74	0.0144				
3			46.28	0.4356				
4			45.56	0.0036				
5			45.96	0.1156				
6			45.72	0.01		0.331663158	◄	=SUM(O1:O20)/19
7			45.59	0.0009				
8			45.75	0.0169		0.331663158	◄	=VAR(N1:N20)
9			45.53	0.0081				
10			45.06	0.3136				
11			44.98	0.4096				
12			44.74	0.7744				
13			44.71	0.8281				
14			45.16	0.2116				
15			45.5	0.0144				
16			45.25	0.1369				
17			45.5	0.0144				
18			46.48	0.7396				
19			46.45	0.6889				
20			46.87	1.5625				
21								

Figure 1-17. Calculating the variance

It sums the squared differences and divides by 19 (one less than the number of values).

In cell Q8 we let Excel do the work by using the VAR function and get the same result.

The most commonly used measure of spread is the standard deviation. Standard deviation is just the square root of the variance, and Excel has the STDEV function to calculate it.

The standard deviation is used in many statistical calculations. Once you have the average and the standard deviation, Excel has functions that can tell you how a value fits into the distribution. This is illustrated in Figure 1-18.

We want to know where 46.75 fits in the distribution, and we know the average and standard deviation. The NORMDIST function gives us the answer. In Figure 1-17 cell Q1 has the average and Q2 has the standard deviation. The formula is:

```
=NORMDIST(46.75,Q1,Q2,TRUE)
```

The first entry is the value we want to test (46.75). Next are the average and standard deviation. Finally, we use the option TRUE to get the cumulative probability for 46.75. If we entered FALSE for this option, the function would return the height of the distribution curve at 46.75.

The NORMDIST function returns a value of 0.9751. This means that 97.51% of the distribution is below 46.75.

The NORMINV function works in the opposite direction. Suppose we need to know what values are in the top 25% of the distribution. The value we need is the one at the 75% point. For the data in Figure 1-17 this formula will find the answer:

```
=NORMINV(0.75,Q1,Q2)
```

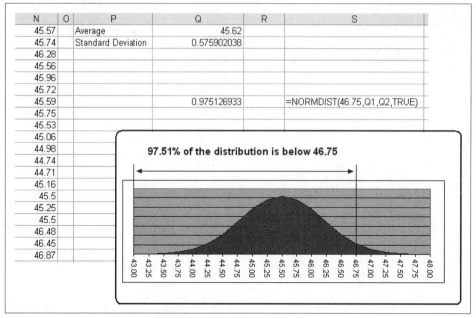

N	O	P	Q	R	S
45.57		Average	45.62		
45.74		Standard Deviation	0.575902038		
46.28					
45.56					
45.96					
45.72					
45.59			0.975126933		=NORMDIST(46.75,Q1,Q2,TRUE)
45.75					
45.53					
45.06					
44.98					
44.74					
44.71					
45.16					
45.5					
45.25					
45.5					
46.48					
46.45					
46.87					

Figure 1-18. Using the average and standard deviation

The first entry is the percentage we are looking for. Next are the average and standard deviation. This function has no TRUE/FALSE option. The formula returns a value of 46. The values 46 and above are the top 25% of the distribution.

Exponential distributions

Our call center gets three calls every ten minutes. The time between calls has a distribution illustrated in Figure 1-19.

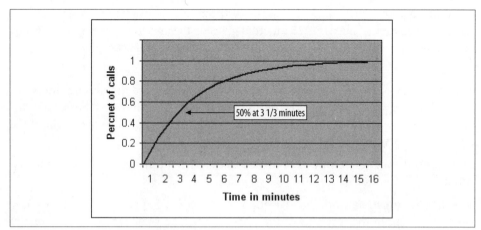

Figure 1-19. Distribution of call times

The curve can start at any point in time. At the instant it begins there is no call, so zero percent of the calls happen in zero time. Half the time the next call comes in within 3 1/3 minutes. The next call arrives with 15 minutes nearly all the time. A wait of 16 minutes is possible but almost never occurs.

In this case we are looking at the time interval between events, and this produces an exponential distribution. Excel lets you calculate probabilities in this distribution with the EXPONDIST function.

Before we can use this function we have to calculate a parameter called Lambda. Lambda is the inverse of the average time. So, if our call center gets 3 calls every 10 minutes, the average time between calls is 3.33... minutes. Lambda is 1 divided by 3.33... which equals 0.3. We used minutes to determine Lambda. Therefore, the results we get from the EXPONDIST function will be in minutes.

Suppose we need to know what percentage of the time the next call will arrive within 4 minutes. The formula is:

    =EXPONDIST(4,0.3,TRUE)

The first entry is 4 because we are interested in the 4 minute interval. Next is Lambda (0.3). The option TRUE tells the function that we want the cumulative probability. This returns a value of 0.698. This means that about 70% of the time the next call arrives within 4 minutes.

This distribution looks forward only. It has no memory. This means that even if there has been no call for the last five minutes, there is still a 70% probability that the next call will arrive in the next 4 minutes. The past does not matter, only the future.

Gamma distribution

The gamma distribution is similar to the exponential, but more general. It allows you to calculate the probability for multiple events.

We get the same result as with EXPONDIST if we use this formula:

    =GAMMADIST(4,1,3.3333,TRUE)

There are two differences from the EXPONDIST entries. In this case Lambda is 0.3, but the GAMMADIST function requires *1/Lambda*. The entry is 3.3333. The *1* is the number of occurrences we want. Here we are interested in the next call, so just one call is involved. If we need to know the probability of getting three calls in the next four minutes, we would enter the formula like this:

    =GAMMADIST(4,3,3.3333,TRUE)

This formula returns a value of 0.1205. There is a 12% chance of getting three calls in the next four minutes.

The GAMMAINV function lets you go the other way. If we want to be 90% sure that the next call will arrive in a certain number of minutes, the formula is:

```
=GAMMAINV(0.9,1,3.333)
```

The 0.9 is the probability we want, and the number of occurrences is one, and 1 divided by Lambda is 3.333. The result is 7.67. That means that there is a 90% chance that the next call will come in during the next 7.67 minutes.

Binomial distribution

Some things have only two possible outcomes. A coin toss is heads or tails, a collections call is successful or not, a new account winds up being uncollectible or it doesn't. For this kind of situation, probability is calculated using a binomial distribution.

If the probability that a collections call will result in a payment is 0.1 and a collector makes 75 calls in a day, what is the probability that the calls will result in exactly 10 payments?

Excel has a function that answers this question. The formula is:

```
=BINOMDIST(10,75,0.1,TRUE)
```

The ten is the number of calls we are looking for. There are 75 calls made, and the probability of success on each call is 0.1. The option TRUE tells the function that we want the probability.

The formula returns a value of 0.873. There is an 8.73% chance that exactly 10 payments will come from the 75 calls.

Correlation

Sometimes we need to know if two groups of numbers are related. Correlation is a measure of how much similarity there is between two groups of numbers. If both groups go up or down by the same amount at the same time there is a positive correlation. If they change at the same time but in the opposite direction there is a negative correlation.

Correlation is always a number between one and negative one, and the groups of numbers being tested must have the same numbers of members. In Excel you can calculate correlation using the CORREL function. An example is shown in Figure 1-20.

Here we have two groups of numbers. The formula in cell E1 is:

```
=CORREL(A2:A12,B2:B12)
```

As the first chart illustrates, the numbers, while not equal, tend to move together. The formula returns a value of 0.68. This is a fairly strong correlation and confirms what we see in the chart; the numbers are related. In the bottom chart the numbers

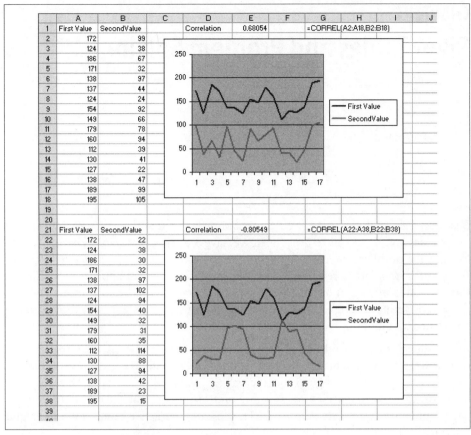

	A	B	C	D	E	F	G	H	I	J
1	First Value	SecondValue		Correlation	0.68054		=CORREL(A2:A18,B2:B18)			
2	172	99								
3	124	38								
4	186	67								
5	171	32								
6	138	97								
7	137	44								
8	124	24								
9	154	92								
10	149	66								
11	179	78								
12	160	94								
13	112	39								
14	130	41								
15	127	22								
16	138	47								
17	189	99								
18	195	105								
19										
20										
21	First Value	SecondValue		Correlation	-0.80549		=CORREL(A22:A38,B22:B38)			
22	172	22								
23	124	38								
24	186	30								
25	171	32								
26	138	97								
27	137	102								
28	124	94								
29	154	40								
30	149	32								
31	179	31								
32	160	35								
33	112	114								
34	130	88								
35	127	94								
36	138	42								
37	189	23								
38	195	15								
39										

Figure 1-20. Positive and negative correlation

are moving at the same time but in the opposite direction. This suggests a negative correlation, and the formula in cell E21 indeed returns a value of –0.805.

A correlation near zero indicates that the number groups are not related.

CHAPTER 2
Pivot Tables and Problem Solving

Business data analysis is a search for relationships. How does advertising impact sales? Does an increase in returns mean we have a quality problem? Whether we are looking for problems or identifying best practices, it all comes down to relationships. Business analysis requires a complex, multidimensional approach. Businesses capture and store large amounts of data. As companies try to become more efficient, the job of sifting through this data looking for valuable insight is becoming more common and important.

Excel is ideal for this kind of work. It can import data from most databases, it can handle almost any statistical or formatting problem, and it has a great pivot table feature. Pivot tables were designed for researching relationships in data. They allow us to try different combinations by dragging and dropping, making it easy to check a large number of relationships quickly. They create interactive tables and charts and can quickly filter the data or change point of view.

In this chapter we use pivot tables to analyze a business process. This is an ad hoc activity and the end product is information, not an application. So, formatting and appearance are not the main concerns. The real goal is to find specific problems or opportunities.

We work with two kinds of data. First, there are categorical items. These elements separate data into well-defined groups. If you look at a customer file, one of the fields might be the customer's ZIP code. It is a number, but it has no real numeric value. Its only purpose is to identify a group or category of customers.

The second type is scalar items. Scalars have a numeric value, like cost or square feet. They can be added up or averaged. In pivot tables we use categoricals and scalars differently.

The sample data for this chapter consists of 10,000 rows of data from an order processing operation. The layout is shown in Figure 2-1.

	A	B	C	D	E	F	G	H	I	J	K
1	Office	Sales Emp #	Customer Number	Order Amount	Action Date	Order Type	Order Status	Commit Days	Order Date	Business Unit	Order Age
2	Atlanta	807788	135350	55.09	8/16/2004	F02	1	15	7/29/2004	126	61
3	Atlanta	806748	181710	9767.68	10/11/2004	H01	2	15	9/21/2004	126	24
4	Atlanta	806748	181710	15120.04	10/11/2004	H01	2	15	9/21/2004	126	24
5	Atlanta	806648	182125	5145.5	9/30/2004	H01	2	15	9/21/2004	126	31
6	Atlanta	806748	181710	790.72	10/26/2004	H01	2	15	10/18/2004	126	14
7	Atlanta	806748	181710	4367.88	10/26/2004	H01	2	15	10/15/2004	126	14
8	Atlanta	806748	182187	3033.08	11/11/2004	F02	2	15	10/28/2004	126	3
9	Atlanta	806748	181927	11134.02	11/11/2004	D01	2	15	11/8/2004	126	3
10	Atlanta	806748	181927	4230.71	11/12/2004	H01	2	15	10/12/2004	126	2
11	Atlanta	806748	2641	38047.53	5/18/2004	D01	2	30	4/2/2004	126	121
12	Atlanta	806748	2641	38047.53	10/28/2004	F02	2	30	4/2/2004	126	12
13	Atlanta	806748	2641	38047.53	10/28/2004	H01	2	30	4/2/2004	126	12
14	Atlanta	807788	136421	390.18	4/22/2004	F02	1	30	4/15/2004	126	138
15	Atlanta	807788	28971	1644.1	5/17/2004	E01	1	30	5/5/2004	126	122
16	Atlanta	807788	28971	1644.1	5/17/2004	F02	1	30	5/5/2004	126	122

Figure 2-1. Order data

It takes too long to handle orders, and we want to find specific problem areas. We also want to find examples of good performance to establish best practices. Pivot tables will provide an excellent tool for exploring this kind of data.

Pivot Table Basics

Pivot tables require data to be arranged in columns with headings. We start by selecting the range of cells or the columns that we want in the pivot table. The pivot table wizard will attempt to find the range for you, if you select a single cell containing data.

Be careful when letting the wizard find the range. The pivot table wizard will stop at an empty row. So, if you are not sure all the rows in your range are used, it is best to select the range you want manually.

Next we click on the Data → Pivot Table PivotChart Report menu option. This starts the pivot table wizard and brings up the dialog in Figure 2-2.

For this example we simply click the Finish button. This accepts all of the defaults, and this is often all you will need. Several options are available at this point, including linking our pivot table to external data or making a PivotChart. For now, just click Finish, which brings us to the display in Figure 2-3.

A newly created pivot table has a few parts. Item 1 is a list of data items in the table. We can drag and drop these items onto the pivot table.

Item 2 is the Pivot Table toolbar. On your system it may show up in a different location. Item 3 is the area where we drag-and-drop row fields. Our selection in this area establishes the order of the rows in the finished table.

Item 4 is the data area. Items dragged to this area are summarized by both row and column. Item 5 is the area for column fields. Selections here determine the horizontal arrangement of the table. The page field area in item 6 is a filtering option, allowing you to add a fourth dimension to the table.

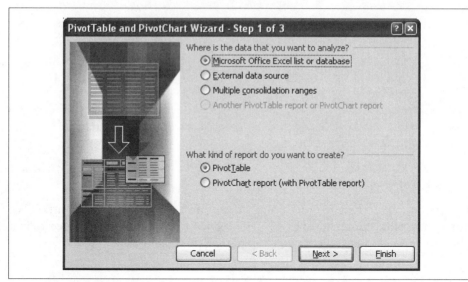

Figure 2-2. The PivotTable Wizard

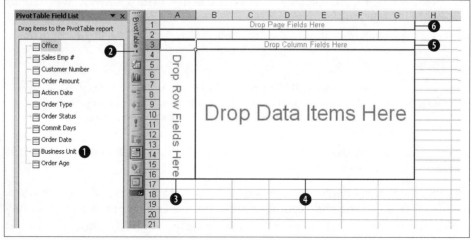

Figure 2-3. The parts of a pivot table

Populating the Table

We start by looking at the average age of orders by location. First, drag the Office data item into the row field area. The results are shown in Figure 2-4. Office is a categorical item. The row, column, and page areas can only use categorical data.

The pivot table is only active when some part of the table is selected. If you select a cell outside the table the field list disappears and the table features are disabled. You can reactivate the pivot table by clicking on any part of it.

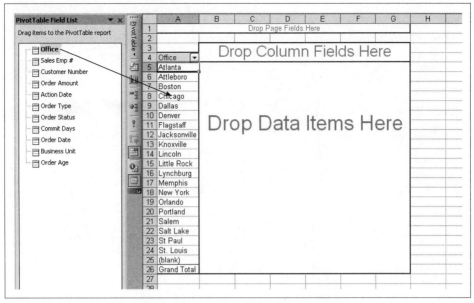

Figure 2-4. Populating the row field area

Scalar items go in the data area, and the next step is to drag the Order Age data item to that area. You can use a categorical item in the data area, but this will make most of the calculations unusable. Excel will try to determine what kind of data you have selected, and it will set a default calculation. In this example the default is Count. We change the Count to the Average as demonstrated in Figure 2-5.

Unfortunately, there is no way for the user to change the default, so you will have to do this every time you move an item to the data area, unless you actually want the default.

Sorting and Filtering

Suppose we want see the locations sorted by average order age. With the interior of the table selected, I click on the Pivot Table button on the toolbar and select Sort and Top 10 as shown in Figure 2-6.

This brings up the sort dialog in Figure 2-7.

Here I select a descending sort on Average of Order Age. In this dialog I could also limit the display to the top few items after the sort. The top ten is the default, but I can select any number of items to show using the options on the right side of the dialog.

In Figure 2-6 the last city is named *(blank)*. This could be useful if we had some blank city names in the data. But we don't. To remove the blank entry, I click on the arrow in cell A4 of Figure 2-6. This displays the dialog in Figure 2-8.

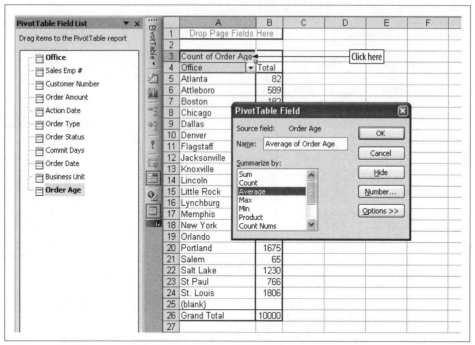

Figure 2-5. Changing from Count to Average

This allows me to control which offices will appear on the table. Here, I have unchecked *(blank)* to exclude it. When OK is clicked, the display looks like Figure 2-9.

There is a big difference in performance. Boston handles orders in about 8.6 days on average while St. Paul takes over 42 days. Some of the difference might be understandable if there is a difference in the kinds or value of orders between the offices.

Multiple Data Items

Next we check to see if the average order amount is related to average order age. First, I drag Order Amount from the field list into the data area. This adds Count of Order Amount as a second data item. To change to the average, I right-click on one of the cells containing data for Count of Order Amount. In Figure 2-10 I right-clicked on cell B7, bringing up a menu dialog.

Selecting the Field Settings option allows us to select how the data is summarized using the dialog in Figure 2-5.

By default, Excel puts the new data item under rather than beside the first one. If you want them side by side, just drag the data item in cell B3 to cell C3 as shown in Figure 2-11.

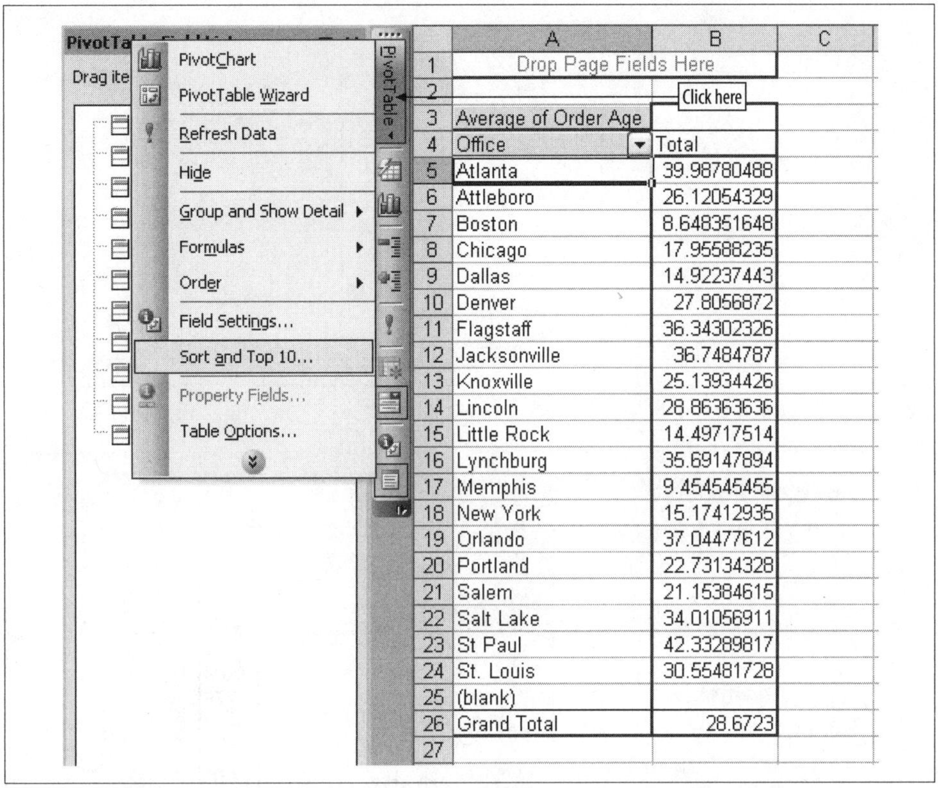

Figure 2-6. The pivot table menu

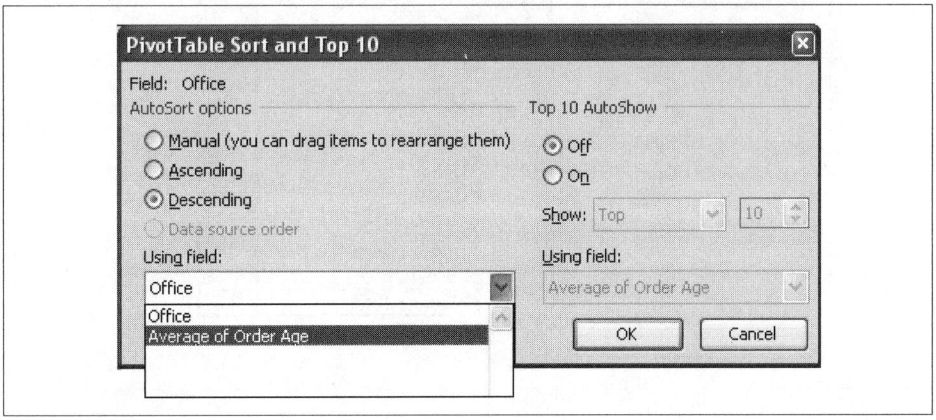

Figure 2-7. Sorting the table

This puts the averages next to each other, making it easy to use Excel functions on the data. I check for linkage between the averages by using the CORREL function as shown in Figure 2-12.

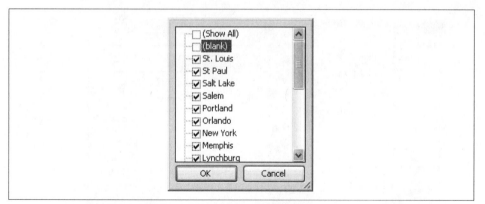

Figure 2-8. Filtering the row fields

	A	B	C
1	Drop Page Fields Here		
2			
3	Average of Order Age		
4	Office	Total	
5	St Paul	42.33	
6	Atlanta	39.99	
7	Orlando	37.04	
8	Jacksonville	36.75	
9	Flagstaff	36.34	
10	Lynchburg	35.69	
11	Salt Lake	34.01	
12	St. Louis	30.55	
13	Lincoln	28.86	
14	Denver	27.81	
15	Attleboro	26.12	
16	Knoxville	25.14	
17	Portland	22.73	
18	Salem	21.15	
19	Chicago	17.96	
20	New York	15.17	
21	Dallas	14.92	
22	Little Rock	14.50	
23	Memphis	9.45	
24	Boston	8.65	
25	Grand Total	28.67	
26			
27			

PivotTable Field List ▼ ✕

Drag items to the PivotTable report

- **Office**
- Sales Emp #
- Customer Number
- Order Amount
- Action Date
- Order Type
- Order Status
- Commit Days
- Order Date
- Business Unit
- **Order Age**

Figure 2-9. The sorted offices

A correlation of −0.3 doesn't explain much. There is a tendency for small orders to be worked in less time. But it cannot account for the differences in performance overall, and we reject the idea that the average size of orders an office processes causes the difference in aging.

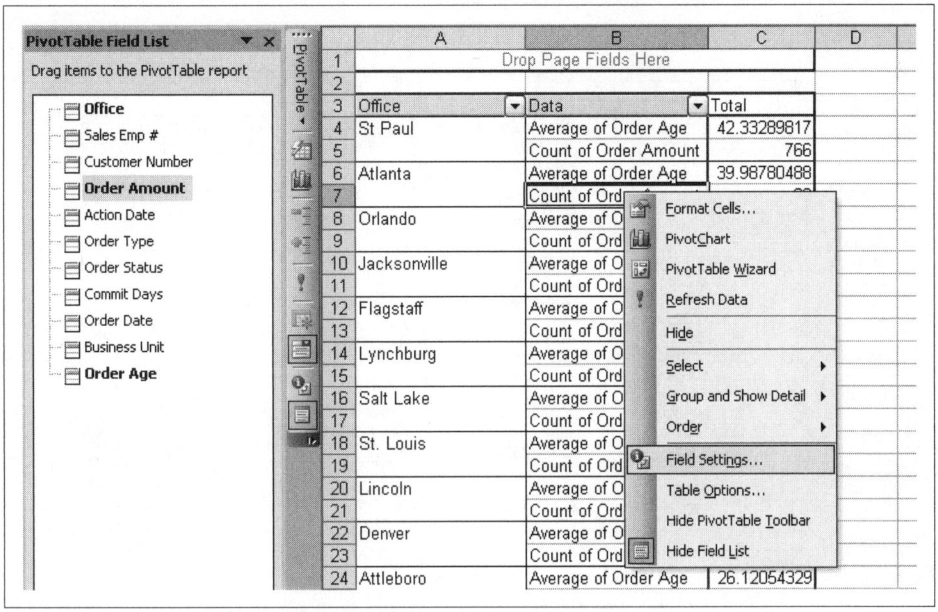

Figure 2-10. Adding a second item to the data area

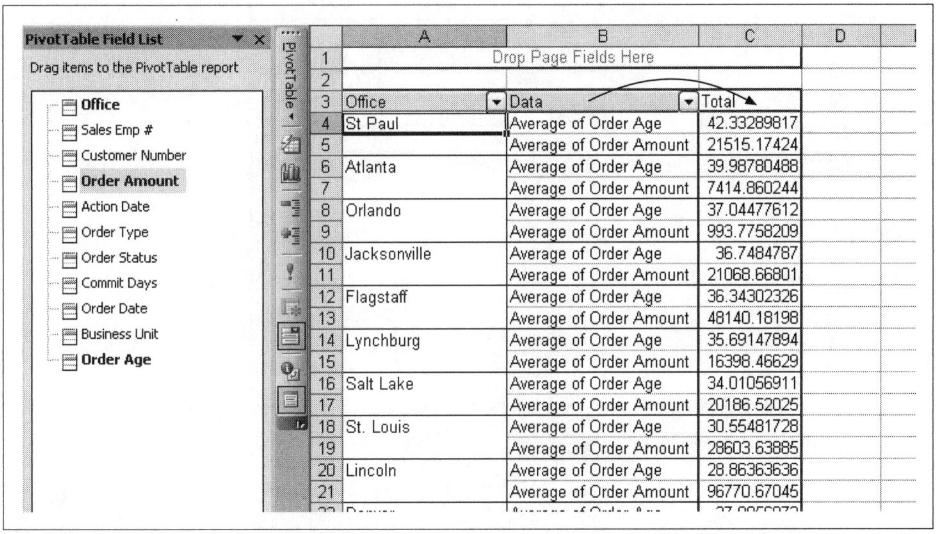

Figure 2-11. Rearranging the table

Working with Rows and Columns

To check the mix of order types in the offices, start by right-clicking on the average order amount and selecting Hide from the menu of table options. This removes the item from the table. Then drag the Order Type item into the column area as shown in Figure 2-13.

	A	B	C	D	E	F	G	H	I	J
1										
2										
3		Data								
4	Office	Average of Order Age	Average of Order Amount							
5	St Paul	42.33289817	21515.17424		-0.30336		=CORREL(B5:B24,C5:C24)			
6	Atlanta	39.98780488	7414.860244							
7	Orlando	37.04477612	993.7758209							
8	Jacksonville	36.7484787	21068.66801							
9	Flagstaff	36.34302326	48140.18198							
10	Lynchburg	35.69147894	16398.46629							
11	Salt Lake	34.01056911	20186.52025							
12	St. Louis	30.55481728	28603.63885							
13	Lincoln	28.86363636	96770.67045							
14	Denver	27.8056872	8252.068626							
15	Attleboro	26.12054329	73317.11197							
16	Knoxville	25.13934426	45847.01978							
17	Portland	22.73134328	42442.77189							
18	Salem	21.15384615	9379.677231							
19	Chicago	17.95588235	48206.17353							
20	New York	15.17412935	31610.12154							
21	Dallas	14.92237443	25747.74251							
22	Little Rock	14.49717514	387937.7309							
23	Memphis	9.454545455	24895.61212							
24	Boston	8.648351648	30492.53231							
25	Grand Total	28.6723	49857.80422							
26										

Figure 2-12. Checking for a link between the averages

PivotTable Field List

Drag items to the PivotTable report

- Office
- Sales Emp #
- Customer Number
- Order Amount
- Action Date
- Order Type
- Order Status
- Commit Days
- Order Date
- Business Unit
- **Order Age**

	A	B	C	D
1	Drop Page Fields Here			
2				
3	Average of Order Age			
4	Office	Total		
5	St Paul	42.33		
6	Atlanta	39.99		
7	Orlando	37.04		
8	Jacksonville	36.75		
9	Flagstaff	36.34		
10	Lynchburg	35.69		
11	Salt Lake	34.01		
12	St. Louis	30.55		
13	Lincoln	28.86		
14	Denver	27.81		
15	Attleboro	26.12		
16	Knoxville	25.14		
17	Portland	22.73		
18	Salem	21.15		
19	Chicago	17.96		
20	New York	15.17		
21	Dallas	14.92		
22	Little Rock	14.50		
23	Memphis	9.45		
24	Boston	8.65		
25	(blank)			
26	Grand Total	28.67		
27				

Figure 2-13. Putting data into the column area

This gives a breakdown by both city and order type. The display is too large to fit in the window on my computer so I used the format menu to show only to two decimal places and auto fit the column widths. Adjusting column widths in pivot tables is almost a waste of time because the pivot table feature resets widths when you make changes to the table. This results in the worksheet displayed in Figure 2-14.

Office	A02	A03	A05	A22	A55	C01	D01	E01	E03	F02	F3	G01	H01	H02	Grand Total
St Paul						34.64	27.84	46.48		42.95		14.00	51.06	10.14	42.33
Atlanta						27.00	69.90	59.00		56.33			15.29	15.42	39.99
Orlando							25.71	38.33		38.64			38.30		37.04
Jacksonville						16.80	38.41	76.68	32.30	41.64			21.14	15.68	36.75
Flagstaff						0.00	42.43	44.80		5.27			61.65	21.47	36.34
Lynchburg	21.00		2.16		10.45	8.39	43.07	73.50	45.48	53.86		28.60	23.94	11.86	35.69
Salt Lake						11.20	33.44	43.32	21.67	52.79			34.84	14.97	34.01
St. Louis			0.00		15.33	17.35	32.92	52.30	41.67	41.27	8.00	77.50	28.82	9.74	30.55
Lincoln							41.29	23.40		19.00			23.88		28.86
Denver						8.00	17.39	42.19		38.35			16.08	46.29	27.81
Attleboro						23.73	27.91	18.69		30.18			26.89	11.30	26.12
Knoxville						55.00	33.67	27.56	11.40	33.87			26.03	6.85	25.14
Portland			4.22	2.50	0.00	6.89	39.34	19.04	19.00	34.09		4.00	14.16	9.20	22.73
Salem						4.00	24.83	36.00		27.64		9.00	9.06	19.57	21.15
Chicago						3.00	14.30	26.57		22.22	8.00		15.52		17.96
New York							15.38	9.98		27.04		7.00	13.98	10.50	15.17
Dallas	12.00					12.67	8.95	53.33		13.83			16.96	14.29	14.92
Little Rock		23.00				13.78	18.44	12.62		18.99			15.70	5.15	14.50
Memphis							10.33	2.00		31.00			8.27		9.45
Boston							14.02	2.33		9.50			7.86	6.11	8.65
Grand Total	12.67	23.00	2.63	2.50	11.00	13.96	32.85	41.88	34.27	38.84	8.00	30.18	28.14	10.91	28.67

Figure 2-14. A table with both city and order type

This demonstrates the real power of the pivot table tool. In seconds I could change this table to look at sales employee numbers, or switch from average order age to average order amount.

We can see in row 25 that there is a difference in age by order type. We can also see the performance differences between the fastest and slowest offices are across the board.

Adding a PivotChart

To highlight the difference between the best and worst performers, I remove all but the two fastest and two slowest offices using the filtering technique shown in Figure 2-8. This results in Figure 2-15 and lets me create a chart to compare the best and worst side by side.

This creates a pivot chart linked to the pivot table. The pivot chart has the field list and pivot menu. It also has all the functionality of the pivot table, as shown in Figure 2-16.

I have the same drag and drop capability on the chart as on the table. If I want to switch from Office to Business Unit, I can drag Office off the chart (it is at the bottom) and replace it with Business Unit. If I make that change on the chart, it is also made on the table, since they are linked.

File Edit View Insert Format Tools Data Window Help

Average of Order Age	Order Type							
Office	C01	D01	E01	F02	G01	H01	H02	Grand Total
St Paul	34.64	27.84	46.48	42.95	14.00	51.06	10.14	42.33
Atlanta	27.00	69.90	59.00	56.33		15.29	15.42	39.99
Memphis		10.33	2.00	31.00		8.27		9.45
Boston		14.02	2.33	9.50		7.86	6.11	8.65
Grand Total	34.43	26.39	43.79	44.01	14.00	40.05	8.97	35.36

Figure 2-15. Adding a PivotChart

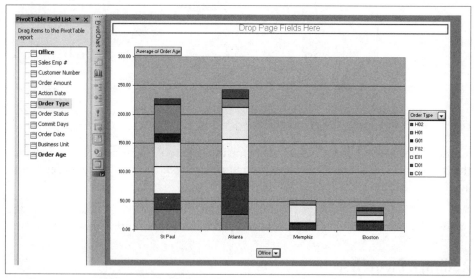

Figure 2-16. Figure 2-16. The pivot chart

Here we see clearly that Memphis and Boston (the best performers) are better than the slower cites for all the order types. The pivot chart has all the power of a normal Excel chart and I can change the chart type by right-clicking in the plot area and selecting a different chart type. I changed to a 100% stacked column chart to look at the order type mix. Then I clicked on the Average of Order Age button just above the plot area on the left and changed from average to count. The result is shown in Figure 2-17.

This chart lets us see how the mix of work differs. When we changed from Average to Count, the pivot table changed automatically. The sort option is enabled on the table so now it is sorting on Count not Average. This changes the order of the cities on the chart.

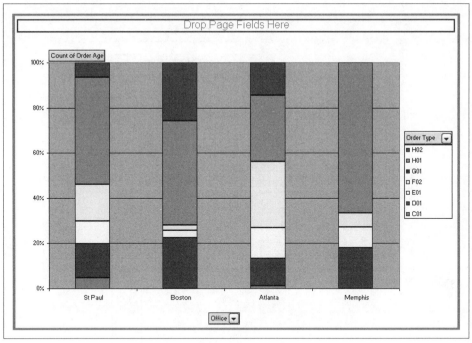

Figure 2-17. Comparing the order type mix

Multiple Layers and Pages

Pivot tables and charts can have multiple layers. Suppose I want to see which customers take the longest for each city. I go to the table and start by taking the filter off City so they all show up on the table. Then I drag Order Type back to the field list and drag Customer Number to the row area as shown in Figure 2-18.

It is important to drag Customer Number to the right side of cell A4. If it is dropped on the left side of A4, Excel tries to arrange cities by customer, which makes no sense. I then use the pivot table menu and select Sort and Top 10. I fill out the sort options as shown in Figure 2-19.

I indicate a descending sort on Average of Order Age, with only the top 5 items showing. The results are shown in the table in Figure 2-20.

Next I want to be able to see this information by order type. I drag Order Type to the page area at the top of the display, as in Figure 2-21.

This creates an interactive display allowing the user to select any Order Type (or all) and see the results in the table immediately. You could drag Customer Number back to the field area and replace it with Sales Emp # or Commit Days to create different views of the data.

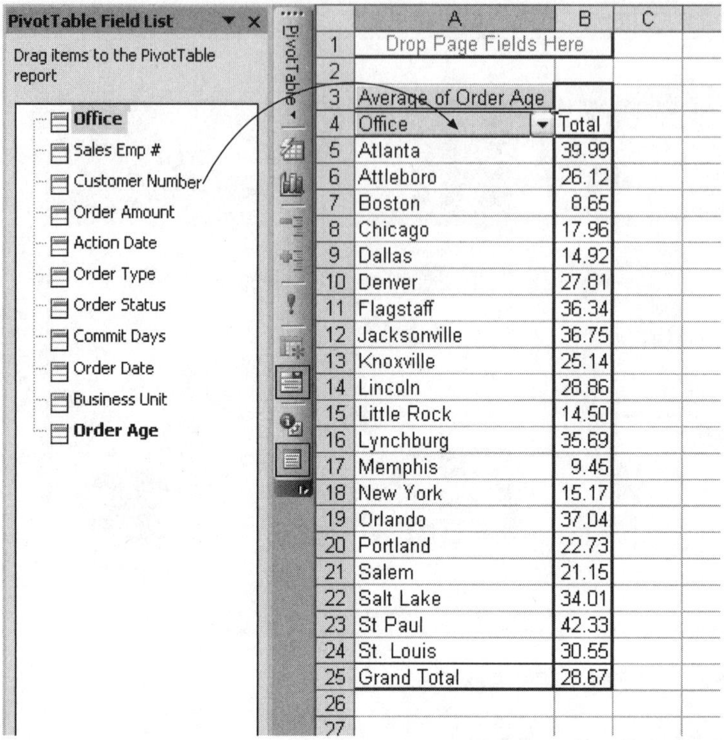

Figure 2-18. Change to a customer-based approach

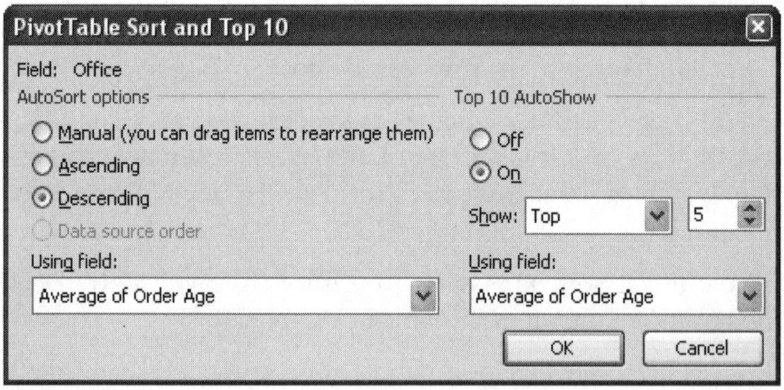

Figure 2-19. Sort and Top 10 options

Drilling Down

Pivot tables have a built-in drill down feature. Suppose we need to see the details for one of the rows in the report from Figure 2-21. The third row for the St. Paul office is

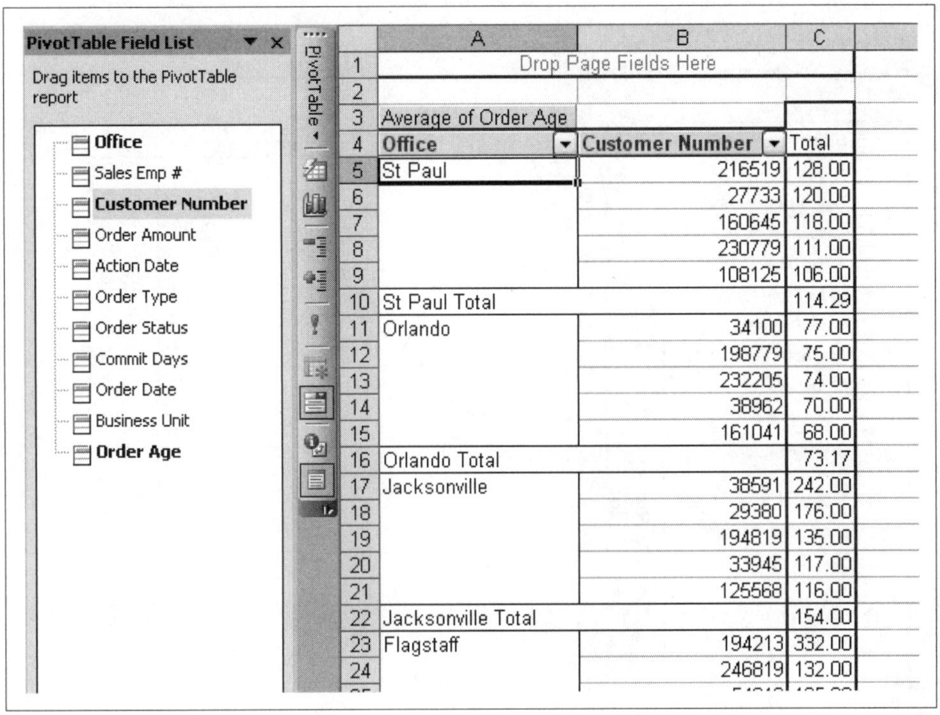

Figure 2-20. The top five customers by city

customer 160645, and their average order age is 118 days. To see the detail, I double click on the number 118 as shown in Figure 2-22.

This adds a new sheet to my workbook containing the orders for this customer. The result is in Figure 2-23. Each time you drill down, you will get a new sheet. So, it is important to delete the new sheet when you finish using it. Features like these make pivot tables ideal for analysis, but they are also a great way to present information in cases where users need flexibility and don't mind interacting with the application.

Changing the Data

You are not limited to the data you get. Sometimes it is helpful to change the form of a data item. You cannot create new information, but you can redefine existing data in ways that make it more useful.

Categorical Information

One of the data items we started with is Action Date. This is categorical information, but there are too many dates. If I use it as the row or column field I get too many categories. I can make this item more useful by changing it into a day of the week. We

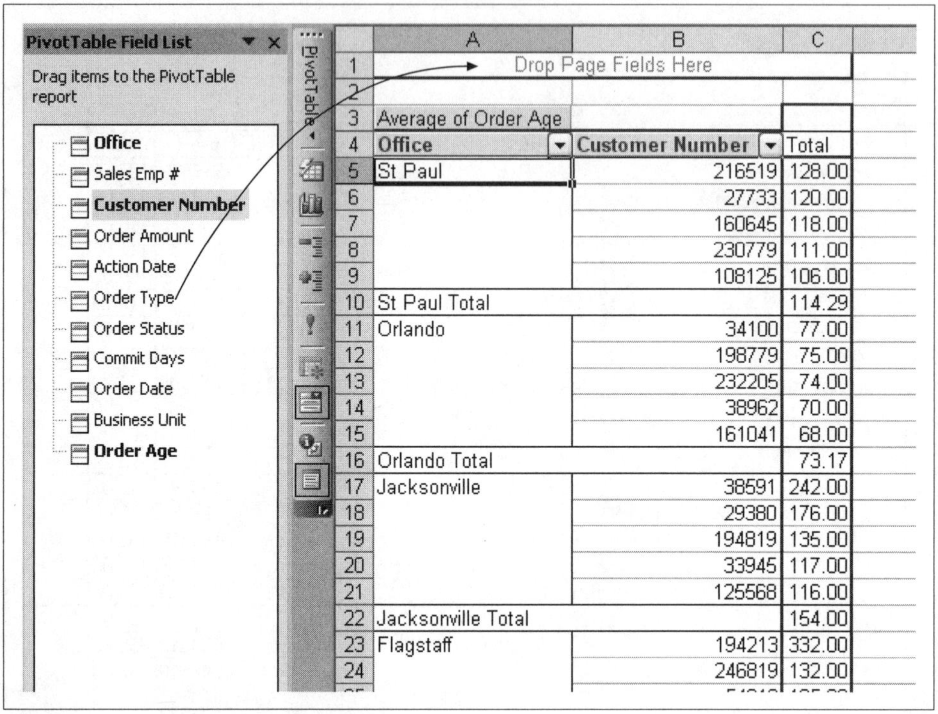

Figure 2-21. Using the page field area

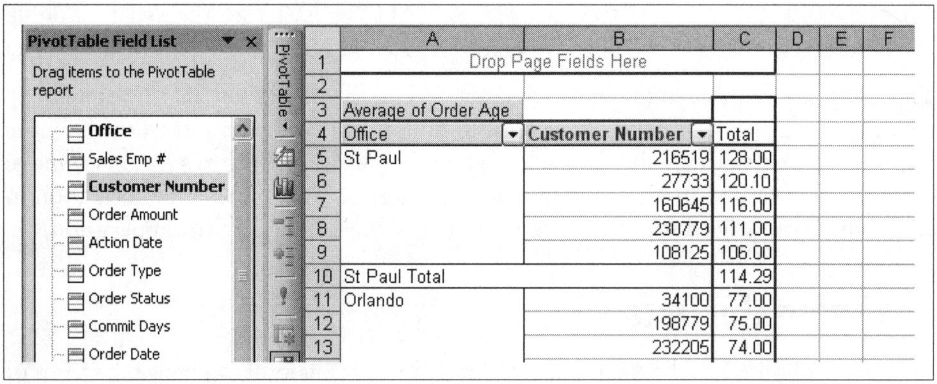

Figure 2-22. Drilling down

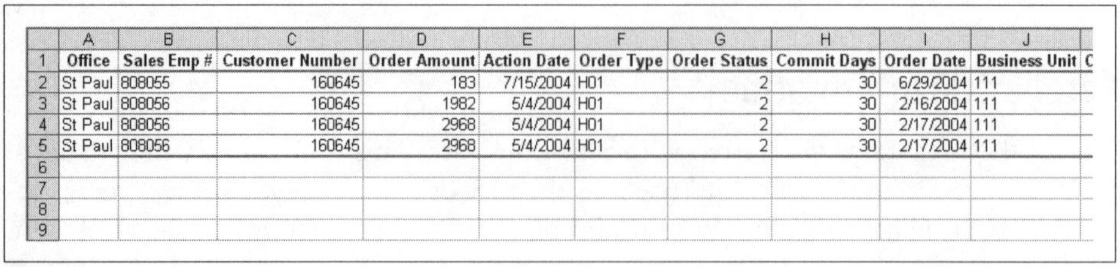

Figure 2-23. The details

might find orders have different characteristics based on the day of the week they are received. I return to the data sheet and add a new column named Weekday, filling it out as shown in Figure 2-24.

	E	F	G	H	I	J	K	L	M	N	O	P
1	Action Date	Order Type	Order Status	Commit Days	Order Date	Business Unit	Order Age	Weekday				
2	11/9/2004	F02	3	30	7/1/2004	126	4	Tue	=TEXT(WEEKDAY(E2),"aaa")			
3	10/29/2004	D01	1	10	9/20/2004	126	12	Fri				
4	11/9/2004	D01	3	30	10/29/2004	126	4	Tue				
5	10/15/2004	H01	1	15	10/7/2004	3L3	21	Fri				
6	10/11/2004	F02	2	30	3/5/2004	111	24	Mon				
7	11/10/2004	H02	2	99	10/27/2004	126	4	Wed				
8	9/20/2004	H01	2	30	9/9/2004	111	38	Mon				
9	11/15/2004	F02	1	30	11/5/2004	131	0	Mon				
10	9/15/2004	E01	2	30	9/2/2004	156	41	Wed				
11	8/6/2004	F02	3	30	8/6/2004	131	68	Fri				
12	11/3/2004	C01	2	30	10/8/2004	111	8	Wed				
13	9/6/2004	F02	1	30	8/26/2004	156	47	Mon				
14	7/28/2004	D01	3	30	7/9/2004	131	74	Wed				
15	8/24/2004	H01	2	30	8/18/2004	111	56	Tue				

Figure 2-24. Adding a new data item

I then go back to the pivot table, click on the pivot table menu and select PivotTable wizard. Clicking on the Back button brings up the dialog in Figure 2-25.

Figure 2-25. Changing the data range for a pivot table

Change the data range to DATA!$A:$L to add the new column, then click Finish, and the new data item appears in the field list.

There are times when you might need to change a scalar item into a categorical. I can convert Order Amount into a categorical item by adding a column that gives its quartile. The formula is shown in Figure 2-26.

The QUARTILE function has two parameters. First is a range that contains a list of numbers. Second is the quartile to be returned. It returns the maximum value of the quartile and the formula in Figure 2-26 returns the quartile number.

The new column holds a value that tells if the order amount is high or low in four steps. This can be used to define groups in the data. Using these two new data items, I built the table in Figure 2-27.

The first quartile is made up of orders with the lowest value. Here we see that the lower value orders are the oldest on average, and this is consistent across all five weekdays.

	E	F	G	H	I	J	K	L	M	N
1	Action Date	Order Type	Order Status	Commit Days	Order Date	Business Unit	Order Age	Quartile		
2	11/9/2004	F02	3	30	7/1/2004	126	4	1		
3	10/29/2004	D01	1	10	9/20/2004	126	12	2		
4	11/9/2004	D01	3	30	10/29/2004	126	4	1		
5	10/15/2004	H01	1	15	10/7/2004	3L3	21	1		
6	10/11/2004	F02	2	30	3/5/2004	111	24	2		
7	11/1	=IF(D2<QUARTILE(D$1:D$10001,1),1,(IF(D2<QUARTILE(D$1:D$10001,2),2,(IF(D2<QUARTILE(D$1:D$10001,3),3,4)))))								
8	9/26/2004	H01	2	30	9/9/2004	111	30	2		
9	11/15/2004	F02	1	30	11/5/2004	131	0	2		
10	9/15/2004	E01	2	30	9/2/2004	156	41	1		
11	8/6/2004	F02	3	30	8/6/2004	131	68	1		
12	11/3/2004	C01	2	30	10/8/2004	111	8	2		
13	9/6/2004	F02	1	30	8/26/2004	156	47	1		
14	7/28/2004	D01	3	30	7/9/2004	131	74	2		
15	8/24/2004	H01	2	30	8/18/2004	111	56	2		
16	11/3/2004	H02	3	30	10/25/2004	126	8	3		
17	11/2/2004	H01	2	1	10/22/2004	111	9	2		
18	8/16/2004	H01	3	30	7/7/2004	131	61	4		
19	10/25/2004	H01	3	30	10/13/2004	156	14	2		

Figure 2-26. Quartile ranking of a numeric item

	A	B	C	D	E	F
1						
2						
3	Average of Order Age	Quartile				
4	Weekday	1.00	2.00	3.00	4.00	Grand Total
5	Mon	31.38	26.59	19.11	17.95	23.66
6	Tue	37.90	35.76	29.62	20.20	31.30
7	Wed	35.62	37.34	29.24	17.04	29.28
8	Thu	35.62	32.07	27.57	24.09	30.01
9	Fri	37.86	33.71	22.58	19.93	28.23
10	Grand Total	35.75	33.27	25.73	19.64	28.59
11						
12						

Figure 2-27. The table using the new data items

Scalar Information

You can also change a categorical into a scalar. This is most commonly done in modeling but it can be useful in research. We want to change Order Type into a scalar. We start by creating the table in Figure 2-28.

We use this table to create a column on the Data sheet. I have named the sheet with the pivot table *PivotSheet*. I add the new column to Data using the formula shown in Figure 2-29.

The VLOOKUP function replaces the Order Type with its average age. This column is linked to the pivot table so I need to copy it and paste special values to convert it to

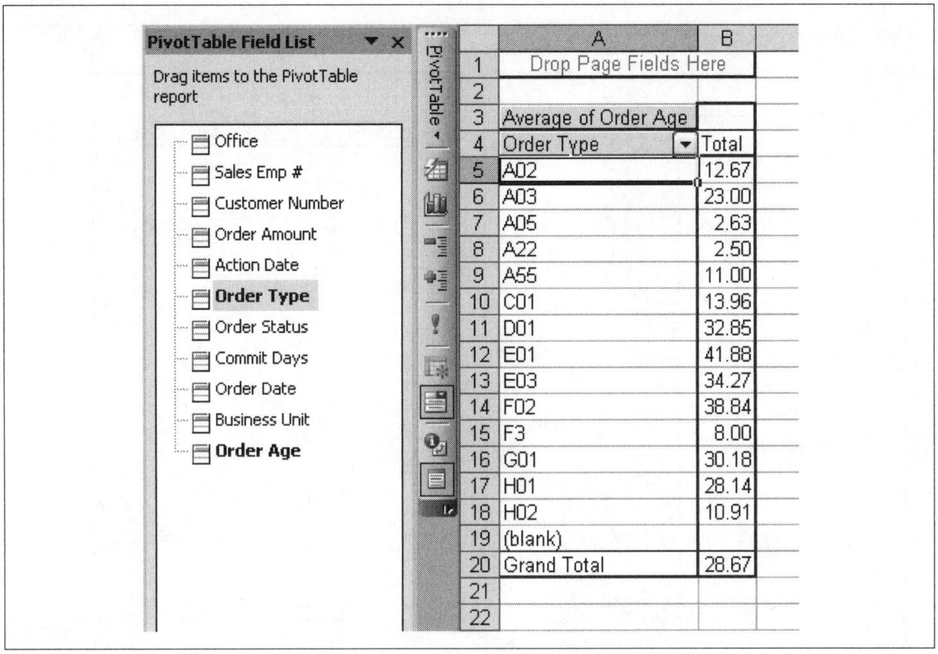

Figure 2-28. Order Type and average Order Age

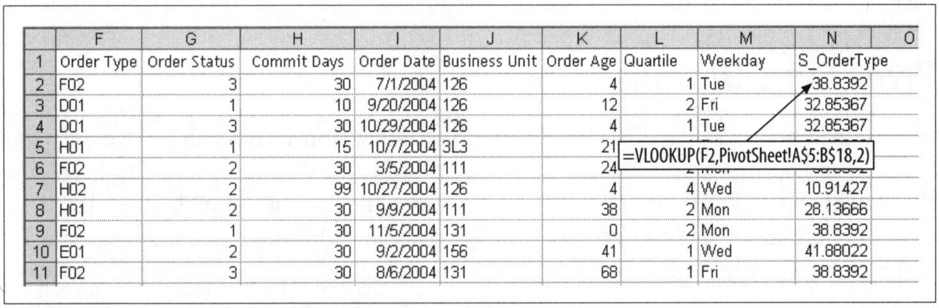

	F	G	H	I	J	K	L	M	N	O
1	Order Type	Order Status	Commit Days	Order Date	Business Unit	Order Age	Quartile	Weekday	S_OrderType	
2	F02	3	30	7/1/2004	126	4	1	Tue	38.8392	
3	D01	1	10	9/20/2004	126	12	2	Fri	32.85367	
4	D01	3	30	10/29/2004	126	4	1	Tue	32.85367	
5	H01	1	15	10/7/2004	3L3	21	=VLOOKUP(F2,PivotSheet!A$5:B$18,2)			
6	F02	2	30	3/5/2004	111	24				
7	H02	2	99	10/27/2004	126	4	4	Wed	10.91427	
8	H01	2	30	9/9/2004	111	38	2	Mon	28.13666	
9	F02	1	30	11/5/2004	131	0	2	Mon	38.8392	
10	E01	2	30	9/2/2004	156	41	1	Wed	41.88022	
11	F02	3	30	8/6/2004	131	68	1	Fri	38.8392	

Figure 2-29. Order type converted to a scalar value

eliminate the formulas. The new column is added to the pivot table using the wizard. The new field, named S_OrderType, gives us a way to compare an office to the average performance for all offices with the mix of order types taken into account. The table in Figure 2-30 demonstrates this.

Here we see St. Louis has an average order age of 30.55. But if St. Louis had average performance for all order types its average age would be 29.06. So, St. Louis is just a little worse than average. The best performer is Boston, on row 22. Its average age of 8.65 is far better than the average for its mix of order types.

This technique allows you to create a standard for comparing different categories, and it gives you a way to be fair when you set goals or measure performance.

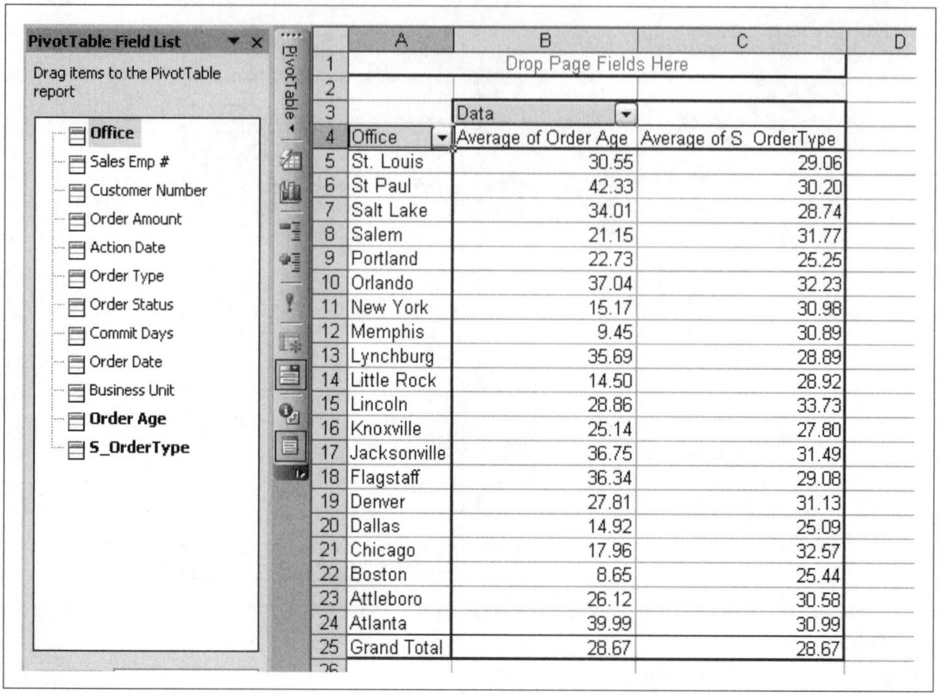

Office	Average of Order Age	Average of S_OrderType
St. Louis	30.55	29.06
St Paul	42.33	30.20
Salt Lake	34.01	28.74
Salem	21.15	31.77
Portland	22.73	25.25
Orlando	37.04	32.23
New York	15.17	30.98
Memphis	9.45	30.89
Lynchburg	35.69	28.89
Little Rock	14.50	28.92
Lincoln	28.86	33.73
Knoxville	25.14	27.80
Jacksonville	36.75	31.49
Flagstaff	36.34	29.08
Denver	27.81	31.13
Dallas	14.92	25.09
Chicago	17.96	32.57
Boston	8.65	25.44
Attleboro	26.12	30.58
Atlanta	39.99	30.99
Grand Total	28.67	28.67

Figure 2-30. Performance by city

Pivot Table Options

In this chapter I have tried to show how pivot tables and charts can be used to analyze business problems, but there are many more features and options. In Step 3 of the PivotTable Wizard there is an Options button. You can launch the wizard by right-clicking anywhere in the pivot table area. The Options button brings up the dialog shown in Figure 2-31.

This gives you control over the general formatting and layout of the table, and the Data source options (bottom left) can be helpful if pivot tables are the end product for your users and you don't want them to have the original data.

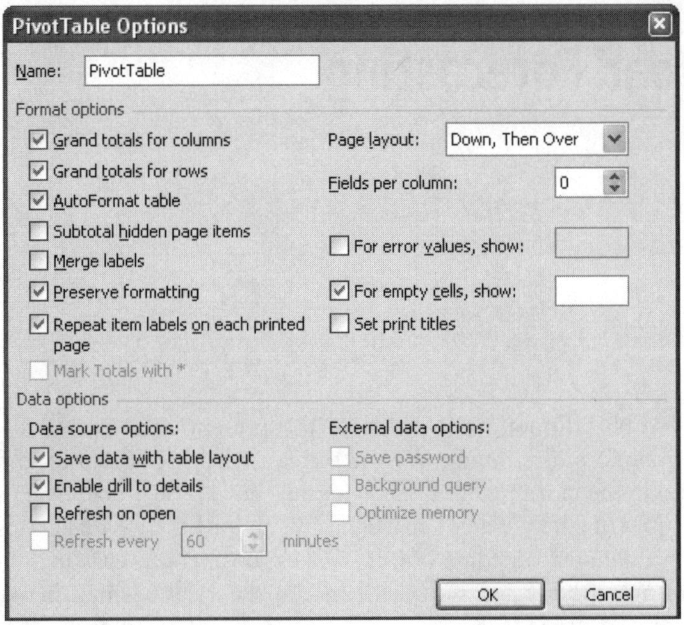

Figure 2-31. The options dialog

CHAPTER 3
Workload Forecasting

Forecasting takes information available in the present and uses it to predict the future. Everyone forecasts things. We use our knowledge of the past to decide what time to get up in the morning, how much food to buy at the grocery, and where to go on vacation. In daily life we don't usually think about how we make these decisions or how we evaluate the outcome of our choices. Business forecasting is more structured. There are specific techniques to model the relationships between present information and a future value.

Few forecasts are exactly right. Some error is expected—some difference between the forecast and the actual value. In most cases, then, it is not enough to make a forecast. We also need to know how accurate the forecast will be. This means that the prediction is not an exact value but a range with a known probability.

This chapter looks at predicting the workload for a typical business process. The example forecasts the volume of calls coming into a call center, but the techniques can be applied to many other problems. This type of forecasting uses only the past values of the item being predicted. Future call volumes are predicted using past call volumes.

This chapter also demonstrates techniques for creating a complete application in Excel. The application uses a combination of organization, workbook functions, formatting, and a little VBA. At the end of the chapter we will have a complete Excel application for predicting workload.

Since this is the first application in the book, we will take a detailed look at the entire process, beginning with the Excel functions and features used to create the application.

The application uses the Excel functions listed in Table 3-1. Most of these functions are discussed as we encounter them in the application. But the INDEX, INDIRECT, and ADDRESS functions are used in several of the applications in the rest of this book and have a unique job. Understanding how they work is critical to understanding this chapter's application, so make sure you have read the explanations of how they work in Chapter 1.

Table 3-1. Excel functions used in this chapter's example application

```
INDEX( )            COL( )            CONFIDENCE( )
INDIRECT( )         SUM( )            INT( )
ADDRESS( )          MIN( )            ABS( )
WEEKDAY( )          IF( )             STANDARDIZE ( )
ROW( )              AVERAGE( )        NORMSDIST( )
MAX( )              STDEV( )
```

The application will also use the Excel features explained in Table 3-2.

Table 3-2. Excel features used in this chapter's example application

Excel feature	Explanation
Formatting	Formatting lets you control the look and feel of the application. It draws attention to important information, while it keeps supporting item in view.
Named Cells and Named Ranges	Named cells and ranges create a simple and clear interface between the parts of the application.
Array Formulas	Array formulas concentrate the logic and avoid the need for multiple columns for a single calculation.
Charting	Charting allows numbers to be presented as pictures. This focuses attention on the meaning and conclusions rather than on the numbers themselves.
VBA	VBA gives you a way to extend and customize the power of Excel.

The Procedure

First we look at the calculations. We need to make the best possible prediction, measure the accuracy, and manage anomalies. Excel provides the tools, but before we start entering formulas we need to understand the data.

Data

This chapter uses data from a call center. It is a five day a week operation, and the data is simply the date and number of incoming calls for each day.

The techniques used can be applied to most workload situations. The goal is to predict a periodic workload that could have an overall trend, and is subject to short-term ups and downs. The accuracy of predictions will be measured and used to set a prediction range with a known probability.

A workload model needs to handle both expected and unexpected shifts in volume. Holidays are expected, but December volumes are not a good predictor for January. Real world workloads are subject to all kinds of unpredictable outside forces. The competition can raise their price, a server can go down, or a snow storm can shut down part of the country. As a result, workloads can go up or down with no warning.

The sample data in this chapter comes from an actual call center and is subject to all the uncertainty of the business environment.

Predictions

Time creates uncertainty. The further into the future we predict, the less accurate we are. This chapter starts with a weekly prediction. The weekly forecast is adjusted as more information is available and becomes an adjusted daily forecast. An hourly forecast is also made, and the daily forecast is adjusted further as actual hourly values are entered.

Find the lag

Lag is the number of observations in a cycle. Many business systems run on a weekly cycle. Mondays look like Mondays; Fridays look like Fridays. If the process runs five days a week, the lag is five. Of course, everything doesn't run on a weekly cycle. Sometimes it is monthly, hourly, or some exotic period. In all cases it is critical to know how many observations there are in a cycle, and usually this is known without examining the data. But if you are not sure, it's best to check.

This example looks at thirty days of call counts for a call center. This is a Monday thru Friday operation, so we expect it to run on a five day cycle. To find the lag we correlate the daily call counts with themselves offset by different numbers of days. The offset with the highest correlation is the lag.

To do this we use the CORREL function. This function takes two arguments. They are both ranges and must have the same number of values. The function gives the correlation between the values in the ranges. The formula in the correlation column is =CORREL(B$2:B$21,B3:B22), and it is filled down for ten cells. Notice that the correlation is high only at five and ten. This confirms that the numbers have a five day cycle. Correlating a list of numbers against itself is called autocorrelation.

The procedure is illustrated in Figure 3-1.

Find the average

The easiest prediction is that each day will have the same volume as the same day in the previous week. But this leads to trouble if last week's call volume was unusual. So, it is better to use a recent average. But even the average can be skewed by a really odd day, and a filtered average tends to do the best job. In a *filtered average* the highest and lowest values are eliminated, and then the remaining numbers are averaged. This gives a good estimate of the true average value.

This is done in two steps. First, build a table that contains values for one weekday (e.g., a list of just Monday values). Then take the sum, subtract the maximum and minimum values, and divide by two less than the number of values.

We use five weeks of data. The first day is Monday 3/2/1998, and there are five Mondays in the list. In practice, the number of weeks giving the most accurate result varies. A balance is required between having enough data to get a good estimate and avoiding seasonal shifts. In most business situations eight weeks works well.

	A	B	C	D	E	F
1	Date	Actual		Cycles	Correlation	
2	2-Mar-98	19,051		1	0.04176153	
3	3-Mar-98	17,589		2	-0.5229394	
4	4-Mar-98	14,773		3	-0.5304882	
5	5-Mar-98	13,751		4	-0.0347171	
6	6-Mar-98	12,055		5	0.89300565	
7	9-Mar-98	17,348		6	-0.0091058	
8	10-Mar-98	16,428		7	-0.464664	
9	11-Mar-98	14,876		8	-0.3444442	
10	12-Mar-98	14,356		9	0.16747496	
11	13-Mar-98	13,154		10	0.87714017	
12	16-Mar-98	17,923		11	0.13182533	
13	17-Mar-98	16,303				
14	18-Mar-98	14,609				
15	19-Mar-98	14,608		=CORREL(B$2:B$21,B3:B22)		
16	20-Mar-98	13,058				
17	23-Mar-98	18,930				
18	24-Mar-98	17,230				
19	25-Mar-98	14,082				
20	26-Mar-98	12,711				
21	27-Mar-98	12,210				
22	30-Mar-98	19,475				
23	31-Mar-98	18,428				
24	1-Apr-98	14,546				
25	2-Apr-98	14,433				
26	3-Apr-98	13,760				
27	6-Apr-98	18,154				
28	7-Apr-98	15,590				
29	8-Apr-98	13,671				
30	9-Apr-98	11,967				
31	10-Apr-98	9,033				
32						

Figure 3-1. Using correlation to find the lag

The INDEX function creates a list of values for one weekday by looking up values in a range. The first argument is a range of cells containing a list of values. The second argument is a number that tells which item in the list is wanted. In this case, we need the row numbers of the Mondays. The first Monday is in row 2, and the first value in the Rows column, cell C2, is 2. The formula in C3 is =C2+5. We add five because that is lag. This formula fills down to C6. In D2 the formula is =INDEX(B$1:B$26,C2). This equates to the second item in the list, B1:B26. This formula also fills down. The formula for the filtered average is =INT((SUM(D2:D6)-(MAX(D2:D6)+MIN(D2:D6)))/3). Five items are being used, but the highest and lowest are eliminated, so we divide by three. The INT function returns the value as an integer. We are dealing with calls, therefore it makes sense to work with integers rather than real numbers. There is no such thing as half a call! In the application, the filtered average is the weekly prediction. Notice that this technique gives us a prediction that is one week in the future. We predicted March 8th on March 1st.

Figure 3-2 shows the calculations.

1	Date	Calls	Rows	Monday Calls	
2	3/2/98	19,051	2		19,051
3	=C2+5	17,589	7		17,348
4	3/4/98	14,773	12		17,923
5	3/5/98	13,751	17		18,930
6	3/6/98	12,055	=INDEX(B$1:B$26,C2)		19,475
7	3/9/98	17,348			
8	3/10/98	16,428		Filtered Average	
9	3/11/98	14,876			18,635
10	3/12/98	14,356			
11	3/13/98	13,154			
12	3/16/98	17,925	=INT((SUM(D2:D6)-(MAX(D2:D6)+MIN(D2:D6)))/3)		
13	3/17/98	16,303			
14	3/18/98	14,609			
15	3/19/98	14,608			
16	3/20/98	13,058			
17	3/23/98	18,930			
18	3/24/98	17,230			
19	3/25/98	14,082			
20	3/26/98	12,711			
21	3/27/98	12,210			
22	3/30/98	19,475			
23	3/31/98	18,428			
24	4/1/98	14,546			
25	4/2/98	14,433			
26	4/3/98	13,760			
27	4/6/98	18,154			
28	4/7/98	15,590			
29	4/8/98	13,671			
30	4/9/98	11,967			
31	4/10/98	9,033			

Figure 3-2. Calculating the filtered average

Adjust for the trend

Trend is the change in average over time. We might expect sales to go up year over year, or complaints to go down. But when the focus is on short-term predictions, these trends often do not mean much. A five percent year-over-year growth rate is less than one tenth of a percent per week. Business systems are not predictable within a range of a tenth of a percent. Consequently, this kind of trend adds no value to the forecast. There are other factors at work, however. In any operation volumes go up and down from week to week. These short-term trends have a significant impact on accuracy of the forecast.

Understanding the trend is essential to building an accurate forecasting model. We calculate the ratio of the predictions (filtered average) to the actuals. In Figure 3-3 the errors are not random. The predictions run low for a few days then high for few days. There is no real trend, just oscillating high and low periods.

	A	B	C	D
1	Date	Actual	Predicted	Predicted/Actual
2	07/17/98	10,773	11,151	1.035
3	07/20/98	17,077	16,881	0.989
4	07/21/98	16,471	15,907	0.966
5	07/22/98	14,192	13,823	0.974
6	07/23/98	12,533	12,732	1.016
7	07/24/98	10,824	11,152	1.03
8	07/27/98	17,056	16,722	0.98
9	07/28/98	16,052	16,138	1.005
10	07/29/98	13,407	13,823	1.031
11	07/30/98	12,415	12,637	1.018
12	07/31/98	10,238	11,036	1.078
13	08/03/98	15,865	16,875	1.064
14	08/04/98	16,033	16,171	1.009
15	08/05/98	15,083	13,729	0.91
16	08/06/98	12,869	12,542	0.975
17	08/07/98	10,864	10,882	1.002
18	08/10/98	14,711	16,809	1.143
19	08/11/98	14,977	16,280	1.087
20	08/12/98	13,255	13,842	1.044
21	08/13/98	11,972	12,572	1.05

Figure 3-3. Analyzing the errors

This means that accuracy can be increased by adjusting based on the previous day's error. If the errors showed significant motion in one direction, it would mean a long-term trend is present. This would require a different approach, such as using a week-over-week growth rate. If the errors have no pattern, it is best to forget the trend and simply use the filtered average as the prediction. In this case we will adjust the filtered average by one half of the error ratio for the previous day. This moves the prediction in the right direction most of the time without overreacting.

Next we calculate the daily adjusted prediction. This value takes the current trend into account and provides improved accuracy. In Figure 3-4 the formula for the adjusted prediction (in D17) is =C16*(1+(B16/C16))/2). This formula multiplies C16 by the value (1+B16/C16))/2), in which B16/C16 is the ratio of the actual and the predicted. But we only want to use half of the ratio. Therefore, the formula averages the ratio with one plus the ratio divided by two. Note that overall the adjusted prediction is 10% more accurate than the filtered average.

The formula for the average error for the Adjusted column is {=AVERAGE(ABS(B3:B16-D3:D16))}. This is an array formula. It creates a vector (a list) of the absolute values of the differences between the actual and predicted. It returns the average of these values. In effect this is the same as creating a new column with =ABS(B3-C3) filled down to row 16, and then taking the average. By using the array formula we get the same answer without adding 14 unnecessary formulas to the worksheet.

	A	B	C	D	E
1	Date	Actual	Filtered Average	Adjusted	Filtered Average/Actual
2	05/27/98	17,169	14,053		1.0454
3	05/28/98	14,371	13,127	14,582	1.0596
4	05/29/98	11,520	11,448	11,990	1.007
5	06/01/98	16,044	17,683	17,739	1.0418
6	06/02/98	15,857	16,457	15,694	0.9513
7	06/03/98	13,972	14,223	13,964	0.9573
8	06/04/98	12,985	13,127	13,011	1.0074
9	06/05/98	11,736	11,300	11,239	0.9917
10	06/08/98	16,535	17,764	18,107	0.9793
11	06/09/98	15,379	16,501	15,930	1.0137
12	06/10/98	13,514	14,273	13,788	1.0182
13	06/11/98	12,692	13,218	12,867	0.967
14	06/12/98	11,657	11,462	11,234	0.969
15	06/15/98	17,405	17,524	17,673	1.0298
16	06/16/98	17,195	16,290	16,235	1.0208
17	**06/17/98**	**14,092**	**14,092**	**14,630**	◀── =C16*(1+(B16/C16))/2)
18					
19	Average Error		659.93	520.95	◀── {=AVERAGE(ABS(B3:B16-D3:D16))}

Figure 3-4. Making a better prediction

Determine the Confidence Interval

The average number of calls per days is about 14,300. Therefore, an average error of 520 equates to around 3.5%. This means that the prediction is really a range.

On the Settings worksheet the user can enter a value for Confidence Level. The application will give the range for the adjusted prediction at that probability. If the confidence level is set at 0.9, the application will display the prediction and a +/- range. There is a 90% probability that the actual value will be in that range.

In Figure 3-4, the adjusted prediction for the next day is 14,630. There is a 90% probability that the actual value will be 14,630 +/- 305. The array formula for this calculation is =`{CONFIDENCE(0.1,STDEV(D3:D16-B3:B16),15)}`. The `CONFIDENCE` function returns the confidence interval. It takes three arguments. The first is the desired confidence level. This is entered as the amount of expected error, so if you want a confidence level of 0.9 the entry is 1-0.9 or 0.1. Next is the standard deviation. In this case it is the standard deviation of the difference between the actual and the adjusted prediction. This is calculated as part of the formula and accounts for this being an array formula. The last argument is the number of values being used. There are 15 values.

Manage Anomalies

Holidays are a problem, as are any large short-term shifts in volume. Not only are they hard to predict, but since the techniques used in this chapter depend on the past, unusual days in the past make accurate prediction difficult. Filtered averaging helps take care of the normal ups and downs. But there are events that are so large and abnormal that they need to be eliminated from the data. Every year, the last two weeks of December are apt to be like this.

When an actual value is entered, the application looks at the prediction error and calculates the probability that the error amount is too great to be part of a normal distribution of errors. This assumes errors are normally distributed.

In the Figure 3-5, the actual value for 06/17/98 has just been entered. The average error amount over the last 15 days was 520.98. The error amount for 06/17/98 is 538. To determine the probability that this value is an anomaly we need the standard deviation of the recent errors. This is calculated by the array formula {=STDEV(D3:D16-B3:B16)}. Here again, we use an array formula to get the answer without creating an additional column of calculations. It is in cell D23. The array formula in D24 is ={AVERAGE(D3:D16-B3:B16)}, which gives the average error. This is different from the value in D19, which is the average error amount, and is based on absolute value.

Next we need to know how many standard deviations from the mean the current error is. The STANDARDIZE function gives this value. The value B17-C17 is the current error. D24 is the average calculated above. And, D23 is the standard deviation from above. The formula =ABS(STANDARDIZE(B17-C17,D24,D23)) in D25 tells how many standard deviations from the mean the current error is.

We need to know what percentage of the distribution is closer to the average than the current error. This will let us calculate the probability that the current error is too large. Using the value returned by the STANDARDIZE function, the formula in D26, which is =NORMSDIST(D25), gives the portion of the distribution between the mean and the value in D23. In the figure, 62% of the population of errors is less than 0.32 standard deviations from the mean.

A forecast can be high or low; therefore, the distribution of errors has two tails. So, the formula in D27, which is =(D26-0.5)*2, gives the final answer. We subtract 0.5 because the NORMSDIST function only considers one tail of the distribution, and multiply by two because the error can occur at either end of the distribution. In this case, only 24% of errors are expected to be smaller than 538. Today is normal. The calculations to do this are shown in Figure 3-5.

If the probability of an anomaly is too high, the value for that day cannot be used for predictions. In the upcoming application, on the Settings worksheet, the user can set a value for Anomaly Detection. If the probability of an anomaly is higher than this setting, the application substitutes the value for the same day in the previous week in all calculations.

	A	B	C	D	E	F
1	Date	Actual	Filtered Average	Adjusted	Filtered Average/Actual	
2	05/27/98	17,169	14,053		1.0454	
3	05/28/98	14,371	13,127	14,582	1.0596	
4	05/29/98	11,520	11,448	11,990	1.007	
5	06/01/98	16,044	17,683	17,739	1.0418	
6	06/02/98	15,857	16,457	15,694	0.9513	
7	06/03/98	13,972	14,223	13,964	0.9573	
8	06/04/98	12,985	13,127	13,011	1.0074	
9	06/05/98	11,736	11,300	11,239	0.9917	
10	06/08/98	16,535	17,764	18,107	0.9793	
11	06/09/98	15,379	16,501	15,930	1.0137	
12	06/10/98	13,514	14,273	13,788	1.0182	
13	06/11/98	12,692	13,218	12,867	0.967	
14	06/12/98	11,657	11,462	11,234	0.969	
15	06/15/98	17,405	17,524	17,673	1.0298	
16	06/16/98	17,195	16,290	16,235	1.0208	
17	**06/17/98**	**14,092**	**14,092**	**14,630**		
18						
19	Average Error		659.93	520.95		
20						
21	Error on 06/17/98			538	=ABS(B17-D17)	
22						
23	Standard Deviation of Error			719.95	{=STDEV(D3:D16-B3:B16)}	
24	Average Error			227.93	{=AVERAGE(D3:D16-B3:B16)}	
25	Standardize			0.32	{=ABS(STANDARDIZE(B17-C17,D24,D23))}	
26	Normsdist			0.62	=NORMSDIST(D25)	
27	**Probability of Anomaly**			**24.84%**	=(D26-0.5)*2	

Figure 3-5. Identifying anomalies

Building an Application

We now understand how this application will work in theory. But, we need to take the theory and turn it into a solution—something we can give to the user. In this section we will build a complete Excel application based on the processes described in the last section.

Design

As we develop an application, things can easily get out of control. Therefore, it is important to start with a plan and some structure. The example has several worksheets, each with its own function.

The Data sheet holds information. It has no formulas. The user is not going to be looking at this sheet, so there is no formatting. This sheet stores the information that drives the application. When new information comes in, it goes on the Data sheet. Keeping the data separate has advantages. If the data source changes, only the interface between the data sheet and the data source needs changing.

All of the logic in the application is on the Workarea sheet. This is the only sheet with workbook functions.

The Display sheet is only concerned with presentation. It is attached to the Workarea sheet by named cells and ranges. There are no formulas, only formatting and information organization.

The Settings sheet contains application options, and there are two specialized sheets: AccuracyChart contains a chart and HourlyForecasts contains a table of hourly predictions. These sheets have no formulas and only hold or display information.

Prediction is the core of the application. But, to make a complete solution there needs to be a structure around it. What will the user see? How will the user interact with the application? These questions are answered by design.

List the Requirements

This is important, and should be shared with users. It forces the developer and the user to think through how the application will be used. In this case there are seven basic requirements:

1. The system will display a full week of predictions.
2. The adjusted prediction for the next day will be shown.
3. Hourly forecasts will be calculated and displayed.
4. The system will provide a twenty day measure of prediction accuracy.
5. A method for entering hourly call volumes will be provided.
6. The system will detect anomalous situations and react to them appropriately.
7. A way of adding new data and deleting/correcting data in the system will be provided.

Consider the Source of Data

The data could come from a variety of sources. It could be in a SQL database, in an XML web service, or it could simply be keyed in. In the sample application the user will key the actual call volume for the previous day into the application. A VBA routine will control the process to ensure that the data is sensible and ends up in the right place. The application will, however, work just as well if the user keys it directly onto the Data sheet.

Figure 3-6 shows the layout of the Data sheet. The user will only provide the Actual value. The rest of the data will come from the application itself. There are no formulas on this sheet and formats play no role. Note that the Anomaly Flag is set for July 3rd.

A VBA routine to delete the last day entered will provide a simple editing scheme. To make the application use a different data source, only the VBA needs to be changed. We will examine the VBA later.

	A	B	C	D	E
1	Anomaly Flag	Date	Actual	Weekly Prediction	Adjusted Prediction
2	0	26-Jun-98	10,733	11,575	11,162
3	0	29-Jun-98	16,138	17,331	16,701
4	0	30-Jun-98	15,082	16,302	15,741
5	0	1-Jul-98	13,049	14,311	13,776
6	0	2-Jul-98	11,006	13,226	12,643
7	1	3-Jul-98	3,235	11,360	10,407
8	0	6-Jul-98	16,628	17,053	16,582
9	0	7-Jul-98	16,569	16,102	15,901
10	0	8-Jul-98	13,771	14,311	14,519
11	0	9-Jul-98	12,445	13,157	12,909
12	0	10-Jul-98	10,931	11,285	10,980

Figure 3-6. Data sheet's layout

Presentation

The next step is to decide what the user will see. There are three things to consider. First, and at this point most important, are the information elements. Information is displayed as blocks of related data. The area that displays the forecasts for each day of the current week is an element. The hourly forecast graph is another. The contents and layout of the elements will guide the development of the logic on the Workarea sheet.

The next consideration is the placement of the elements. Related elements should support each other. Principal elements should be prominently placed. The last thing to consider is the formatting. A simple color scheme that puts the emphasis on the content is best. Placement and formatting are easy to change.

Figure 3-7 shows the main display, which looks and behaves like the home page of a web site, helping the user understand how the application works. The web page is an established metaphor and tells the user what to expect and how to interact with the application. Areas that display information retain an Excel look. This is another use of an established metaphor. Notice that only the information is displayed as black on white. Headings and labels use lower contrast. The emphasis is on the information.

The area on the left is set apart by using a different background color. It contains the navigation buttons and displays summary information. The main section shows the detailed forecasts.

The display is based on black, gray, and white. Colorful displays can cause problems. People are better at distinguishing the difference between light and dark than between colors. Some color combinations cause eye strain, and some users will be color vision deficient. If the display is printed, information represented by color can be lost.

The information shown on this sheet is actually on the Workarea sheet. All the references are to named cells and ranges. This has several advantages. It makes changing

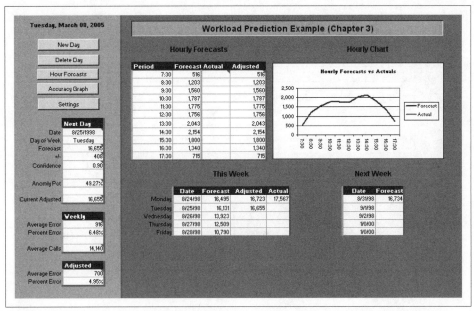

Figure 3-7. Application's main display

the display sheet easy. Areas on the sheet can simply be cut and pasted anywhere. It also preserves the application's organization. You know there is no logic on this sheet, only formatting.

Two additional display areas complete the application: a chart showing the accuracy of the predictions during the last twenty days and a table showing hourly predictions for the whole week. They will not fit on this sheet. So, two additional sheets are used. As with the Display sheet, they reference information on the Workarea sheet.

Figure 3-8 shows the accuracy chart.

The hourly forecasts are shown in Figure 3-9.

Conventions and Names

This application is complex. Using names for important values simplifies formulas and makes the application easier to understand. It also aids in troubleshooting or enhancing the logic. Another way to keep things from getting out of hand is following a set of conventions for the Workarea sheet. There are a few simple rules. Information from the Data sheet is displayed in blue font. Information to be displayed has a gray background. Information to be stored on the Data sheet has a blue background. Calculation areas have a border. Calculated values that are used in other calculations or macros are in Column A and are named.

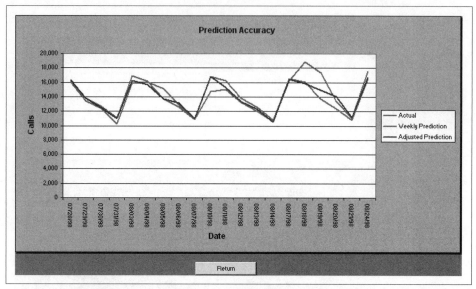

Figure 3-8. Accuracy chart

	Sunday	Monday	Tuesday	Wednesday	Thursday	Friday	Saturday
Hourly Forecasts for the Week Starting Monday 08/24/1998							
7:30		511	660	522	442	440	
8:30		1,191	1,524	1,129	948	900	
9:30		1,545	1,805	1,454	1,281	1,147	
10:30		1,770	2,007	1,700	1,491	1,324	
11:30		1,758	1,879	1,555	1,436	1,221	
12:30		1,739	1,682	1,509	1,366	1,198	
13:30		2,024	1,816	1,679	1,524	1,294	
14:30		2,133	1,730	1,538	1,462	1,178	
15:30		1,782	1,496	1,378	1,233	1,013	
16:30		1,328	1,002	944	857	702	
17:30		708	525	509	463	368	

Figure 3-9. Hourly forecasts

Named Values and Ranges on Settings

The Settings sheet, shown in Figure 3-10, contains options that can be changed by the user.

The application uses named cells and ranges to isolate the interfaces between sheets. These name cells and ranges are defined on the Settings sheet.

Heading (B1)

> This is the heading that appears at the top of the Display sheet.

	A	B	C	D	E	F	G	H	I	J	K
1	Heading	Workload Prediction Example (Chapter 3)			Sunday	Monday	Tuesday	Wednesday	Thursday	Friday	Saturday
2	Lag	5		7:30	0	0.03102	0.040952	0.037551	0.035409	0.040785	0
3	Work Item	Calls		8:30	0	0.072252	0.094491	0.081134	0.075831	0.083451	0
4	Confidence Level	0.9		9:30	0	0.093715	0.11194	0.104503	0.102436	0.106373	0
5	Anomaly Detection	0.999		10:30	0	0.10733	0.124467	0.122103	0.119256	0.122759	0
6				11:30	0	0.106624	0.116518	0.111733	0.114839	0.113231	0
7				12:30	0	0.105455	0.104304	0.108432	0.109232	0.111107	0
8				13:30	0	0.122718	0.112581	0.120613	0.121888	0.119947	0
9				14:30	0	0.129346	0.107272	0.110491	0.116936	0.109205	0
10				15:30	0	0.108088	0.092776	0.099011	0.098599	0.093951	0
11				16:30	0	0.080511	0.062129	0.067858	0.068543	0.065082	0
12				17:30	0	0.04294	0.032571	0.036572	0.03703	0.034109	0
13											
14											
15			Return								
16											

Figure 3-10. The Settings sheet

Lag (B2)

Lag is the number of values per cycle in the data. The sample data uses a five-day week so Lag is 5. The application is designed to work with any value from 2 to 7.

Work Item (B3)

This is the name of the work item. In the sample data it is Calls, but depending on the work being done it could be checks, orders, cars, or any unit or work. This value is used in headings and labels.

Confidence Level (B4)

The confidence level determines the probability used to set the range for the adjusted prediction.

Anomaly Detection (B5)

The application calculates the probability that the actual value for the day is an anomaly. This user-set value is used to decide if the current value should be ignored.

HourlyDist (E2:K12)

This area contains the expected work distribution during the day. It uses an 11-hour workday, but any number of divisions is possible. For each day of the week, several weeks of hourly data were used to determine what percentage of the daily calls arrived during each hour. This table contains that distribution, and is used to generate the hourly forecasts.

Periods (D2:D12)

These are the labels for the items in HourlyDist. In the sample data they are hours taken on the half hour.

The Named Values on the Workarea Sheet

The first part of the Workarea sheet is shown in Figure 3-11.

The Workarea sheet contains all the logic. The named values from this sheet are described in Table 3-3.

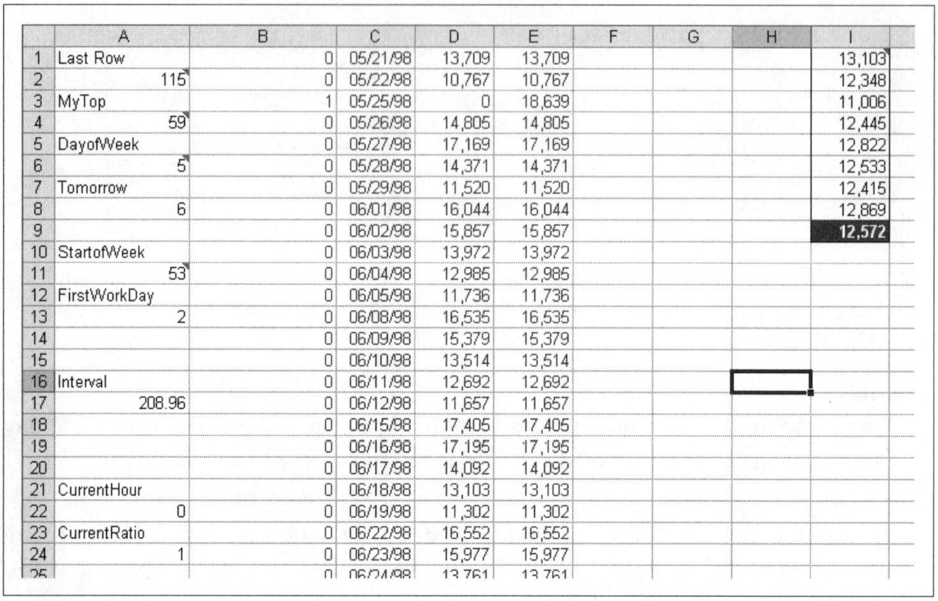

	A	B	C	D	E	F	G	H	I
1	Last Row	0	05/21/98	13,709	13,709				13,103
2	115	0	05/22/98	10,767	10,767				12,348
3	MyTop	1	05/25/98	0	18,639				11,006
4	59	0	05/26/98	14,805	14,805				12,445
5	DayofWeek	0	05/27/98	17,169	17,169				12,822
6	5	0	05/28/98	14,371	14,371				12,533
7	Tomorrow	0	05/29/98	11,520	11,520				12,415
8	6	0	06/01/98	16,044	16,044				12,869
9		0	06/02/98	15,857	15,857				12,572
10	StartofWeek	0	06/03/98	13,972	13,972				
11	53	0	06/04/98	12,985	12,985				
12	FirstWorkDay	0	06/05/98	11,736	11,736				
13	2	0	06/08/98	16,535	16,535				
14		0	06/09/98	15,379	15,379				
15		0	06/10/98	13,514	13,514				
16	Interval	0	06/11/98	12,692	12,692				
17	208.96	0	06/12/98	11,657	11,657				
18		0	06/15/98	17,405	17,405				
19		0	06/16/98	17,195	17,195				
20		0	06/17/98	14,092	14,092				
21	CurrentHour	0	06/18/98	13,103	13,103				
22	0	0	06/19/98	11,302	11,302				
23	CurrentRatio	0	06/22/98	16,552	16,552				
24	1	0	06/23/98	15,977	15,977				
25		0	06/24/98	13,761	13,761				

Figure 3-11. The Workarea sheet

Table 3-3. Descriptions of the named values from the Workarea sheet

Named value	Formula	Description
`Last_Row` (cell A2)	`={MAX((ROW(Data!B1:B2000)*(Data!B1:B2000<>"")))}`	This is the row number of the last row used on the Data sheet. It is an array formula that multiplies row numbers by a truth value (1 or 0) that is 0 if the cell in that row is empty. This value is used to locate the part of the Data sheet to be used and to determine what row to put new data on.
`MyTop` (cell A4)	`=Last_Row-56`	The calculations require 56 days of data. This value is one row above the first row to be used on the Data sheet. It is one row above so that a formula using this value can be filled down. It controls the row numbers of data being linked between the Data and Workarea sheets.
`DayofWeek` (cell A6)	`=WEEKDAY(C56)`	Dates from the Data sheet are in column C. Since 56 rows are used, the last day entered will be in C56. This formula gives the day of the week for the last day entered. The application displays predictions for this week and next week. To do this it has to be able to find the row with the first workday of the week. DayofWeek is used in these calculations and for display.

Table 3-3. Descriptions of the named values from the Workarea sheet (continued)

Named value	Formula	Description
FirstWorkDay (cell A13)	={MIN(WEEKDAY(C49:C56))}	In the sample data the work week starts on Monday. But a workweek could start on any day. The application uses the minimum value of WEEKDAY over eight days to determine what day the workweek starts on. The value is also used to find the beginning of the current weeks.
StartofWeek (cell A11)	=56-((DayofWeek-FirstWorkDay))	This is the row where the current week starts on the Workarea sheet. It is used in week-related formulas.
Interval (cell A17)	={CONFIDENCE(1-Confidence_Level,STDEV(G37:G56-D37:D56),20)}	This is the confidence interval for the adjusted prediction. It is an array formula. Column G contains the adjusted predictions and column D the actual values. The sample size is 20. Confidence_Level is a named value on the Setting sheet. Interval is a display item.
CurrentHour (cell A22)	={IF(SUM(T48:T58)<1,0,MAX((T48:T58>0)*ROW(T48:T58)))}	When the user enters hourly actual call volumes, they are linked to the T column on the Workarea sheet. The application adjusts the forecast during the day as hourly actuals are entered. CurrentHour keeps up with the entry of hourly information. It points to the last hour entered.
CurrentRatio (cell A24)	=IF(CurrentHour=0,1,INDIRECT("U"&A22)/INDIRECT("V"&A22))	This compares the expected volume to the volume for today (up to the current hour). The ratio tells if the day (so far) is high or low and by how much. This value is used to adjust the current day's hourly forecasts.
Prediction (cell I9)	=INT((SUM(I1:I8)-(MAX(I1:I8)+MIN(I1:I8)))/6)	This is the weekly prediction, the filtered average. It is based on the calculation area above it (I1:I8), which contains the actual values for the current day of the week for the last eight weeks. This value is copied to the D column on the Data sheet when new data is entered.
Anomaly (cell L43)	=IF(L42>=Anomaly_Detection,1,0)	This is the anomaly flag for the current actual value. It is the result of the calculation area above it (L38:L42). Anomaly_Detection is a user-set value on the Settings sheet. This value is copied to the A column on the Data sheet.
Adjusted Prediction (cell G57)	=IF(F56=0,"",F57*((1+(E56/F56))/2))	This is the adjusted prediction for the current day. The weekly prediction for this day (F57) is multiplied by half the error ratio for the previous day. This value is copied to the E column on the Data sheet.

Named Ranges on Workarea

In this section we look at the named ranges on Workarea. Each area manages a set of data and calculations for one piece of the logic. They also arrange the data to fit the needs of the display sheet.

This part of Workarea is shown in Figure 3-12.

H	I	J	K	L	M	N	O	P	Q
	13,103								
	12,348					ThisWeek			
	11,006			1	Monday	08/03/98	16,875	16,265	15,865
	12,445			1	Tuesday	08/04/98	16,171	15,687	16,033
	12,822			1	Wednesday	08/05/98	13,729	13,670	15,083
	12,533			1	Thursday	08/06/98	12,542	13,160	12,869
	12,415			1	Friday	08/07/98	10,882	11,024	0
	12,869			0			0		
Preditction	12,572			0			0		
				Eight weeks of values for the current day of the week					
						NextWeek			
						08/10/98	16,809		
						08/11/98	16,280		
						08/12/98	13,842		
						08/13/98	12,572		
						08/14/98	0		

Figure 3-12. Thisweek and Nextweek

ThisWeek (M3:Q9)

This area contains the day of the week, date, weekly prediction, adjusted prediction, and actual value for each day of the current week. The calculation area in column L is a set of flags that tell which days are in use. The basic formula in this area is =IF(L3=1,INDIRECT("workarea!C" & StartofWeek + ROW(A1)-1),""). A reference to a cell is built inside the INDIRECT function. It starts as a literal specifying the Workarea sheet's column C. It uses StartofWeek and a row number to get the correct row. This formula fills down. Data is pulled from columns C, F, G, and D. The formula in column M, =IF(L3=1,TEXT(WEEKDAY(N3),"dddd"),""), returns the name of the day of the week. The WEEKDAY function returns a number, and the TEXT function translates the number into the day of the week.

NextWeek (N15:O21)

This area contains the dates and weekly predictions for next week. It uses the same basic technique as ThisWeek. The formula is =IF(L3=1,INDIRECT("workarea!C" & Lag + StartofWeek + ROW(A1)-1),""). The only difference is that Lag is added to StartofWeek.

HourlyNextWeek (Z20:AG31)

These are the hourly forecasts for the whole week. This area is displayed on the Hourly sheet. The calculation area to the left links to the HourlyDist area on Settings. The values in S20:Y20 are the weekly predictions for each of the seven days of the current week. To get the hourly forecast, the prediction for the day is multiplied by the distribution value for each hour of the day.

Figure 3-13 contains the HourlyNextWeek part of the Workarea sheet.

							HourlyNextWeek						
0	16875	16171	13729	12542	10882	0	Sunday	Monday	Tuesday	Wednesday	Thursday	Friday	Saturday
0	0.03102	0.040952	0.037551	0.035409	0.040785	0	7:30	0	523	662	515	444	443	0
0	0.072252	0.094491	0.081134	0.075831	0.083451	0	8:30	0	1219	1528	1113	951	908	0
0	0.093715	0.11194	0.104503	0.102436	0.106373	0	9:30	0	1581	1810	1434	1284	1157	0
0	0.10733	0.124467	0.122103	0.119256	0.122759	0	10:30	0	1811	2012	1676	1495	1335	0
0	0.106624	0.116518	0.111733	0.114839	0.113231	0	11:30	0	1799	1884	1533	1440	1232	0
0	0.105455	0.104304	0.108432	0.109232	0.111107	0	12:30	0	1779	1686	1488	1369	1209	0
0	0.122718	0.112581	0.120613	0.121888	0.119947	0	13:30	0	2070	1820	1655	1528	1305	0
0	0.129346	0.107272	0.110491	0.116936	0.109205	0	14:30	0	2182	1734	1516	1466	1188	0
0	0.108088	0.092776	0.099011	0.098599	0.093951	0	15:30	0	1823	1500	1359	1236	1022	0
0	0.080511	0.062129	0.067858	0.068543	0.065082	0	16:30	0	1358	1004	931	859	708	0
0	0.04294	0.032571	0.036572	0.03703	0.034109	0	17:30	0	724	526	502	464	371	0

Figure 3-13. HourlyNextWeek

Hours (R48:S58)

Times and hourly predictions for the current day are in this range. This works like HourlyNextWeek, but it is only for the current day. So, it has to find the right column in Settings. The formula is `=INDIRECT("Settings!" & ADDRESS(ROW(A2),DayofWeek+4))`. Here the Settings sheet is the target, but both the row and column are calculated. The `ADDRESS` function inside of an `INDIRECT` provides the flexibility to read from any row or column. 4 is added to `DayofWeek` because the hourly distribution value starts in the fifth column of Settings.

AdjustedHourly (W48:W58)

This area contains the adjusted hourly forecast for the current day. It works with Hours to build the hourly area on the Display sheet. As the user enters actual hourly values, they appear in column T. Column U keeps a running total for the day and column V does the same for the predicted hourly values. CurrentRatio contains the total volume entered so far divided by the expected volume for the same hours. The hourly forecasts are adjusted by multiplying them by CurrentRatio.

Figure 3-14 shows the part of Workarea that deals with the hourly calculations.

Weekly (H60:H63)

The values in this area give the average weekly prediction error and error percentage over the last 20 days. It also contains the average number of daily calls during that period.

	Hours					AdjustedHourly
0.035409	7:30	390	0	0	390	390
0.075831	8:30	835	0	0	1225	835
0.102436	9:30	1129	0	0	2354	1129
0.119256	10:30	1314	0	0	3668	1314
0.114839	11:30	1265	0	0	4933	1265
0.109232	12:30	1204	0	0	6137	1204
0.121888	13:30	1343	0	0	7480	1343
0.116936	14:30	1289	0	0	8769	1289
0.098599	15:30	1086	0	0	9855	1086
0.068543	16:30	755	0	0	10610	755
0.03703	17:30	408	0	0	11018	408

Figure 3-14. Hours and AdjustedHourly

NextDay (H67:H75)

This is summary information about the current day. It gives the adjusted forecast, the confidence interval, the probability of anomaly, and the most recent adjusted forecast based on the hourly actual values.

Adjusted (J60:J61)

This is the 20 day average error and error percent for the adjusted forecast.

The part of Workarea that handles the error calculations is shown in Figure 3-15.

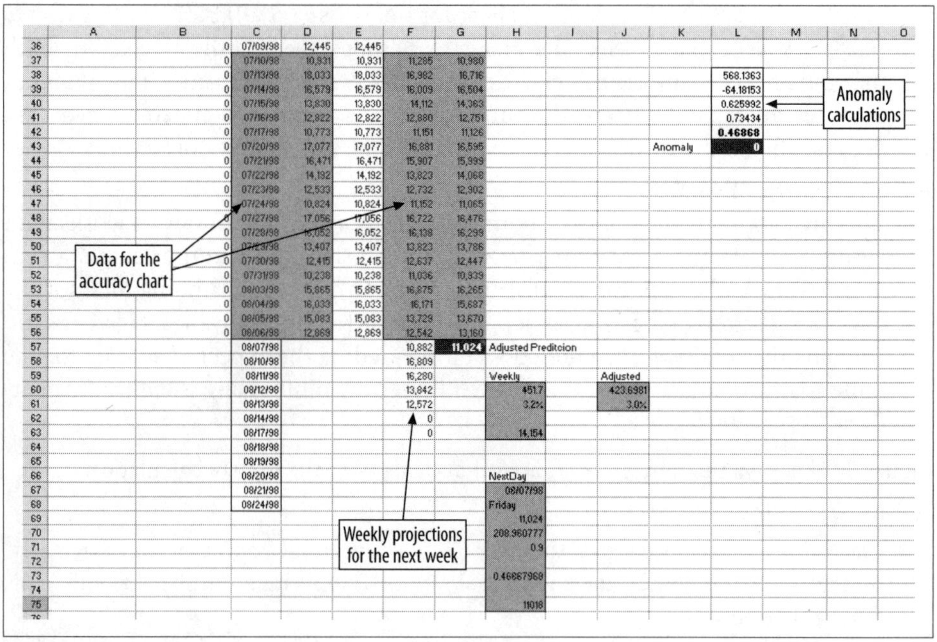

Figure 3-15. Areas and Links on Workarea

Other Important Links on Workarea

(C37:D56) & (F37:G56)

These ranges link to the chart on the AccuracyChart sheet, and link back to the Data sheet.

(T48:T85)

This area links to H7:H17 on the Display sheet. This is where the user enters the actual hourly values. This information feeds the calculations that adjust the hourly forecasts as the day progresses.

Linking to the Data

We now know what the Workarea sheet has to do. It is time to build the logic. The first step is to link the Workarea to the data on the Data sheet. To handle all the possible lags and days of the week, the INDIRECT function is used. The calculations use eight weeks of history and there can be up to seven workdays in a week. So, 56 days of history must be available.

The Last_Row named cell on the Workarea sheet contains the row number of the last row used on the Data sheet. The application needs to start 55 rows above the last row. MyTop contains the starting row number. The data starts in cell B1. The formula is =INDIRECT("Data!A" & MyTop + ROW(A1)). It references column A on the Data sheet. Note that MyTop points to the cell one row above the first one needed. This allows the formula to be copied down. Row(A1) is added to MyTop. Row(A1) is one, but as the formula copies down A1 becomes A2, A3, etc. This gives the correct row for each value. The cells in columns C and D work the same way. The three columns are filled down to row 56.

Column E masks anomalies. If the anomaly flag is set in column B, the actual value for that day is ignored, and the value from the previous week is substituted. The formula is =IF(B1=0,D1,INDIRECT("Data!C" & (MyTop + ROW(A1)-Lag))). This also fills down to row 56. This is the value used in the prediction calculation.

Predictions from the last 20 days are used for several calculations and for a chart. So, we need to bring them onto Workarea. The weekly predictions are in the range F37:F63 and the adjusted predictions are in G37:G56. These cells use the same formula as in columns B, C, and D, but reference a different column on the Data sheet. The weekly predictions in column F fill down to 63 because we are predicting a week into the future.

These formulas keep Workarea linked to the Data sheet. When new information is added to the Data sheet, Workarea automatically updates, and all of the values are ready to use.

Visual Basic

This application uses Visual Basic for Applications (VBA). VBA is a powerful tool and is easily over-used. In general, it is best to do as much as possible on the workbook and only use VBA for things that Excel cannot do. The code is in Module One (the default module for a spreadsheet) and can be viewed using the Visual Basic Editor. To reach the editor, select Tools → Macro → Visual Basic Editor. You can also launch the editor by pressing Alt-F11.

VBA is not necessary for the application to work. The most complex VBA operation is adding a new day's data, and that can be done manually by going to the bottom of the Data sheet and typing the values in. In this application VBA is used for three things.

First, for navigation, there are buttons on the sheets that move the user between sheets and ensure the view is set to the top left corner. This works like the sheet tabs, but gives flexibility in securing the application and helps make the application a complete package. Navigation code looks like this.

```
Sub AccuracyChart( )

'******************
' Navigation
' This macro takes the user to
' the AccuracyChart worksheet and selects
' cell A1.
'******************

Sheets("AccuracyChart").Select
Range("A1").Select
End Sub
```

This code only does two things. It selects the sheet and then it selects cell A1.

Next, this macro adds a new day to the Data sheet. This can easily be modified to use an automated data source such as an SQL database. The variable NewActual could be populated by any method. This may look like a fairly involved routine, but actually it merely moves data around. All the calculations are done by Excel.

```
Sub AddDay( )

'****************************************
' This routine allows the user to
' enter the actual for the next day.
' The entry is checked and if it
' is valid the new data is moved to the
' Data sheet.
'****************************************

Dim myItem As String
Dim myDate As Date
Dim NewActual As Variant
```

```
Dim NextRow As Integer
Dim Anomaly As Double
Dim Prediction As Integer
Dim AdjustedPrediction As Integer
Dim TheLag As Integer

myItem = Range("Item").Value          ' Read the item from Settings
myDate = Range("workarea!c57").Value  ' Get the next date

' Use an input box to allow the user to enter the next actual
NewActual = InputBox("Please enter the number of " & LCase(myItem) & _
" for " & myDate & ".", "Enter Actual", 0)

' If cancel or no entry quit
If NewActual = "0" Or NewActual = "" Then Exit Sub
If Not IsNumeric(NewActual) Then            ' Is the value a number?
    MsgBox ("The Actual must be a number.") ' If not put up a message
    Exit Sub                                ' and quit
End If
If Val(NewActual) < 0 Then           ' Is the value less than zero?
    MsgBox ("The Actual cannot be negative.")
    Exit Sub
End If

' Is the value not an integer?
If Val(NewActual) <> Int(Val(NewActual)) Then
    MsgBox ("The Actual must be an integer.")
    Exit Sub
End If
NextRow = Range("Last_row").Value + 1  ' Get the row number of the next
                                       ' row on the Data sheet
Range("data!b" & NextRow).Value = myDate     ' put the new date on the sheet
Range("data!c" & NextRow).Value = NewActual ' put the new actual on the sheet
TheLag = Range("Lag").Value  ' get the lag from Settings

' Prediction will update when the new actual is put on the Data sheet
Prediction = Range("Prediction").Value

' Anomaly will also update automatically
Anomaly = Range("Anomaly").Value

' The anomaly goes on the Data sheet next
' since it is used as part of the calculation
' of the adjusted forecast
Range("data!a" & NextRow).Value = Anomaly

' get the adjusted forecast
AdjustedPrediction = Range("AdjustedPrediction").Value

' The weekly prediction goes one lag down from the current day
Range("data!d" & NextRow + TheLag).Value = Prediction

' the adjusted prediction is put on the next row
Range("data!e" & NextRow + 1).Value = AdjustedPrediction
```

```
' clear the area where the hourly actuals are entered
Range("h7:h17").ClearContents
Range("a1").Select ' select A1
End Sub
```

The last macro allows the user to delete the data for the last day entered. This provides a simple editing capability. All this does is find the cells populated when the last day was entered then selects and clears them.

```
Sub DeleteDay()

'*****************************************
' This sub deletes the last day. All that is
' necessary is to remove the last entry from
' the Data sheet.
'*****************************************

Dim LastRow As Integer
Dim TheLag As Integer

LastRow = Range("Last_row").Value  ' First we need to know where the
                                   ' last row is. The number of the
                                   ' last row used on the data sheet
                                   ' is in a named cell on the workarea
                                   ' sheet. This statement stores the
                                   ' row number in a variable called
                                   ' LastRow
Sheets("data").Select  ' All of the data to be deleted is on the
                       ' the data sheet. So we start by selecting
                       ' that sheet.
' The data is in columns A-E. We need only build a reference to
' the cells and clear the contents.
' For columns A,B, and C the data
' to be deleted is in LastRow. So,
' we can clear them at the same time.
Range("data!a" & LastRow & ":c" & LastRow).ClearContents
TheLag = Range("Lag")     ' To determine the row of the last
                          ' weekly prediction we need to know the
                          ' lag. Lag is a named cell on the Settings
                          ' sheet.

' This section deletes the last weekly
' prediction. It is one Lag below the
' LastRow.
Range("data!d" & LastRow + TheLag).ClearContents

' The last adjusted prediction is one
' row below LastRow
Range("data!e" & LastRow + 1).ClearContents
Sheets("display").Select      ' Return to the Display sheet
Range("h7:h17").ClearContents  ' clear the area where the
    ' hourly actuals are entered.
Range("a1").Select
End Sub
```

With Workarea and the VBA complete, it is time to build the application's user interface.

Formatting

Formatting in this application uses mainly backgrounds and borders. However, there is some conditional formatting on the Display sheet. In the ranges G23:J28 and M23:M28, the number of rows that will contain data varies with the number of workdays in the week. Therefore, a conditional format is set to include those cells in the display if they are used and to gray them out if they are not.

The hourly sheet is just patterns and borders, as shown in Figure 3-16.

Hourly Forecasts for the Week Starting Monday 08/24/1998							
	Sunday	Monday	Tuesday	Wednesday	Thursday	Friday	Saturday
7:30		511	660	522	442	440	
8:30		1,191	1,524	1,129	948	900	
9:30		1,545	1,805	1,454	1,281	1,147	
10:30		1,770	2,007	1,700	1,491	1,324	
11:30		1,758	1,879	1,555	1,436	1,221	
12:30		1,739	1,682	1,509	1,366	1,198	
13:30		2,024	1,816	1,679	1,524	1,294	
14:30		2,133	1,730	1,538	1,462	1,178	
15:30		1,782	1,496	1,378	1,233	1,013	
16:30		1,328	1,002	944	857	702	
17:30		708	525	509	463	368	

| Return |

Figure 3-16. Hourly Sheet

This sheet may be over-formatted, but it shows how metaphor can imply function and guide user expectations.

Running the Application

The application was written using Excel 2002. It uses no third party software. There are some formatting issues if it is run in Excel 95, but all the logic works even in that older version of the software.

Start by opening the application to the Display sheet. In the Next Day area on the left, the value for Current Adjusted is 11,024. That is the adjusted prediction for the current day. The hourly forecasts for the first three hours are 390, 835, and 1,129. Suppose that the actual call counts for those hours are 500, 1,000, and 1,300. In Figure 3-17, in item 1 those volumes have been entered as the actuals for those hours. In item 2, the Hourly Chart is now showing that the day is higher than the forecast. If the first three hours are higher than expected, in this case about 19% higher, we would expect the rest of the day to be high as well. The Current Adjusted has increased to 13,106. In the Hourly Forecasts area the adjusted hourly forecasts have also been increased.

The main display is described in Figure 3-17.

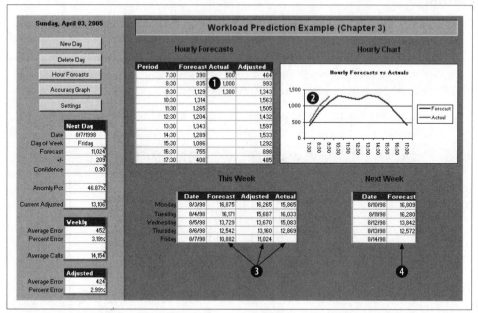

Figure 3-17. Using the Display Sheet

The current day is Friday 9/7/1998. That is the day in the Next Day area on the left. In the This Week area the full current week is shown. Item 3 points to the current day. The Forecast and Adjusted cells are filled in because they are predictions. Actual is blank since this is the day that is now working. In item 4, the Forecast for next Friday is not filled in. This is because we are predicting a week out and cannot predict next Friday until the Actual for this Friday is entered.

Use the Hour Forecast button to view the hourly predictions for the current week. The Accuracy Graph button displays a chart showing the weekly predictions, the adjusted predictions, and the actual values for the last 20 days.

The sample data ends on 8/6/98. The next week of call volumes is:

    10,864
    14,711
    14,977
    13,255
    11,972

Click the NewDay button and enter 10,864, the value for the next day. The display will update automatically. This is illustrated in Figure 3-18.

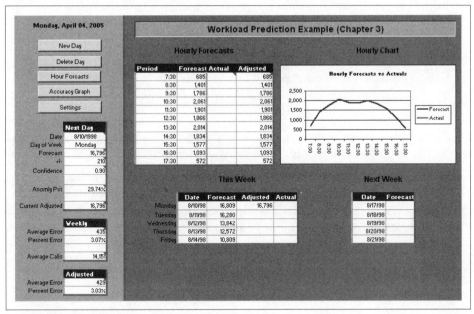

Figure 3-18. The Next Day

Monday 8/10/1998 is now the working day, and all the viewing areas are reset to the beginning of the week. The Delete Day button will remove the last entered day from the application. So if you mistyped 10,864 or just want to go back to Friday, press Delete Day.

 The application is just an Excel workbook, so when new data is entered it is important to save changes just as you would with any Excel project.

Customizing the Application

To use the application with your data, the Data sheet should be cleared, and 56 days of dates and actual volumes should be pasted into columns B and C starting in row 2. Row 1 contains headings. Change the Settings sheet for the heading, item, lag, and sensitivity as needed. It will take one more full cycle of data for all the features to populate. It is easiest to enter this week using the AddDay macro, but the values can be typed directly into the Data sheet.

The application is self-contained, and needs no other software except Excel. Later in the book we look at more advanced prediction techniques that could be incorporated into this project by changing the Workarea sheet. It is possible to enhance the application in many ways:

- A staffing model could be built by adding a new worksheet and some new logic on Workarea. A new entry for units of work per day can be added to Settings and used to calculate required staff.

- The AddDay macro could be enhanced to update the HourlyDist range on Settings. This would keep the expected hourly work distribution current.

- The Accuracy Chart could be replaced with a Pivot Chart, allowing prediction accuracy to be analyzed in more detail.

- The Display sheet can be reformatted and information elements can be moved by Cut and Paste. Changing the information elements themselves is more complex and requires changes to the Workarea.

The key to successfully modifying the application is to follow the conventions. Keep the logic on Workarea. If you need to introduce a new data item put it on the Data sheet. New parameters go on Settings. Be sure to name everything you use.

CHAPTER 4

Modeling

In the last chapter we used the past to predict the future. This works well for simple situations, but things are often more complicated. Most things depend on other things. Forecasting stock prices, credit scoring, predicting the weather, and designing a direct mail campaign all depend on independent data that influences the thing being predicted. If you want to predict tomorrow's weather in Chicago, you have to consider today's weather further west. They are connected.

In this chapter we look at using Excel to model a complex situation. We consider selecting independent data items and preparing them for use. It is not always easy to decide what value to predict, so we examine this process. Finally, we go through the steps and techniques needed to build a working model.

Regression

For more complex kinds of problems, a technique called regression is used. Excel has a regression tool from Tools → Data Analysis → Regression. If Data Analysis is not showing up on the Tools menu, select Add-Ins and check Analysis ToolPak.

The first example predicts a stock price. We have 223 days of technical data for a stock including the opening price, the high, the low, the closing price, and the volume for each day. We predict tomorrow's closing price using this information.

We build a model using regression. But we will need a way to know if our model is any good. So, we start by making a simple prediction. Then we can compare the accuracy of our model to the simple prediction. If our model is not more accurate than the simple prediction, it does not add any value and we might as well just use the simple prediction. For the simple prediction, we assume the closing stock price tomorrow will be the same as today's closing price. Figure 4-1 shows the setup.

The array formula in cell I7 gives the average error amount for the prediction. On average we are off by about $0.46 everyday. But we have six pieces of information about the stock, not just the closing price, so next we make the prediction using all six.

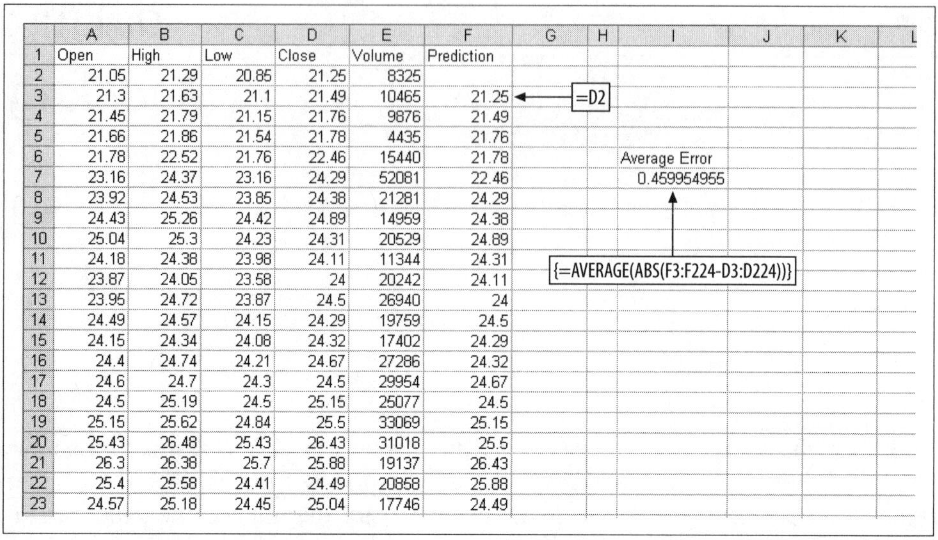

Figure 4-1. A simple prediction

In Figure 4-1, cell H3 contains `=D2`, and cell I7 shows the Average Error value 0.459954955 computed with `{=AVERAGE(ABS(F3:F224-D3:D224))}`.

	A	B	C	D	E	F	I
1	Open	High	Low	Close	Volume	Prediction	
2	21.05	21.29	20.85	21.25	8325		
3	21.3	21.63	21.1	21.49	10465	21.25	
4	21.45	21.79	21.15	21.76	9876	21.49	
5	21.66	21.86	21.54	21.78	4435	21.76	
6	21.78	22.52	21.76	22.46	15440	21.78	Average Error
7	23.16	24.37	23.16	24.29	52081	22.46	0.459954955
8	23.92	24.53	23.85	24.38	21281	24.29	
9	24.43	25.26	24.42	24.89	14959	24.38	
10	25.04	25.3	24.23	24.31	20529	24.89	
11	24.18	24.38	23.98	24.11	11344	24.31	
12	23.87	24.05	23.58	24	20242	24.11	
13	23.95	24.72	23.87	24.5	26940	24	
14	24.49	24.57	24.15	24.29	19759	24.5	
15	24.15	24.34	24.08	24.32	17402	24.29	
16	24.4	24.74	24.21	24.67	27286	24.32	
17	24.6	24.7	24.3	24.5	29954	24.67	
18	24.5	25.19	24.5	25.15	25077	24.5	
19	25.15	25.62	24.84	25.5	33069	25.15	
20	25.43	26.48	25.43	26.43	31018	25.5	
21	26.3	26.38	25.7	25.88	19137	26.43	
22	25.4	25.58	24.41	24.49	20858	25.88	
23	24.57	25.18	24.45	25.04	17746	24.49	

We assume all six metrics add some value to the prediction. Each metric is multiplied by a weight, and then they are added up. An additional value, called the intercept, is added to the sum to get the final prediction. Figure 4-2 below shows how the problem is set up in Excel.

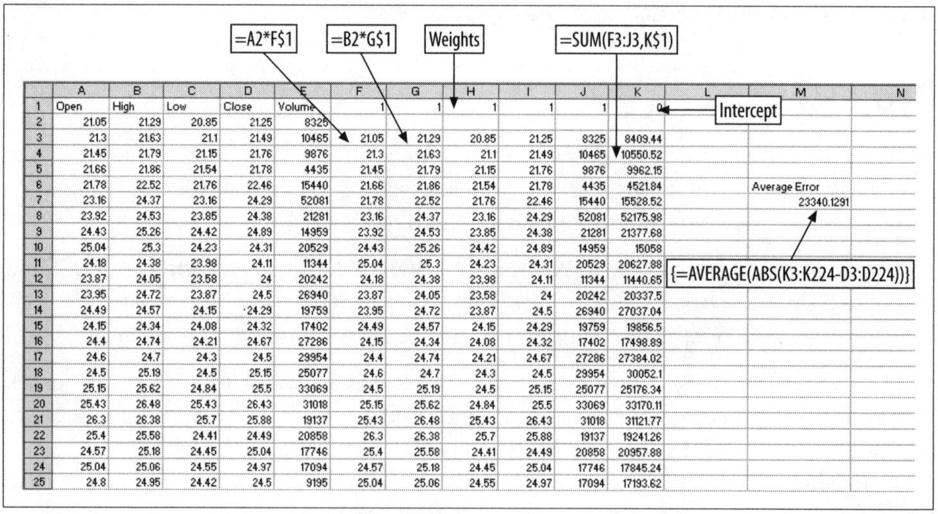

Figure 4-2. Setup for a regression model

In Figure 4-2, annotations show: `=A2*F$1`, `=B2*G$1`, Weights, `=SUM(F3:J3,K$1)`, Intercept (cell K1), and the Average Error `{=AVERAGE(ABS(K3:K224-D3:D224))}` = 23340.1291.

	A	B	C	D	E	F	G	H	I	J	K	M
1	Open	High	Low	Close	Volume	1	1	1	1	1	0	
2	21.05	21.29	20.85	21.25	8325							
3	21.3	21.63	21.1	21.49	10465	21.05	21.29	20.85	21.25	8325	8409.44	
4	21.45	21.79	21.15	21.76	9876	21.3	21.63	21.1	21.49	10465	10550.52	
5	21.66	21.86	21.54	21.78	4435	21.45	21.79	21.15	21.76	9876	9962.15	
6	21.78	22.52	21.76	22.46	15440	21.66	21.86	21.54	21.78	4435	4521.84	Average Error
7	23.16	24.37	23.16	24.29	52081	21.78	22.52	21.76	22.46	15440	15528.52	23340.1291
8	23.92	24.53	23.85	24.38	21281	23.16	24.37	23.16	24.29	52081	52175.98	
9	24.43	25.26	24.42	24.89	14959	23.92	24.53	23.85	24.38	21281	21377.68	
10	25.04	25.3	24.23	24.31	20529	24.43	25.26	24.42	24.89	14959	15058	
11	24.18	24.38	23.98	24.11	11344	25.04	25.3	24.23	24.31	20529	20627.88	
12	23.87	24.05	23.58	24	20242	24.18	24.38	23.98	24.11	11344	11440.65	
13	23.95	24.72	23.87	24.5	26940	23.87	24.05	23.58	24	20242	20337.5	
14	24.49	24.57	24.15	24.29	19759	23.95	24.72	23.87	24.5	26940	27037.04	
15	24.15	24.34	24.08	24.32	17402	24.49	24.57	24.15	24.29	19759	19856.5	
16	24.4	24.74	24.21	24.67	27286	24.15	24.34	24.08	24.32	17402	17498.89	
17	24.6	24.7	24.3	24.5	29954	24.4	24.74	24.21	24.67	27286	27384.02	
18	24.5	25.19	24.5	25.15	25077	24.6	24.7	24.3	24.5	29954	30052.1	
19	25.15	25.62	24.84	25.5	33069	24.5	25.19	24.5	25.15	25077	25176.34	
20	25.43	26.48	25.43	26.43	31018	25.15	25.62	24.84	25.5	33069	33170.11	
21	26.3	26.38	25.7	25.88	19137	25.43	26.48	25.43	26.43	31018	31121.77	
22	25.4	25.58	24.41	24.49	20858	26.3	26.38	25.7	25.88	19137	19241.26	
23	24.57	25.18	24.45	25.04	17746	25.4	25.58	24.41	24.49	20858	20957.88	
24	25.04	25.06	24.55	24.97	17094	24.57	25.18	24.45	25.04	17746	17845.24	
25	24.8	24.95	24.42	24.5	9195	25.04	25.06	24.55	24.97	17094	17193.62	

The formula in F3 multiplies the opening price in column A by the weight in cell F1. We start in row 3 because that is where we started in the calculations in Figure 4-1. This way we can compare the accuracy of the regression to the simpler method for exactly the same days. This formula fills right to column J, and down to the end of the data at row 224.

In cell K3, the weighted metrics are summed with the intercept. The value in K3 is the prediction. The weights are all 1, the intercept is 0, and the average error is a little on the high side. Next we set the weights and intercept using Excel's regression tool. When Regression is clicked on the Data Analysis sub-menu, the dialog in Figure 4-3 is displayed.

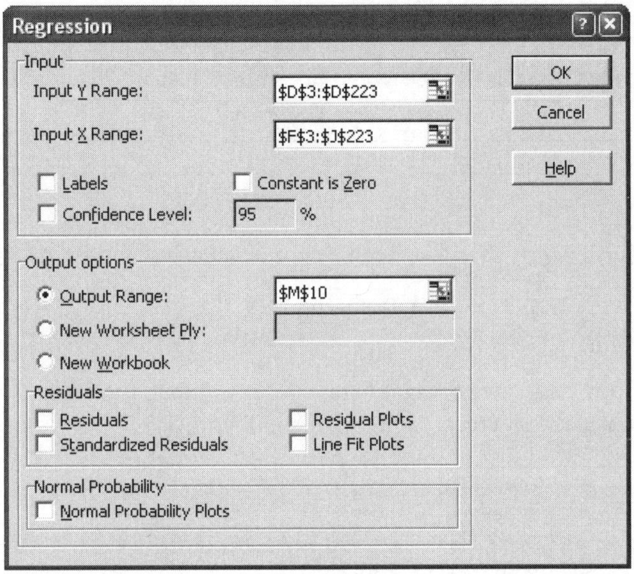

Figure 4-3. Regression dialog

The Input Y Range is the value we want to predict. Here it is the next day's closing stock price from Figure 4-2. The Input X Range contains the metrics used to make the prediction. The Output Range is selected as the output option and cell M10 is entered. This means that the Regression tool will put its output in a cell range starting at M10, as shown by the results in Figure 4-4.

In the Regression results, item 1, R Square, tells us the model has predictive ability. This value is always between 0 and 1. The higher the value the better, and 0.97666 is about as good as it gets. Item 2 is the intercept. Item 3 is the weight for the first metric, Opening Price. The other weights are below in the same column.

Item 4, P value, tells us how much importance each of the metrics has in the model. With this item, low values are good. The P Value for the first metric, Opening Price, is over 0.8. This is too high and suggests Opening Price is not adding much value to the prediction. So, it makes sense that the weight for opening prices is small, 0.048.

Figure 4-4.

SUMMARY OUTPUT

Regression Statistics	
Multiple R	0.988261893
R Square	0.976661568
Adjusted R Square	0.976118814
Standard Error	0.6267159
Observations	221

ANOVA

	df	SS	MS	F	Significance F
Regression	5	3533.884228	706.7768455	1799.454572	3.0442E-173
Residual	215	84.44615617	0.392772819		
Total	220	3618.330384			

	Coefficients	Standard Error	t Stat	P-value	Lower 95%	Upper 95%	Lower 95.0%	Upper 95.0%
Intercept	0.50470261	0.29581497	1.706142894	0.089425489	-0.078365534	1.087770754	-0.07836553	1.087770754
X Variable 1	0.048314657	0.195480372	0.247158608	0.805021329	-0.336988283	0.433617596	-0.33698828	0.433617596
X Variable 2	-0.364066136	0.235739501	-1.544357793	0.123972287	-0.828722111	0.100589839	-0.82872211	0.100589839
X Variable 3	0.302087282	0.232303638	1.300398412	0.194856656	-0.155796411	0.759970975	-0.15579641	0.759970975
X Variable 4	1.002684341	0.20525407	4.885086172	2.01773E-06	0.598116887	1.407251795	0.598116887	1.407251795
X Variable 5	4.413E-06	3.25582E-06	1.355420551	0.176705782	-2.0044E-06	1.08304E-05	-2.0044E-06	1.08304E-05

Figure 4-4. Regression results

The best metric is variable 4, the Closing Price. It has a P value of 0.000002 and has the highest weight.

Next we use Copy and Paste Special (Transpose) to move the weights to the model, and copy and paste the intercept. This results in Figure 4-5.

Figure 4-5.

	A Open	B High	C Low	D Close	E Volume	F 0.048315	G -0.364066	H 0.302087	I 1.002684	J 4.41E-06	K 0.504703	L	M
2	21.05	21.29	20.85	21.25	8325								
3	21.3	21.63	21.1	21.49	10465	1.017024	-7.750968	6.29852	21.30704	0.036738	21.41306		
4	21.45	21.79	21.15	21.76	9876	1.029102	-7.874751	6.374042	21.54769	0.046182	21.62696		
5	21.66	21.86	21.54	21.78	4435	1.036349	-7.933001	6.389146	21.81841	0.043583	21.85919		
6	21.78	22.52	21.76	22.46	15440	1.046495	-7.958486	6.50696	21.83846	0.019572	21.95771		Average Error
7	23.16	24.37	23.16	24.29	52081	1.052094	-8.198769	6.573419	22.52029	0.068137	22.52007		0.448322743
8	23.92	24.53	23.85	24.38	21281	1.118967	-8.872292	6.996341	24.3552	0.229834	24.33276		
9	24.43	25.26	24.42	24.89	14959	1.155687	-8.930542	7.204782	24.44544	0.093913	24.47399		
10	25.04	25.3	24.23	24.31	20529	1.180327	-9.196311	7.376971	24.95681	0.066014	24.88852		
11	24.18	24.38	23.98	24.11	11344	1.209799	-9.210873	7.319575	24.37526	0.090595	24.28905		
12	23.87	24.05	23.58	24	20242	1.168248	-8.875932	7.244053	24.17472	0.050061	24.26585		
13	23.95	24.72	23.87	24.29	26940	1.153271	-8.755791	7.123218	24.06442	0.089328	24.17915		
14	24.49	24.57	24.15	24.29	19759	1.157136	-8.999715	7.210823	24.56577	0.118886	24.5576		
15	24.15	24.34	24.08	24.32	17402	1.183226	-8.945105	7.295408	24.3552	0.087197	24.48063		
16	24.4	24.74	24.21	24.67	27286	1.166799	-8.86137	7.274262	24.38528	0.076795	24.54647		
17	24.6	24.7	24.3	24.5	29954	1.178878	-9.006996	7.313533	24.73622	0.120413	24.84675		
18	24.5	25.19	24.5	25.15	25077	1.188541	-8.992434	7.340721	24.56577	0.132187	24.73948		
19	25.15	25.62	24.84	25.5	33069	1.183709	-9.170826	7.401138	25.21751	0.110665	25.2469		
20	25.43	26.48	25.43	26.43	31018	1.215114	-9.327374	7.503848	25.56845	0.145934	25.61067		
21	26.3	26.38	25.7	25.88	19137	1.228642	-9.640471	7.68208	26.50095	0.136882	26.41278		
22	25.4	25.58	24.41	24.49	20858	1.270675	-9.604065	7.763643	25.94947	0.084452	25.96888		
23	24.57	25.18	24.45	25.04	17746	1.227192	-9.312812	7.373951	24.55574	0.092046	24.44082		
24	25.04	25.06	24.55	24.97	17094	1.187091	-9.167185	7.386034	25.10722	0.078313	25.09617		
25	24.8	24.95	24.42	24.5	9195	1.209799	-9.123497	7.416243	25.03703	0.075436	25.11971		
26	24.32	24.84	24.32	24.67	21782	1.198203	-9.08345	7.376971	24.56577	0.040578	24.60277		
27	24.7	24.73	24.25	24.6	21069	1.175012	-9.043403	7.346763	24.73622	0.096124	24.81542		
28	24.35	24.73	24.2	24.56	18862	1.193372	-9.003356	7.325617	24.66603	0.092978	24.77935		
29	24.6	25.09	24.55	25.04	30360	1.176462	-9.003356	7.310512	24.62593	0.083238	24.69749		
30	24.55	24.68	24.2	24.43	12062	1.188541	-9.134419	7.416243	25.10722	0.133979	25.21626		
31	24.31	24.68	24.31	24.65	10190	1.186125	-8.985152	7.310512	24.49558	0.05323	24.565		

Figure 4-5. Regression Model

The average error is \$0.448 per day. This is just a little better than the \$0.46 average error for the simple prediction, because the regression model is using more information. The six metrics working together do a better job.

But are these the best metrics? We have more past information and could consider how many days in a row the stock has been up or down, where the price is with respect to the 50 day moving average, or any number of other things. Selecting good metrics is critical.

Regression assumes the relationships are linear. What if they aren't? Are we sure that tomorrow's closing price is the best thing to predict? Perhaps it is better to predict how much the stock price will change or whether it will move more than 2%. Some things are easier to predict, some metrics work better in a model. To make a good model you have to make good choices.

Understanding how to use regression is just the beginning. To go further, we'll use a different but analogous example.

Defining the Problem

We start with a question. Can we predict the results of a dog race? The first challenge is to figure out what the question means. We could predict which dog is most likely to win, or finish in the top two or three positions. We could predict the first and second dogs in a race. But predicting which dog will win may not be the point. The real issue is probably money. If we are looking at dog races, we want to know which bets are most likely to be profitable, so we need to predict how much a dog will pay along with its chances of winning.

We can build a model to predict this, but how will we know if the model is any good? In this case it's easy. If we can make a profit using the model, then it is good; otherwise, it is useless. If we build a credit scoring model, we have the same problem. It is not enough to identify accounts that are most risky. As a group these accounts may still be profitable, and a model would need to consider the impact to the bottom line, not just the level of risk. The same problem occurs when modeling stock prices. What do we really need to know? If we are trading options, we don't need to know the future price of the stock. All we need is the probability that it will trade above or below a price in a given period of time.

There is another important consideration here. Some things are easier to model than others. For example, if we try to build a model that predicts which dog will win in a race, we are trying to identify one winner out of eight dogs. When we look at the data there will be seven times more losers than winners. This makes modeling difficult. It is easier to get a good result when there is an even mix of outcomes in the data.

Next we consider the data used to build the model. What data is available? In most business situations there will be historical data. If we are modeling collections calls to increase dollars collected per call, we will need data on past collections calls and their outcomes. For stocks there is plenty of historical data available. With dog races, the data is on the racing form.

Which metrics are best at predicting the value we are interested in? Since we are looking at dog racing, presumably we want to know if a dog is in the habit of winning races. The racing form tells us how many races each dog has been in and how many first, second, and third places the dog has achieved.

It also has detailed information about each dog's last six races. From this information we take the number of first places the dog has out of the last six races and the fastest speed the dog has run in the last six races.

Perhaps starting position makes a difference. The dog in the first position starts on the inside and that could be an advantage. And what about experience? If a dog has run more races maybe they will have a better chance.

Racing forms are available on the Internet at several betting and track web sites. The report extracting macro explained in Chapter 9 was used to extract data from racing forms for 6,204 races. Each race has eight dogs so there are 52,032 rows of data, one for each dog.

Most of the data items come straight from the form, but in two cases some logic is involved. First is running speed. On the racing form the running time for each of the dog's last six races is given. But not all races are the same length. The distance for each race is given, so we could divide the distance by the time to get running speed. But converting race distances (as they appear on the form) into yards is difficult. There is an easier way.

We convert the running time to a ratio by dividing the dog's time by the average time for all dogs running that distance. The technique is shown in Figure 4-6.

We have a list of distances and average times taken from historical data in columns A and B of Figure 4-6. For each dog's last six races we have the distance and the time. We use the LOOKUP function to find the average time for a race of that distance and then divide the dog's time by the average time. In Figure 4-6, the dog has run a 550 yard race about 1% faster than average. This technique eliminates the need to understand data like the distance given as RP. It is probably a race course name, but knowing that still doesn't give us the distance in yards. Converting the times to ratios makes the actual distance unimportant.

This works for much more than dog races. If you are modeling a direct mail campaign, you might have response rates by ZIP code from previous mailings. This is good information but there are thousands of ZIP codes and, since ZIP codes have no numeric meaning, they cannot be used directly in a model. You can, however, substitute ratios for the ZIP codes and use the ratios in the model. This technique can convert most categorical items into metrics that can be used in a model.

	A	B	C	D	E	F	G	H
1	Distance	Average Time		Race Distance	550			
2	5-16	31.75729128		Race Time	31.02			
3	3-8	39.10262385		Average Time	31.30001	←	=LOOKUP(E1,A2:A16,B2:B16)	
4	7-16	44.99146678		Ratio	0.991054			
5	1650	31.98365854						
6	RP	30.83216179						
7	550	31.30000632			=E2/E3			
8	1699	33.20719972						
9	685	39.67822198						
10	583	33.37612768						
11	660	38.11767241						
12	3-16	17.52606154						
13	5/16	31.76225564						
14	2050	40.7087234						
15	PC	31.50127413						
16	KC	39.45375						
17								
18								
19								

Figure 4-6. Substituting a ratio

In our example, the ratios for the dog's six previous races are calculated and the lowest ratio (best time) is kept. We don't use an average because we are interested in how fast the dog can run under ideal conditions. The second calculated item is the number of first places the dog has scored out of the last six races. This is a number from zero to six.

The rest of the data comes straight from the racing form and is shown in Figure 4-7.

The race number in column A is just a number to keep the races separate. Next is the dog number, which is also the position number. Dog 1 starts on the inside next to the rail. Dog 8, on the outside, has the longest distance to run. Column C, Races, is the number of races the dog has run. A big number here means the dog is older and more experienced. Column D, Wins, is the total number of times the dog has come in first. Column E, WinCnt, is the number of races out of the last six the dog has won; this is a measure of how well the dog has done recently.

There are inconsistencies in this data. On row 28 in Figure 4-7 the data tells us the dog has won two out of its six most recent races, but Races for this dog is 0, meaning it has never been in a race. Modeling requires large amounts of data. In this example we have over 50,000 rows and before we are done we will wish we had more. Inconsistencies in data are a common problem. In this case some of the information, probably recorded by hand, is simply wrong. Our options are to eliminate suspicious rows or to use them. It is a judgment call, and in this case we will use what we have.

The BestSpeed column is the lowest ratio for the dog in its last six races. PlacePay is the amount the dog paid as a place bet. A place bet pays if the dog comes in first or

	A	B	C	D	E	F	G	H
1	Race	Dog	Races	Wins	WinCnt	BestSpeed	PlacePay	
2	1	1	21	2	0	1.0021923	0.00	
3	1	2	20	3	0	1.00339686	3.80	
4	1	3	14	1	0	0.99556723	0.00	
5	1	4	0	0	0	1.00972079	0.00	
6	1	5	18	1	0	1.00490256	0.00	
7	1	6	19	1	0	1.00159003	0.00	
8	1	7	20	1	0	0.99436268	0.00	
9	1	8	0	0	0	1.0067094	7.20	
10	2	1	14	3	2	0.97629431	3.80	
11	2	2	12	2	2	0.99044786	0.00	
12	2	3	1	0	0	0.99014672	0.00	
13	2	4	1	0	2	0.98291938	0.00	
14	2	5	21	3	1	0.99285698	0.00	
15	2	6	24	3	0	0.98713533	0.00	
16	2	7	19	2	0	0.98502735	6.00	
17	2	8	0	0	2	0.99165242	0.00	
18	3	1	1	0	1	0.99135128	0.00	
19	3	2	1	0	1	0.98261824	0.00	
20	3	3	1	0	1	0.97629431	5.00	
21	3	4	1	0	0	0.99677179	0.00	
22	3	5	20	2	0	0.98562963	0.00	
23	3	6	1	0	1	0.98502735	0.00	
24	3	7	22	6	1	0.97810114	0.00	
25	3	8	1	0	1	0.97599317	6.40	
26	4	1	15	2	0	1.00580598	0.00	
27	4	2	20	1	1	0.99135128	0.00	
28	4	3	0	0	2	1.00082359	2.40	
29	4	4	10	1	0	1.00430028	0.00	

Figure 4-7. Historical racing data

second, so there are two paid amounts in each race. In the first race a $2.00 bet on dog 3 paid $3.80 and on dog 8 it paid $7.20.

The problem is now defined: to predict the amount that a place bet will pay using the available data. Our model is a success if it results in an average payout above $2.00.

Refining Metrics

BestSpeed tells us how fast a dog can run, but not how that speed compares to the speeds of the other dogs in a race. There are eight dogs in each race and one is the fastest. We need a way to rank the dogs in each race by speed. We start by sorting the data by Race and BestSpeed, as in Figure 4-8.

We insert a column between BestSpeed and PlacePay and label it SpeedRank. For the first race we enter the numbers 1-8. Then in cell G9 we enter the formula =G2, and fill this formula down to the bottom of the data, as in the Figure 4-9. Next, Copy and Paste Special (Values) on the G column.

	A	B	C	D	E	F	G	H
1	Race	Dog	Races	Wins	WinCnt	BestSpeed	PlacePay	
2	1	1	21	2	0	1.0021923	0.00	
3	1	2	20	3	0	1.00339686	3.80	
4	1	3	14	1	0	0.99556723	0.00	
5	1	4	0	0	0	1.00972079	0.00	
6	1	5	18	1	0	1.00490256	0.00	
7	1	6	19	1	0	1.00159003	0.00	
8	1	7	20	1	0	0.99436268	0.00	
9	1	8	0	0	0	1.0067094	7.20	
10	2	1					3.80	
11	2	2					0.00	
12	2	3					0.00	
13	2	4					0.00	
14	2	5					0.00	
15	2	6					0.00	
16	2	7					6.00	
17	2	8					0.00	
18	3	1					0.00	
19	3	2					0.00	
20	3	3					5.00	
21	3	4					0.00	
22	3	5					0.00	
23	3	6					0.00	
24	3	7					0.00	
25	3	8					6.40	
26	4	1	15	2	0	1.00580598	0.00	
27	4	2	20	1	1	0.99135128	0.00	
28	4	3	0	0	2	1.00082359	2.40	
29	4	4	10	1	0	1.00430028	0.00	

Sort dialog:

Sort by: Race — Ascending / Descending

Then by: BestSpeed — Ascending / Descending

Then by: — Ascending / Descending

My list has: Header row / No header row

Options... | OK | Cancel

Figure 4-8. Sort each race by BestSpeed

We also need a ranking by how often the dogs win. For this we use the Races and Wins columns. We create a new column called WinRatio. The value is Wins divided by Races for each dog. If a dog has no races, we set this value to zero since we cannot divide by zero. We then sort by Races and WinRatio and build a WinRank column just as we built SpeedRank. The setup is shown in Figure 4-10.

Once the WinRank column is filled down and columns H and I are copied and pasted as values, the data is ready to use.

Analysis

We still do not know if the metrics can predict the payout. We hope the data can make the prediction, but we need more information about the relationships in the data. The Pivot Table tool makes it easy to explore these relationships. We select all rows for columns B thru J. Then we select PivotTable and PivotChart Report from the Data menu. The PivotTable dialog opens up, and we select Pivot Chart Report as in Figure 4-11.

Figure 4-9. Adding the SpeedRank column

	A Race	B Dog	C Races	D Wins	E WinCnt	F BestSpeed	G SpeedRank	H PlacePay
2	1	7	20	1	0	0.99436268	1	0.00
3	1	3	14	1	0	0.99556723	2	0.00
4	1	6	19	1	0	1.00159003	3	0.00
5	1	1	21	2	0	1.0021923	4	0.00
6	1	2	20	3	0	1.00339686	5	3.80
7	1	5	18	1	0	1.00490256	6	0.00
8	1	8	0	0	0	1.0067094	7	7.20
9	1	4	0	0	0	1.00972079	8	0.00
10	2	1	14	3	2	0.97629431	1	3.80
11	2	4	1	0	2	0.98291938	2	0.00
12	2	7	19	2	0	0.98502735		6.00
13	2	6	24	3	0	0.98713533	=G2	0.00
14	2	3	1	0	0	0.99014672		0.00
15	2	2	12	2	2	0.99044786		0.00
16	2	8	0	0	2	0.99165242		0.00
17	2	5	21	3	1	0.99285698		0.00
18	3	8	1	0	1	0.97599317		6.40
19	3	3	1	0	1	0.97629431		5.00
20	3	7	22	6	1	0.97810114		0.00
21	3	2	1	0	1	0.98261824		0.00
22	3	6	1	0	1	0.98502735		0.00
23	3	5	20	2	0	0.98562963		0.00

Figure 4-10. Adding the WinRank column

	A Race	B Dog	C Races	D Wins	E WinCnt	F BestSpeed	G SpeedRank	H WinRank	I WinRatio	J PlacePay	K	L
2	1	2	20	3	0	1.00339686	5	1	0.15	3.80		
3	1	1	21	2	0	1.0021923	4	2	0.0952381	0.90		
4	1	3	14	1	0	0.99556723	2	3	0.07142857	=IF(C2=0,0,D2/C2)		
5	1	5	18	1	0	1.00490256	6	4	0.05555556	0.00		
6	1	6	19	1	0	1.00159003	3	5	0.05263158	0.00		
7	1	7	20	1	0	0.99436268	1	6	0.05	0.00		
8	1	8	0	0	0	1.0067094	7	7	0	7.20		
9	1	4	0	0	0	1.00972079	8	8	0	0.00		
10	2	1	14	3	2	0.97629431	1	1	0.21428571	3.80		
11	2	2	12	2	2	0.99044786	6		0.16666667	0.00		
12	2	5	21	3	1	0.99285698	8		0.14285714	0.00		
13	2	6	24	3	0	0.98713533	4		0.125	0.00		
14	2	7	19	2	0	0.98502735	=H2 3		0.10526316	6.00		
15	2	4	1	0	2	0.98291938	2		0	0.00		
16	2	3	1	0	0	0.99014672	5		0	0.00		
17	2	8	0	0	2	0.99165242	7		0	0.00		
18	3	7	22	6	1	0.97810114	3		0.27272727	0.00		
19	3	5	20	2	0	0.98562963	6		0.1	0.00		
20	3	8	1	0	1	0.97599317	1		0	6.40		
21	3	3	1	0	1	0.97629431	2		0	5.00		
22	3	2	1	0	1	0.98261824	4		0	0.00		
23	3	6	1	0	1	0.98502735	5		0	0.00		
24	3	1	1	0	1	0.99135128	7		0	0.00		
25	3	4	1	0	0	0.99677179	8		0	0.00		

After Finish is clicked, the Pivot Chart is displayed. We are interested in the relationships between the payout and the other metrics. So, we drag PlacePay to the Data area in the center of the chart, labeled as Item 1 in Figure 4-12. By default the count

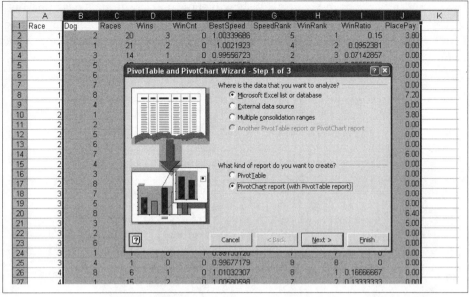

Figure 4-11. Setting up a Pivot Chart

of the data item, PlacePay, is displayed. We change to average by double-clicking on the Count of PlacePay button and selecting Average (Item 3). Next we drag Dog to the Category area at the bottom (Item 2).

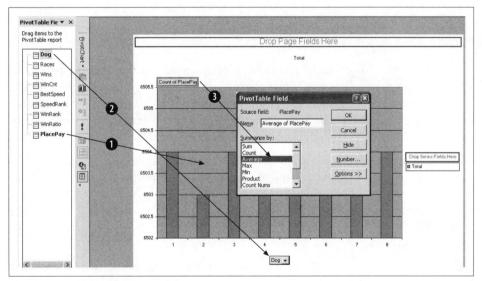

Figure 4-12. Configuring the Pivot Chart

This results in the chart in Figure 4-13, showing how post position relates to payout. On average, the dog in position 1 pays more. So, if you bet dogs running in position 1, you will lose less money. The minimum bet is $2.00, thus there is a profit if the average of PlacePay is more than $2.00.

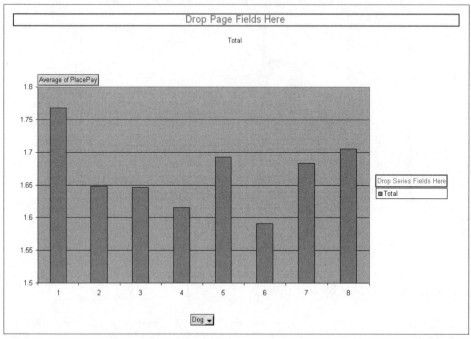

Figure 4-13. Post position and Payout

We use this chart to check the relationship between our metrics and the payout to find ones with the greatest predictive power. The metric Dog is dragged back to the list of metrics and the other metrics are dragged to the category box one by one. Races, Wins, and BestSpeed look odd because they have a large number of possible values. The metric that gives the best result is WinCnt, the number of wins out of the last six races.

In Figure 4-14, which displays WinCnt, there are two important pieces of information. First, there is a definite increase for values five and six. And second, this metric comes closest to making a profit. The bar for WinCnt five is above $1.90. Of all the metrics WinCnt is the most predictive and powerful. But it still cannot make a profitable betting decision.

WinCnt is our best metric. But how well does it predict the payout when combined with other metrics? To check, we change the chart. We drag Dog to the series area on the right side of the chart as shown in Item 1 of Figure 4-15. Then we right-click on the data region (Item 2), and select Chart Type from the dialog. We select Surface chart as shown.

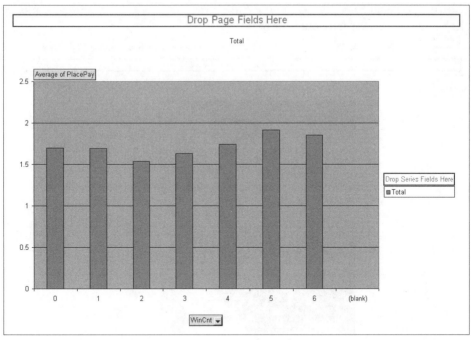

Figure 4-14. WinCnt and Payout

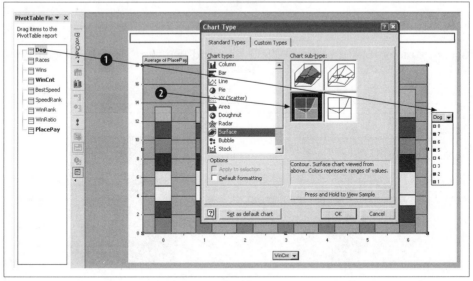

Figure 4-15. Setting up the surface chart

The result is Figure 4-16, and we see two regions of profitability; i.e., two areas where the average payout is over $2.00. The fact that there are two areas suggests that either we do not have enough data to get a good representation or the relationship between

WinCnt, Dog, and PlacePay is complex. Either way, we now know a profitable model can be built if we can figure out how to do it.

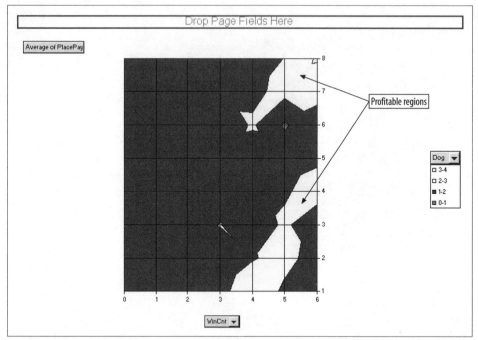

Figure 4-16. WinCnt and Dog have two profitable regions

Checking the other metrics with WinCnt we find two more, SpeedRank and Winrank, with profitable regions, as shown in Figure 4-17.

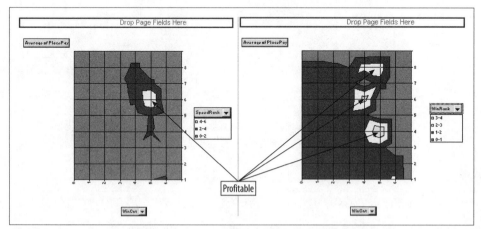

Figure 4-17. More profitable territory

Before we start building a model, we need to make the problem as simple as possible. Regression is a good tool but it needs all the help it can get. In all the charts in Figures 4-16 and 4-17, the profitable areas have a WinCnt of four or higher. In Figure 4-15 we see that WinCnt is the best predictor. We can simplify the problem by only looking at dogs that have a WinCnt of four or higher. This group is the closest to profitable to start with, and we already know that by combining it with other metrics it is possible to make a profit.

We eliminate the rows that have a WinCnt less than four by using a filter. First, we build the criteria for the filtering operation. In Figure 4-18 the criteria is in cell range K1:K2. It is simply the column heading of the column to be filtered and the condition that we want (i.e., greater than 3). Next we select Data → Filter → Advanced Filter and the dialog box in Figure 4-18 is displayed. Since we are eliminating tens of thousands of rows, we use the "Copy to another location" option. The List range is the range of cells that contain the data we are looking at. The Criteria range points to the criteria in K1:K2. "Copy to" is the location that the filtered data will be in. After OK is clicked, a copy of columns A–J will be in columns M–V. The data in M–V will only have rows with a WinCnt of four or more. We then delete columns A–L and are left with the data we want. Earlier we saw an inconsistency between Races and WinCnt, and now Races is out of the model.

	A	B	C	D	E	F	G	H	I	J	K	L	M
1	Race	Dog	Races	Wins	WinCnt	BestSpeed	SpeedRank	WinRank	WinRatio	PlacePay	WinCnt		
2	1	1	21	2	0	1.0021923	4	2	0.0952381	0.00	>3		
3	1	2	20	3	0	1.00339686	5	1	0.15	3.80			
4	1	3	14	1	0	0.99556723	2	3	0.07142857	0.00			
5	1	4	0	0	0	1.00972079	8	8	0	0.00			
6	1	5	18	1	0	1.00490256	6	4	0.05555556	0.00			
7	1	6	19	1					0.05263158				
8	1	7	20	1					0.05	0.00			
9	1	8	0	0					0	7.20			
10	2	1	14	3					0.21428571	3.80			
11	2	2	12	2					0.16666667	0.00			
12	2	3	1	0					0	0.00			
13	2	4	1	0					0	0.00			
14	2	5	21	3					0.14285714	0.00			
15	2	6	24	3					0.125	0.00			
16	2	7	19	2					0.10526316	6.00			
17	2	8	0	0					0	0.00			
18	3	1	1	0					0	0.00			
19	3	2	1	0					0	0.00			
20	3	3	1	0					0	5.00			
21	3	4	1	0	0	0.99677179	6	6	0	0.00			
22	3	5	20	2	0	0.98562963	6	2	0.1	0.00			
23	3	6	1	0	1	0.98502735	5	6	0	0.00			
24	3	7	22	6	1	0.97810114	3	1	0.27272727	0.00			
25	3	8	1	0	1	0.97590217	1	3	0	5.40			

Advanced Filter

Action
○ Filter the list, in-place
● Copy to another location

List range: A1:J52033
Criteria range: K1:K2
Copy to: M1

☐ Unique records only

OK   Cancel

Figure 4-18. Filtering the Data

This leaves us with 710 rows. We are looking at results for the place bet, so in the general population 25% of the dogs would win. There are eight dogs in a race and two will win the place bet, since the place bet covers both first and second. The filtered population, dogs that have won at least four of their last six races, wins the place bet 47% of the time. This means that about half of the rows in the filtered data have a payout. This is important because regression works best when there is a good mix of values in the data. The average payout for the general population is $1.67, but for the filtered group it is $1.78.

Building the Model

We need to limit the number of metrics. If we use too many, the model will *over-train*. If this happens, the model will be overly influenced by unusual or isolated data. There might be one or two dogs that win with a very high payout. Two out of seven hundred doesn't mean much. But regression is not a magic formula, and it is not guaranteed to find the relationships in the data. It is just a mathematical technique that draws a bunch of lines based on the best fit to the data. With too much flexibility it will, in effect, memorize the data rather than learn how to solve the problem.

To guard against this we test the results. The data is separated into two groups. One group is used to build the model and the other is used for testing. If we get good results when we build the model but worse results when we test, the model is over-trained and useless.

We have 710 data items. We will use 449 to build the model and the remaining 261 will be reserved for testing. We have already used WinCnt to limit the data. We now build a worksheet with just the columns needed for the model. We know that Dog (running position), SpeedRank, and WinRank are the metrics to use. But there is a problem with Dog. In Figure 4-16 we see that Dog produces two distinct profitable regions. This seems to mean that the middle positions are less profitable than one, two, seven, and eight. Since we know that this situation exists, we should make a change in the Dog metric. Figure 4-19 shows the resulting sheet.

	A	B	C	D	E	F	G
1	Dog	Dog-4	SpeedRan	WinRank	PlacePay	Random	
2	5	1	=ABS(A2-4)	2	0.00	0.397583	=RA
3	1	3	1	8	0.00	0.805016	
4	8	4	1	1	0.00	0.269975	
5	4	0	6	6	5.40	0.639475	
6	8	4	5	2	0.00	0.492684	
7	4	0	1	1	0.00	0.357043	
8	8	4	2	1	3.20	0.231857	
9	2	2	1	1	4.20	0.28301	
10	2	2	3	7	0.00	0.654576	
11	6	2	1	1	2.60	0.798003	
12	1	3	1	1	2.80	0.403592	
13	7	3	3	2	8.00	0.886656	
14	6	2	3	2	3.60	0.061669	

Figure 4-19. Model data

We insert a new column named Dog-4 containing the absolute value of the difference between the dog's running position and 4.

We need to be sure the rows are assigned to the model and test groups randomly. Therefore, we add a new column called Random and fill it with random numbers. Next we sort the data on Random. This will ensure that each row has the same chance of being assigned to the model group or the test group. After sorting on the Random column, it is deleted.

We start the model like we did the stock example in Figure 4-2. The resulting sheet is shown in Figure 4-20.

	A	B	C	D	E	F	G	H	I
1	Dog	Dog-4	SpeedRan	WinRank	PlacePay	1	1	1	0
2	5	1	3	2	0.00	1	2	2	5
3	1	3	1	8	0.00	3	1	1	5
4	8	4	1	1	0.00	4	1		
5	4	0	6	6	5.40	0	6	6	12
6							5	2	11
7							1	1	2
8							2	1	7
9							1	1	4
10							3	7	12
11							1	1	4
12							1	1	5
13							3	2	8
14							3	2	7
15							1	1	6
16							3	1	5
17							1	2	4
18							2	1	5
19							3	1	6
20							5	1	8
21							3	1	7
22							2	2	5
23							6	1	10
24							1	1	5
25							1	1	6
26							5	1	10
27	7	3	1	1	0.00	3	1	1	5
28	6	2	5	1	0.00	2	5	1	8

Cell F3 note: =B2*F$1

Cell H3 note: =SUM(F2:H2,I$1)

Regression dialog:

Input
Input Y Range: $E$2:$E$450
Input X Range: $F$2:$H$450
☐ Labels   ☐ Constant is Zero
☐ Confidence Level: 95 %

Output options
◉ Output Range: $M$1
○ New Worksheet Ply:
○ New Workbook

Residuals
☐ Residuals   ☐ Residual Plots
☐ Standardized Residuals   ☐ Line Fit Plots

Normal Probability
☐ Normal Probability Plots

OK   Cancel   Help

Figure 4-20. Regression setup

The calculations in columns F–I could be handled in a single column using the SUMPRODUCT function, or even reduced to a single cell using an array formula. But, keeping the calculations separate makes this process easier to understand. We have 710 rows of data but in the Input Ranges we only use rows 2–450. The Y Range is PlacePay in column E. The regression output is shown in Figure 4-21.

In Item 1, the overall performance of the model is low. In general, the metrics are not great at predicting the payout. But R Square measures the model's performance

SUMMARY OUTPUT								
Regression Statistics								
Multiple R	0.10304644							
R Square	0.01061857 ← ❶							
Adjusted R Squa	0.00394858							
Standard Error	2.37930755							
Observations	449							

ANOVA								
	df	*SS*	*MS*	*F*	*ignificance F*			
Regression	3	27.03730722	9.012436	1.591992	0.190573	❷		
Residual	❸ 445	2519.191468	5.661104					
Total	448	2546.228775						

	Coefficients	Standard Error	*t Stat*	*P-value*	Lower 95%	Upper 95%	ower 95.0%	pper 95.0%
Intercept	1.1885645	0.277790509	4.278636	2.3E-05	0.64262	1.734509	0.64262	1.734509
X Variable 1	0.15884143	0.093003452	1.707909	0.088351	-0.02394	0.341622	-0.02394	0.341622
X Variable 2	0.05982476	0.06086003	0.982989	0.326147	-0.05978	0.179434	-0.05978	0.179434
X Variable 3	0.0314417	0.083752134	0.375414	0.707532	-0.13316	0.196041	-0.13316	0.196041

Figure 4-21. Regression output

across all 449 rows. We are interested in setting a threshold that divides the dogs into two groups, and only one group has to be profitable. The model can do this without a complete understanding of the relationships. A high value for R Square would be better, but this may be good enough.

The P-values in Item 2 for Dog-4 are encouraging.

Item 3 gives the weights and intercept. We copy and paste them into the model resulting in Figure 4-22. The values in column I are the scores. A high value in column I means our model predicts that the dog is more likely to be a profitable bet.

Is it? We find out by testing. We need to know if there is a score above which we can bet profitably. We used 449 rows to set the weights, so there are 449 scores to consider. Perhaps the top half is profitable.

To make testing easy, we start by creating logic to analyze the model's performance.

Analyzing the Results

To see if the model is working, we rank the dogs by their scores and only consider half of them, the ones with the highest scores. The mid-point is not likely to be the best threshold, and we will want to experiment with different splits. So, the sheet shown in Figure 4-23 is set up to allow different percentages to be tested.

The number 50 is entered in cell L1. This indicates that we are going to test a 50% split. In cell L2, we calculate how many of the 449 model dogs are in the top half. The formula is =INT(450*(L1/100)). The result is 225.

Figure 4-22. Model with scores

	A	B	C	D	E	F	G	H	I
1	Dog	Dog-4	SpeedRan	WinRank	PlacePay	0.158841	0.059825	0.031442	1.188565
2	5	1	2	2	0.00	0.1588	Scores 0.11965	0.062883	1.529939
3	1	3	1	8	0.00	0.476524	0.059825	0.251534	1.976447
4	8	4	1	1	0.00	0.635366	0.059825	0.031442	1.915197
5	4	0	6	6	5.40	0	0.358949	0.18865	1.736163
6	8	4	5	2	0.00	0.635366	0.299124	0.062883	2.185937
7	4	0	1	1	0.00	0	0.059825	0.031442	1.279831
8	8	4	2	1	3.20	0.635366	0.11965	0.031442	1.975021
9	2	2	1	1	4.20	0.317683	0.059825	0.031442	1.597514
10	2	2	3	7	0.00	0.317683	0.179474	0.220092	1.905814
11	6	2	1	1	2.60	0.317683	0.059825	0.031442	1.597514
12	1	3	1	1	2.80	0.476524	0.059825	0.031442	1.756355
13	7	3	3	2	8.00	0.476524	0.179474	0.062883	1.907446
14	6	2	3	2	3.60	0.317683	0.179474	0.062883	1.748605
15	8	4	1	1	4.40	0.635366	0.059825	0.031442	1.915197
16	5	1	3	1	3.40	0.158841	0.179474	0.031442	1.558322
17	5	1	1	2	0.00	0.158841	0.059825	0.062883	1.470114
18	6	2	2	1	8.40	0.317683	0.11965	0.031442	1.657339

Figure 4-23. Test setup

Formula box (over E/F columns): =IF(I2>=K$3,E2,0)

	K	L	M
1	Percent to Test	50	50
2	Target Score	225	=INT(450*(L1/100))
3	Target Score Value	1.71716335	=LARGE(I2:I450,L2)
5	The Model Building Group	The Model Building Group	
6	Dogs bet	230	=COUNTIF(I2:I450,">=" & L3)
7	Total Winnings	$430.90	{=SUM(E2:E450 *(I2:I450 >= L3))}
8	Average Payout	$1.87	=L7/L6
9	Wins	104	=COUNTIF(J2:J450,">,0")
10	Win Percentage	45%	=L9/L6
11	Win Average Amount	$4.14	=L7/L9
12	Net Profit (Loss)	($29.10)	=(L8-2)*L6
14	The Test Group	The Test Group	
15	Dogs bet	129	=COUNTIF(I451:I711,">=" & L3)
16	Total Winnings	$246.40	{=SUM(E451:E711 *(I451:I711 >= L3))}
17	Average Payout	$1.91	=L16/L15
18	Wins	59	=COUNTIF(J451:J711,">,0")
19	Win Percentage	46%	=L18/L15
20	Win Average Amount	$4.18	=L16/L18
21	Net Profit (Loss)	($11.60)	=(L17-2)*L15
23	Results for all Dogs	Results for all Dogs	
24	Dogs bet	710	710
25	Total Winnings	$1,239.50	=SUM(E2:E711)
26	Average Payout	$1.75	=L25/L24
27	Wins	331	=COUNTIF(E2:E711,">,0")
28	Win Percentage	47%	=L27/L24
29	Win Average Amount	$3.74	=L25/L27
30	Net Profit (Loss)	($180.50)	=(L26-2)*L24

The threshold for this test is the 225th highest score. The formula in L3 is =LARGE(I2:I450,L2). This gives the value we need. With these formulas in place we can easily test any percentage. If we enter 15 in cell L1, the value in L3 gives us the value to test the top 15%.

In the range L6:L12 are details of the model's performance for the top 449 rows. The first formula is =COUNTIF(I2:I450,">=" & L3). This counts the number of scores equal to or greater than the threshold. It tells how many bets we make if we bet the top half of the scores.

In column J, the formula =IF(I2>=L$3,E2,0) gives the payout for each dog. If the dog's score is less than the threshold, it is not bet and the payout is zero. To get the total payout for the model group, we use the formula =SUM(J2:J450) in cell L7.

We get the average payout by dividing L7 by L6. In this case it is $1.87 in cell L8. The number of wining bets is calculated in cell L9 using =COUNTIF(J2:J450,">0"). The win rate, the percentage of bets that win, is in L10. The formula is =L9/L6.

We also want to know the average amount of a winning payout. We get it with =L7/L9 in L11. Finally, the formula =(L8-2)*L6 in cell L12 gives the total profit or loss for the 449 model dogs. We subtract 2 because the bet is $2.00 and we are interested in the profit.

The same details for the test group are in the range L15:L21. We can now compare the performance of the model group and the test group. If they are not similar, the model may be over-trained.

To test the effectiveness of the model we need to see how it compares to the whole population. In cells L24:L30 we calculate the same details for all dogs. The formulas in this area are a little different because we do not consider the threshold in this area. Here we want to see what would happen if we just bet all the dogs.

In Figure 4-24 we consider the results.

In Item 1 the average payout for all dogs is $1.75, but for the top 50% scores the results are better. The model group paid out $1.87 and for the test group it was $1. 91. This is good news for two reasons. It suggests that the model is working and that it is not over-trained.

Item 2 shows that the percentage of wins is a bit lower for the dogs in the top 50%. This is probably because the model is finding the dogs with higher payouts. Item 3 shows this clearly. The average amount paid for a winner is $3.74 overall, but for the top scoring dogs it is above $4.00.

The model works, but is not profitable at 50%. The next step is to find a profitable threshold.

We started with tens of thousands of rows, but now we are down to a modest amount of information. We know the model is capable of making good predictions and there is no evidence of over-training. We need to know how the model's performance changes as we change the threshold.

We test this by changing the value in cell L1. Starting with 50 and working down to 5 in steps of 5, we build Figure 4-25.

Item 1 is the threshold being tested. The Profit/Loss amounts for both groups are added together (Item 2), building an area to populate a chart. We add the amount together because the groups are small. At the 5% threshold there are only three wins in the test group.

K	L	M
	The Model Building Group	
Dogs bet	230	
Total Winnings	$430.90	
Average Payout	$1.87	
Wins	104	
Win Percentage	45%	
Win Average Amount	$4.14	
Net Profit (Loss)	($29.10)	
		❶ ❷ ❸
	The Test Group	
Dogs bet	129	
Total Winnings	$246.40	
Average Payout	$1.91	
Wins	59	
Win Percentage	46%	
Win Average Amount	$4.18	
Net Profit (Loss)	($11.60)	
	Results for all Dogs	
Dogs bet	710	
Total Winnings	$1,239.50	
Average Payout	$1.75	
Wins	331	
Win Percentage	47%	
Win Average Amount	$3.74	
Net Profit (Loss)	($180.50)	

Figure 4-24. Results at 50%

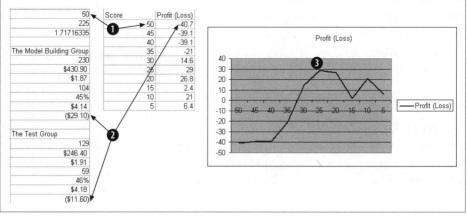

Figure 4-25. Finding the threshold

In Item 3 we can see the overall shape of the curve. The profit tops out at about 25%, and that is probably the best threshold for the model.

Testing Non-Linear Relationships

Regression assumes that the relationships in the data are linear. This is usually a safe assumption, but sometimes you can get a more accurate model if you allow for non-linear relationships. We can use the solver to test the potential value of using non-linear terms in the model.

We start by inserting a row at the top of the worksheet, setting it up as shown in Figure 4-26.

	E	F	G	H	I	J	K	L
1		1	1	1			Correlation	0.103046443
2	PlacePay	0.158841	0.059825	0.031442	0	Payout if Bet	Percent to Test	50
3	0.00	0.158841	0.11965	0.062883	0.341374	0	Target Score	225
4	0.00	0.476524	0.059825	0.251534	0.787883	0	Target Score Value	0.528598846
5	=(B3^F$1)*F$2		0.059825	0.031442	0.726632			
6			0.358949	0.18865	0.547599		=CORREL(I3:I451,E3:E451)	The Model Building Group
7	0.00	0.635366	0.299124	0.062883	0.997373	0	Dogs bet	230
8	0.00	0	0.059825	0.031442	0.091266	0	Total Winnings	$430.90
9	3.20	0.635366	0.11965	0.031442	0.786457	3.2	Average Payout	$1.87
10	4.20	0.317683	0.059825	0.031442	0.408949	0	Wins	104
11	0.00	0.317683	0.179474	0.220092	0.717249	0	Win Percentage	45%
12	2.60	0.317683	0.059825	0.031442	0.408949	0	Win Average Amount	$4.14
13	2.80	0.476524	0.059825	0.031442	0.567791	2.8	Net Profit (Loss)	($29.10)
14	8.00	0.476524	0.179474	0.062883	0.718882	8		
15	3.60	0.317683	0.179474	0.062883	0.560041	3.6	The Test Group	
16	4.40	0.635366	0.059825	0.031442	0.726632	4.4	Dogs bet	129
17	3.40	0.158841	0.179474	0.031442	0.369757	0	Total Winnings	$246.40
18	0.00	0.158841	0.059825	0.062883	0.28155	0	Average Payout	$1.91
19	8.40	0.317683	0.11965	0.031442	0.468774	0	Wins	59
20	0.00	0.317683	0.179474	0.031442	0.528599	0	Win Percentage	46%
21	0.00	0.317683	0.299124	0.031442	0.648248	0	Win Average Amount	$4.18

Figure 4-26. Setup to test non-linear relationships

This is a classification problem. We are dividing the population of dogs into two groups. As long as we can set a good threshold, we do not care how well the model predicts the exact value.

This means the intercept is not adding any value. The model will do just as well without it because we are only interested the correlation between the score and the payout. If we substitute a zero for the intercept in cell I2, the performance of the model does not change.

The results in Figure 4-26 are exactly the same as in Figure 4-23. Only the threshold is different. In row one of columns F, G, and H we enter 1. We change the formula in F3 from =B3*F$1 to =(B3^F$1)*F$2), and fill this new formula across to column H and down to row 712.

At the top of the L column we add the formula =CORREL(I3:I451,E3:E451) to measure the correlation between the scores in column I and the payouts in column E. The value is 0.103. This means the scores are positively correlated with the payouts, but the correlation is not especially strong.

We want to see if changing the values in F1:H1 can increase the correlation. For this we use the Solver, which is on the Tools menu. If the Solver does not appear as one of the items on the Tools menu, it may be necessary to select Add-Ins and make sure the Solver Add-In is checked.

The Solver dialog is filled out as shown in Figure 4-27.

	E	F	G	H	I	J	K	L
1		1	1	1			Correlation	0.103046443
2	PlacePay	0.158841	0.059825	0.031442	0	Payout if Bet	Percent to Test	50
3	0.00	0.158841	0.11965	0.062883	0.341374	0	Target Score	225
4	0.00	0.478						0.528598846
5	0.00	0.635						
6	5.40						e Model Building Group	
7	0.00	0.635						230
8	0.00							$430.90
9	3.20	0.635						$1.87
10	4.20	0.317						104
11	0.00	0.317						45%
12	2.60	0.317						$4.14
13	2.80	0.478						($29.10)
14	8.00	0.478						
15	3.60	0.317					e Test Group	
16	4.40	0.635						129
17	3.40	0.158						$246.40
18	0.00	0.158841	0.059825	0.062883	0.28155	0	Average Payout	$1.91
19	8.40	0.317683	0.11965	0.031442	0.468774	0	Wins	59
20	0.00	0.317683	0.179474	0.031442	0.528599	0	Win Percentage	46%
21	0.00	0.317683	0.299124	0.031442	0.648248	0	Win Average Amount	$4.18

Solver Parameters

Set Target Cell: $L$1

Equal To: ⦿ Max ◯ Min ◯ Value of: 0

By Changing Cells: $F$1:$H$2

Subject to the Constraints:

[Solve] [Close] [Guess] [Options] [Add] [Change] [Delete] [Reset All] [Help]

Figure 4-27. The Solver dialog

The target cell is L1. This is the cell with the correlation formula and is the value we want to improve. Equal to Max is selected because we want the highest value possible for correlation.

The By Changing Cells field is set to the range F1:H2. This means Solver is allowed to change the values in this range to get the maximum possible value in L1.

In Figure 4-28 the results are compared to the best results for the non-linear model.

	A	B	C
1		Non-Linear Model	Linear Model
2	Correlation	0.16976891	0.103046443
3	Percent to Test	25	25
4	Target Score	112	112
5	Target Score Value	0.510780042	1.876004782
6			
7		The Model Building Group	The Model Building Group
8	Dogs bet	113	119
9	Total Winnings	$257.80	$260.20
10	Average Payout	$2.28	$2.19
11	Wins	52	56
12	Win Percentage	46%	47%
13	Win Average Amount	$4.96	$4.65
14	Net Profit (Loss)	$31.80	$22.20
15			
16		The Test Group	The Test Group
17	Dogs bet	72	68
18	Total Winnings	$140.60	$142.80
19	Average Payout	$1.95	$2.10
20	Wins	30	31
21	Win Percentage	42%	46%
22	Win Average Amount	$4.69	$4.61
23	Net Profit (Loss)	($3.40)	$6.80
24			

Figure 4-28. Comparing results

In Item 1 the correlation is increased from 0.103 to 0.1976. This is a significant increase and could mean the model will now do a better job. In Item 2 the Profit for the model group has gone up from $22.20 to $31.80. That is great, but the test group in Item 3 tells a different story. In the test group the profit of $6.80 has turned into a loss of $3.40. This suggests that the additional flexibility of the non-linear terms has caused the model to over-train.

In this case the linear model is the right one to use.

CHAPTER 5

Measuring Quality

In the last two chapters we looked at measuring quantity. Now we turn to quality. Sampling and statistical analysis have been used to measure quality in manufacturing since the 1920s. Years ago it relied on small samples and simple calculations, but today we can do more. With modern technology we can look at thousands of pieces of work and the complexity of calculations is no longer an issue.

In this chapter we use Statistical Process Control techniques to build an application to measure quality. We will go through the techniques and calculations, and then use them to build an application. We will also look at the data requirements for this kind of project.

In earlier projects we used VBA to make the application interact with the user, but Excel can interact without VBA. This project uses controls to bring the application to life. Controls are easy to use and we will include four of them in the project.

The basic problem is always the same. We start with data that contains the answer to a question. We find the answer and give it to the user.

This chapter uses the following Excel functions and features, shown in Tables 5-1 and 5-2.

Table 5-1. Excel functions used in this chapter

INDEX( )	ROW( )	IF( )
INDIRECT( )	MAX( )	AVERAGE( )
ADDRESS( )	STDEV( )	LN( )
INT( )	SUM( )	EXP( )

The INDEX, INDIRECT, and ADDRESS functions are vital to understanding the application, and they are explained in Chapter 1.

Table 5-2. Excel features used in this chapter

Controls	Named Ranges	Charting
Named Cells	Array Formulas	

Statistical Process Control

This chapter's example is a check processing operation. The number of checks varies by day of the week as does the amount of money deposited. These are measures of quantity and can be forecasted and monitored using techniques in Chapter 3. But quality is as important as quantity. If something is going wrong in the operation (e.g., if payments are being misapplied, or check numbers are being recorded incorrectly), we need to know.

Choosing Metrics

When monitoring a manufacturing process we can measure the diameter of a bolt, the weight of a bottle of shampoo, or the percent of electrical components failing a test. These are things that do not vary by day of the week, and a significant change in any of them can mean trouble. In our check processing operation we need to use metrics that behave this way.

First, we consider potential problem areas. Checks received for payment need to be processed quickly, so we measure the average age of the checks. Customers are supposed to send a remittance slip with their check, and we will measure the percentage of payments received that contain only a check and the average number of pages of remittance information per check. Money is important, so we measure both the average check amount and the average amount per remittance page. Finally, we need to monitor the accuracy of our data capture process. For this we look at the percentage of checks that have a valid invoice number, the average number of digits in the check number, and the average number of digits in the check amount.

If any of these metrics shows a significant change we need to find the reason. Avoiding metrics based on volume or day of the week keeps the focus on quality.

This concept can be applied to almost any operation. In a call center you might look at average talk time, percentage of calls abandoned, and percentage of calls transferred. In an invoicing area it could be average value, average lines, and product mix.

X and S Charts

The process, like forecasting, is simply predicting what each metric should be, knowing how accurate the prediction is, and using this to set control limits for each metric. The prediction is the recent average. We don't consider lag since these metrics are not cyclic. We don't correct for the trend. If there is a trend, we want to know. We are looking for trends.

We use two kinds of metrics. First is the average. In the example we look at the average number of pages per check. Second is the standard deviation. For some metrics we need to know if the amount of variation is changing. With number of pages per check, the average could be steady, yet we could be getting more really high and low page counts.

Results are displayed on a chart like the one in Figure 5-1.

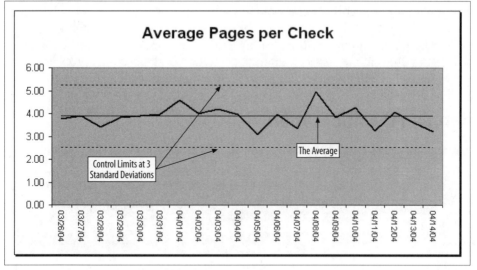

Figure 5-1. Statistical Process Control chart

Charts dealing with averages are called *X charts*. Those dealing with standard deviation are called *S charts*. Years ago there were also charts that looked at the range (the difference between the highest and lowest measurement). They were called *R charts*, and were used because the calculations are simpler. Finding standard deviations by hand for hours every day is not as much fun as you might think.

Today the distinction between X and S charts doesn't mean much. The terminology evolved before PCs and Excel. Statistical Process Control was a complex and labor intensive proposition. The metrics had to be manually collected and the calculations done by hand. Today you can probably collect all your metrics from automated sources and Excel takes care of the calculations.

The control limits are usually set three standard deviations from the average. This means that 99.7 percent of the time the metric will be within the control limits if there is not a problem. This also means that three times in every thousand tests there is a false positive.

Of course, you don't have to use three standard deviations. Three is commonly used because it gives good results and because that's what everyone else uses. But you can use a different number. The number of standard deviations used to set the control limits is called the sigma. It is a trade off. A low sigma is good at detecting problems, but it is also good at producing false positives. A high sigma means less work tracking down false alarms but a better chance of missing something important.

We assume the metrics are normally distributed. In the real world few things really are, but it is easier to assume that they are normal than it is to figure out what is actually going on. There are times, however, when a different distribution gives better results.

The application will let the user choose to use either a normal or *log normal distribution*. In a log normal distribution, the measures are skewed to the high end of the range. Using a log normal distribution to set the limits makes the application more sensitive to drops in the metric. It improves detection of skipped digit problems. This can be helpful in monitoring keying or OCR operations, for example.

Running the Application

The main display of the application is shown in Figure 5-2.

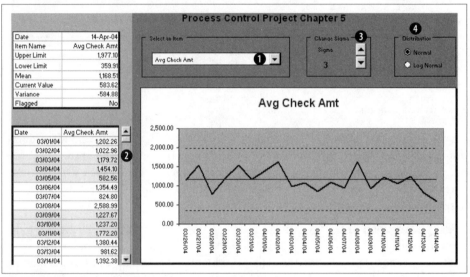

Figure 5-2. Application Main Display

The application has only four options. First, the sample data contains 11 metrics. Use the combo box control (Item 1) to select the one you want. The chart and data area in the upper left update automatically.

All the dates and values for the selected metric appear in the scroll area. Use the scroll bar (Item 2) to move the data up or down.

The application is set to a sigma of three. The control limits are set at three standard deviations from the average. If you want to change the sigma, use the spinner control (Item 3).

Finally, if you want the control limits to be set using a log normal distribution, use the radio buttons (Item 4).

If the metric is out of control limits, it will be flagged as shown by Item 1 in Figure 5-3. The metric is the standard deviation of the number of digits in the check amount. The current value for this metric is 1.63. That is above the upper control limit of 1.54. The chart (Item 2) shows the metric is outside the control limits.

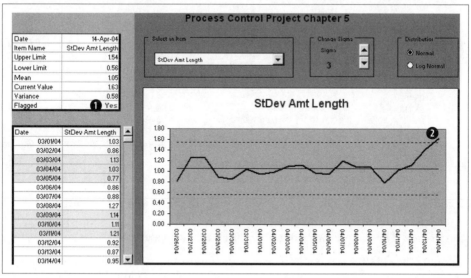

Figure 5-3. Main display with out of control item

What does it mean? The dollar amount of a check is a number. Here we are measuring the number of digits in the amounts of all the checks processed today. The high standard deviation tells us there is an unexpectedly high amount of variation in the metric today. We need to look at the information capture process for this metric. Perhaps a data entry person is skipping digits or an OCR process is having a problem. We are probably getting the check amount wrong some of the time. We can either look into it now, or wait until the monthly close and see if the CFO asks about it.

Application Design

The application contains three worksheets. A sheet named Data holds the data. It has no formulas and no real formatting. It is just a place for the information. All the calculations are done on the Workarea sheet. It references the Data sheet, does all of the calculations, and builds named display ranges. The Display sheet uses the named ranges on Workarea, formatting, and a chart to present the results to the user. This sheet also uses controls to allow the user to interact with the application.

The Data Sheet

The Data sheet is shown in Figure 5-4.

	A	B	C	D	E	F	G	H	I
1	Date	Avg Check Amt	Average Pages per Check	Avg Value per Page	Pct Check Only	Valid Inv Num Pct	Avg Ck num Length	Avg Amt Length	StDev Pgs St
2	03/01/04	$ 1,202.26	4.27	$ 281.56	4.00	93.39	4.71	5.33	0.64
3	03/02/04	$ 1,022.96	3.66	$ 279.50	6.00	90.82	4.96	5.30	0.92
4	03/03/04	$ 1,179.72	4.01	$ 294.20	6.00	89.85	4.74	5.39	0.76
5	03/04/04	$ 1,454.10	3.76	$ 386.73	7.00	92.64	4.82	5.29	0.95
6	03/05/04	$ 582.56	3.31	$ 176.00	18.00	88.98	4.86	4.77	0.71
7	03/06/04	$ 1,354.49	3.87	$ 350.00	13.00	92.63	4.83	5.21	0.56
8	03/07/04	$ 824.80	3.58	$ 230.39	12.00	89.82	4.75	4.99	0.80
9	03/08/04	$ 2,588.99	4.63	$ 559.18	6.00	97.02	4.67	5.40	1.09
10	03/09/04	$ 1,227.67	3.95	$ 310.80	9.00	93.71	4.72	5.33	0.99
11	03/10/04	$ 1,237.20	4.44	$ 278.65	8.00	95.19	4.73	5.34	1.25
12	03/11/04	$ 1,772.20	7.15	$ 247.86	9.00	95.15	4.35	5.30	1.17
13	03/12/04	$ 1,380.44	4.09	$ 337.51	7.00	93.86	4.82	5.20	1.01
14	03/13/04	$ 981.62	3.16	$ 310.64	9.00	93.00	4.95	5.36	0.50
15	03/14/04	$ 1,392.38	4.29	$ 324.56	11.00	92.55	4.84	5.26	0.96
16	03/15/04	$ 1,565.69	3.55	$ 441.04	1.00	85.33	5.02	5.40	0.69

Figure 5-4. The Data sheet

Headings are in row one. Dates go in column A and the metrics fill out the columns to the right. The sample application will handle up to 25 metrics and up to 1,000 days of data. These limits are arbitrary and can easily be increased.

Changing the data is also simple. The new data must be arranged the same way, with headings and dates. Just select and clear the entire sheet. Don't delete the columns, just clear them. Then paste your data onto the sheet starting in cell A1. The formulas on Workarea do the rest. Everything updates automatically.

The Workarea Sheet

All the logic and calculations are on the Workarea sheet. A few conventions are used to make this sheet easier to understand. Some ranges on this sheet are linked to the Data sheet, and they are in blue font. Named ranges used on the Display sheet have a grey background. Ranges that are used together, but not named, have a border. An example is the cells used to populate the chart. All the intermediate calculations are in column A and the results are named. Values set by controls on the Display sheet are bold and in red font.

The layout of Workarea is shown in Figure 5-5.

Item 1 is the range that populates the chart on the Display sheet. The first two columns reference the Data sheet. Item 2 is a named range called DisplayData. This data appears in the upper-left part of the Display sheet. Item 3 is also a named range. It is called ScrollArea and feeds the scrolling area on Display.

Item 4 is a range that references the column headings in row 1 of the Data sheet. It appears in the combo box on Display and allows the user to select a metric. The combo box sets the value in cell A9. The number in cell A9 is the row of the item

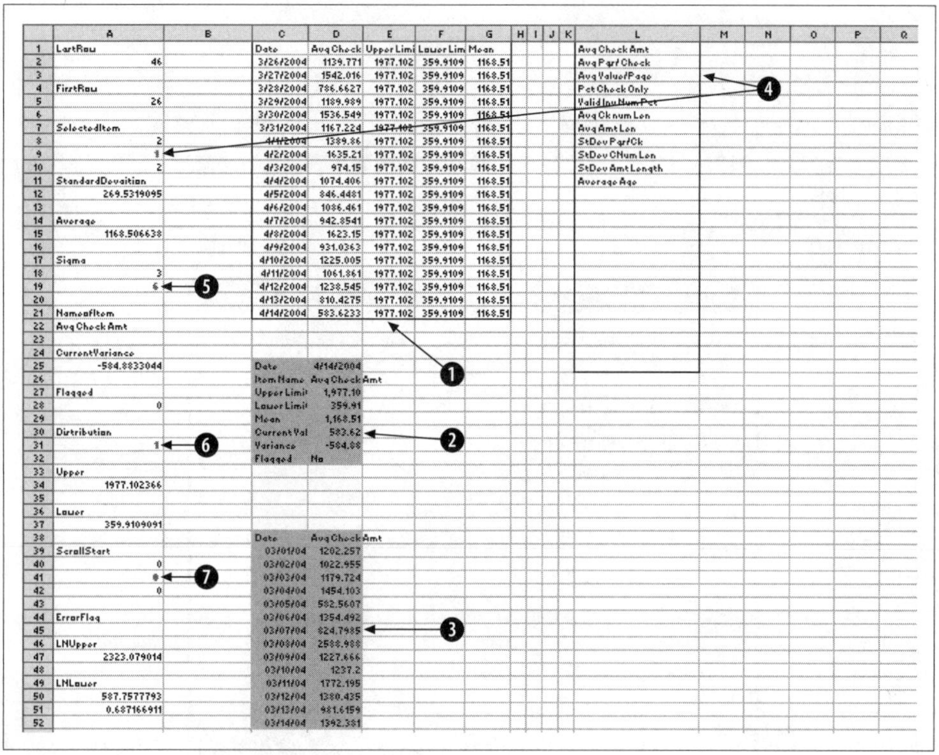

Figure 5-5. Layout of Workarea

selected. In Figure 5-5 the value is 1. This means the first item, Average Check Amount, has been selected.

If the user changes the sigma, the spinner control sets the value in cell A19 (Item 5). The option boxes handle changes in the distribution. The option boxes both link to cell A31 (Item 6). When the first option box is checked, A31's value is 1; if the second is checked, the value is 2.

Item 7, cell A41, is set by the scroll bar control. The value is set to a number from 0 to 100, indicating how far down the scroll bar is.

The calculations are in column A. The named cells show their name above them. For example, cell A2 is named LastRow, so the cell A1 contains the name LastRow.

The Controls on the Display Sheet

The Display sheet contains four controls. The combo-box control lets the user select an item from a list. Controls are on the Forms toolbar. (To display the Forms toolbar, select View → Toolbars.) Then check Forms.

To use a combo box, we need a list of items to select from. In the example in Figure 5-6, we start by clicking on the combo box on the toolbar (Item 1).

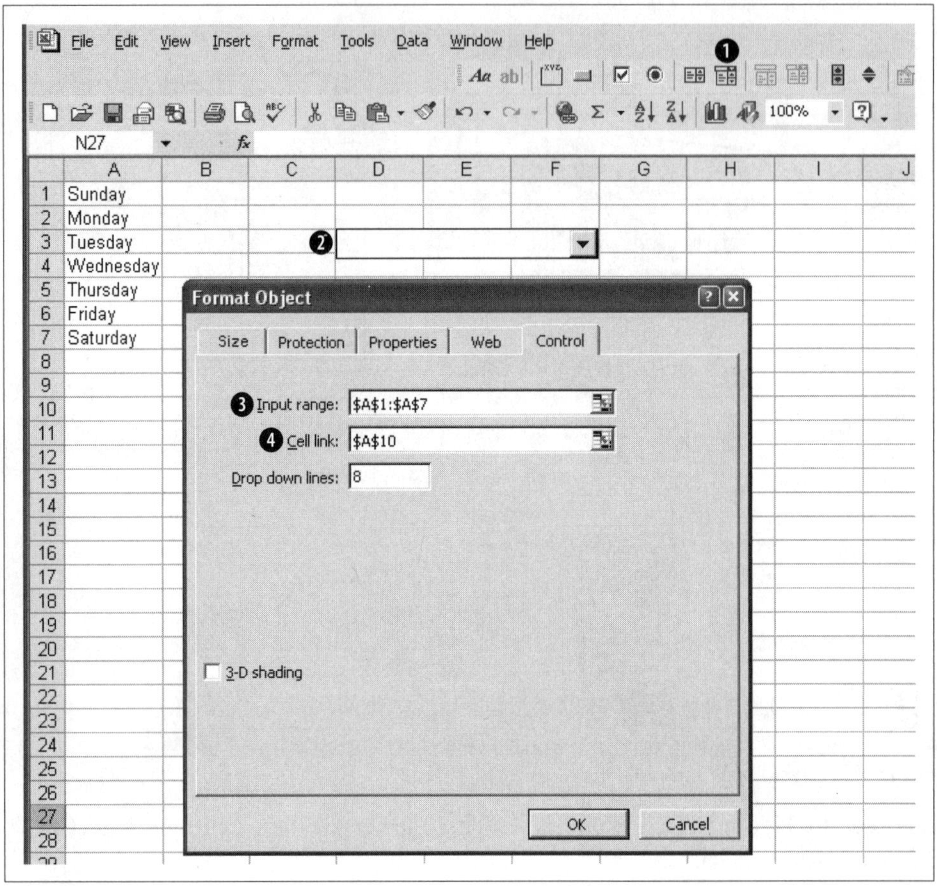

Figure 5-6. Setting up a combo box

We then draw the box on the worksheet (Item 2). Use the mouse to select the location. Hold the left mouse button down and drag the mouse to indicate the size box you want. When you release the mouse button, the combo box will be there.

Right-click on the combo box and select Format Control. The Format Object box in Figure 5-6 will display. Enter the cell range to be displayed in the Input range box (Item 3). In Figure 5-6 the user will select a day of the week. The names of the days are in the range A1:A7.

Item 4 is the Cell link. When the user selects an item from the list, the combo box will put a number in this cell. The number tells which item was selected.

Figure 5-7 shows how the combo box works. When the user clicks on the box, the list is displayed. In this case Tuesday has been selected. The number 3 in cell A10 tells us the user selected the third item.

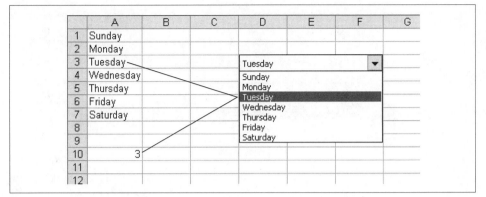

Figure 5-7. Using the combo box

Figure 5-8 shows how the scrollbar is set up. Item 1 is the scrollbar control on the Forms toolbar. You drag and drop the control on the worksheet. In Figure 5-8 the link cell is A10. Item 2 shows how the link is set and how it works. The scrollbar is halfway down and the value in A10 is 50. In the Format Control window, the Minimum value is 0 and the Maximum is 100, so halfway is 50.

The spinner control (Item 1) in Figure 5-9 is set up like the scrollbar. They just look different. The option box (Item 2) is similar. In the project there are two option boxes, and they link to the same cell. The value in the linked cell tells which option box is selected. Excel keeps up with how many option boxes there are and only allows one of them to be selected at a time.

There are also group boxes (Item 3) on the Display sheet. They don't do anything in this application, and here they are just for looks. They are generally used to group radio button controls, and handle the logic that allows only one radio button to be checked.

Linking the Workarea Sheet to the Data Sheet

The Data sheet contains a lot of information, but we only use a small part of it at any given time. The user selects the column using the selector on the display sheet. The area of interest is the last 20 rows in that column. We know that the dates are in column A of Data, and we need the last 20 rows.

Figure 5-10 shows how we reference the data. LastRow, cell A2, keeps up with the last row on Data that is used. It is an array formula that multiplies the row numbers times a list of truth values (0 or 1) that are 1 for the rows that contain information. The row numbers of empty rows are multiplied by 0, so they become 0. The Maximum is the highest row that has anything in it.

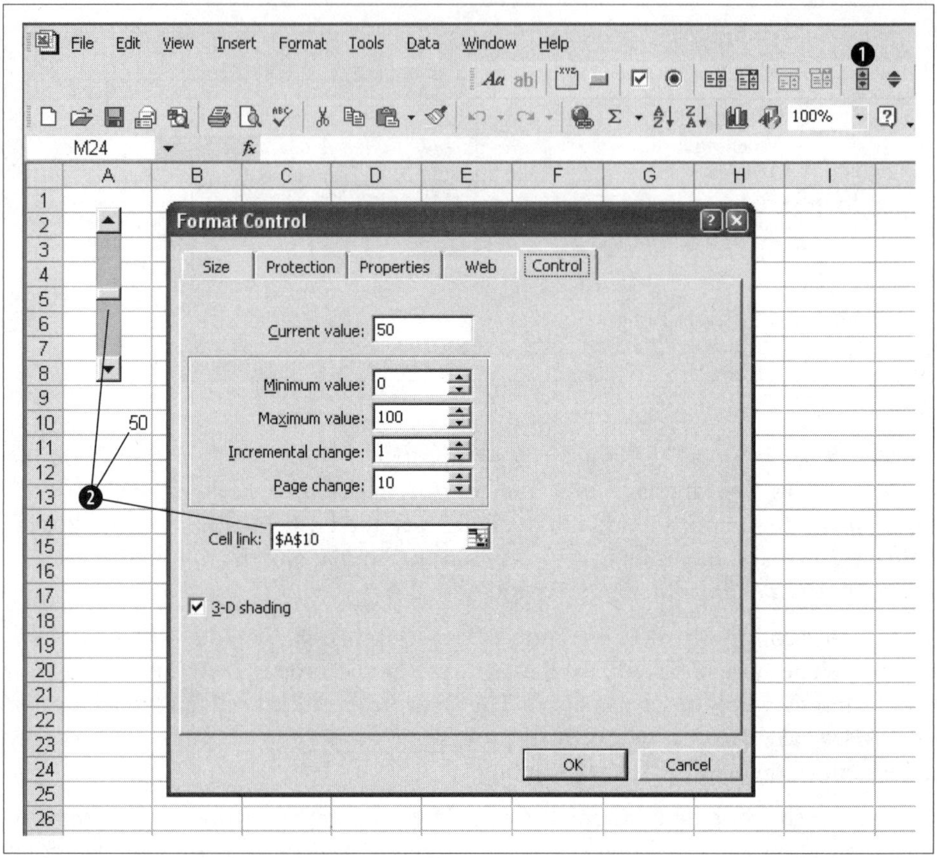

Figure 5-8. Setting up and using a scrollbar

Figure 5-9. Other controls

We do not just want the last row, but the last 20 rows. The first row that we will use is 20 rows above LastRow. So, FirstRow, in cell A5, is equal to LastRow-20. These calculations on Workarea are shown in Figure 5-10.

The dates are in column C, but what about the metric? The combo box sets a value in cell A9 telling us which metric was chosen. But on the Data sheet the first column, column A, is for dates, so we have to add one to the value in A9. This gives us SelectedItem in cell A8. It is the column number of the metric we need.

The dates are referenced in column C using the INDEX function. The range is the first 1,000 rows of column A on the Data sheet. The formula in C2 uses FirstRow + ROW(A1) to reference the correct item in the range. =ROW(A1) has a value of 1. As this

Figure 5-10. Connecting to the Data sheet

	A	B	C	D
1	LastRow		Date	Avg Check A
2	46 ◄— {=MAX((Data!A1:A1000<>"")*ROW(Data!A1:A1000))}		3/26/2004	1139.77074
3			3/27/2004	1542.01601
4	FirstRow		3/28/2004	786.662692
5	26 ◄— =LastRow-20		3/29/2004	1189.98927
6			3/30/2004	1536.54947
7	SelectedItem	=INDEX(Data!A$1:A$1000,FirstRow+ROW(A1))	3/31/2004	1167.22405
8	2 ◄— =A9+1		4/1/2004	1389.86021
9	1		4/2/2004	1635.21
10		=INDIRECT("data!"&ADDRESS(FirstRow+ROW(A1),SelectedItem))	4/3/2004	974.15
11	StandardDeviation		4/4/2004	1074.40555
12	269.5319095		4/5/2004	846.448136
13			4/6/2004	1086.4613
14	Average		4/7/2004	942.854054
15	1168.506638		4/8/2004	1623.15036
16			4/9/2004	931.036291
17	Sigma		4/10/2004	1225.00457
18	3		4/11/2004	1061.86085
19	6		4/12/2004	1238.54507
20			4/13/2004	810.4275
21	NameofItem		4/14/2004	583.623333

formula fills down, the A1 becomes A2, A3, and so on. FirstRow is deliberately set to one row above the first cell so the formula will fill down.

For the metrics we use the INDIRECT function because it allows us to reference both row and column. The formula in D2 uses ADDRESS to build the reference and INDIRECT to get the value. The parameters for the ADDRESS function are row and column number. The row number is calculated just like the INDEX formula in column C. The column number is SelectedItem.

Calculations on the Workarea Sheet

The next part of Workarea is shown in Figure 5-11.

We use the numbers in the range D2:D20 to set the control limits. The value in D21 is the current value, the one we are checking. Therefore, we do not use it to set the limits.

The formula in A12 returns the standard deviation of the range. In A15 we get the average.

Cell A19 is set by the spinner control and can be from 0 to 12 in increments of 1. We are going to let the user select a sigma in the range 0 to 6 in increments of one half. The formula in A18 divides the set value by 2 and returns the sigma used in the calculations.

Cell D21 contains the current value. The named value Average is the average of the last 19 days. CurrentVariance is the difference between D21 and Average. This part of Workarea is in Figure 5-12.

The named values Upper and Lower are the control limits. In Figure 5-12 cell A28 (named Flagged) checks the current value of cell D21. If the value is higher than

10		
11	StandardDevaition	
12	269.5319095	◄——— =STDEV(D2:D20)
13		
14	Average	
15	1168.506638	◄——— =AVERAGE(D2:D20)
16		
17	Sigma	
18	3	◄——— =A19/2
19	6	
20		
21	NameofItem	
22	Avg Check Amt	◄——— =D1
23		
24	CurrentVariance	
25	-584.8833044	◄——— =D21-Average
26		

Figure 5-11. Calculations on Workarea

Upper or Lower then the value is set to 1. This indicates the current value is out of the control limits.

The calculation of Upper depends on the distribution selection. If it is normal, the named value Distribution is 1. In that case Upper is =Average + (Sigma * StandardDeviation), which is the named value NUpper. Otherwise it is based on the log normal distribution. The named value LNUpper has the value. A similar technique is used for Lower. It is either based on the Average, Sigma, and Standard Deviation, NLower, or it uses the log normal calculation LNLower.

The scrolling area on Display is controlled by the value ScrollStart. It is the row number of the first row of Data shown in the scrolling area. When the user moves the scrollbar, a value from 0 to 100 is set in cell A41. This value tells how far down the scrollbar is. The formula in cell A42 uses this value to decide what row on Data should be the first of the 15 rows of the scroll area.

The scrolling calculations work from the bottom up, so it is possible to get a row number that is less than 1. That would cause an error, and the formula in cell A40 takes the maximum of the value in A42 and 1. 1 is subtracted from the answer to simplify the formulas in Scrollarea.

Cell A51 contains an array formula that calculates the standard deviation based on the log of the values in D2:D20 and multiplies the answer by sigma. This value is added to the log of the average to obtain log normal upper limit in A47 (LNUpper). The EXP function is applied to the result turning it back into a value for the chart. If the value in A51 is an error, there are values in the range D2:D20 that are not positive real numbers and the Log cannot be taken. If this is the case and log normal distribution is selected, an error message is built in cell A45 (ErrorFlag). In an error condition, the normal distribution limit is used.

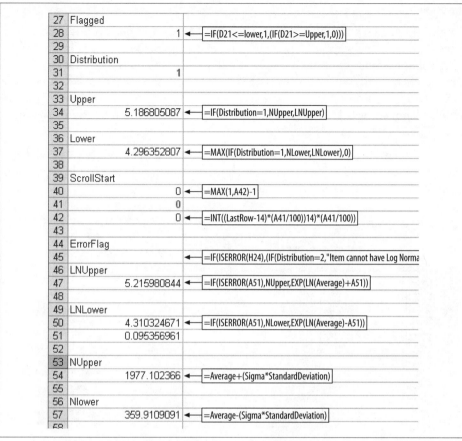

27	Flagged	
28	1	← =IF(D21<=lower,1,(IF(D21>=Upper,1,0)))
29		
30	Distribution	
31	1	
32		
33	Upper	
34	5.186805087	← =IF(Distribution=1,NUpper,LNUpper)
35		
36	Lower	
37	4.296352807	← =MAX(IF(Distribution=1,NLower,LNLower),0)
38		
39	ScrollStart	
40	0	← =MAX(1,A42)-1
41	0	
42	0	← =INT((LastRow-14)*(A41/100))14)*(A41/100))
43		
44	ErrorFlag	
45		← =IF(ISERROR(H24),(IF(Distribution=2,"Item cannot have Log Norma
46	LNUpper	
47	5.215980844	← =IF(ISERROR(A51),NUpper,EXP(LN(Average)+A51))
48		
49	LNLower	
50	4.310324671	← =IF(ISERROR(A51),NLower,EXP(LN(Average)-A51))
51	0.095356961	
52		
53	NUpper	
54	1977.102366	← =Average+(Sigma*StandardDeviation)
55		
56	NLower	
57	359.9109091	← =Average-(Sigma*StandardDeviation)
58		

Figure 5-12. More calculations on Workarea

The calculations in A50 (LNLower) are for the lower log normal limit. They are the same as A47 except the value in A51 is subtracted from the average.

The named values NUpper and NLower are in cells A54 and A57. They are the upper and lower control limits based on a normal distribution.

Isolating the calculations keeps the application simple. There are several things going on with the control limits, but each part of Workarea only does one thing. It is important to break multi-step processes down to basic elements. If you can understand how each step works, you can build the entire process.

The Display Sheet

The most complex part of the Display sheet is the scroll.

The scroll

Figure 5-13 shows how the scroll area works. The data is on the Data sheet. The dates (Item 1) are always in column A. The metric to be displayed is in one of the other columns. Since the dates are in A, the formula in item 3 can use the INDEX function. ScrollStart tells which row to start with, and adding =ROW(A1) makes it possible to fill the formula down. The metric in item 2 is the one to be displayed. The column is identified by SelectedItem and the row by ScrollStart in the formula shown in item 4. This range is named ScrollArea.

On the Display sheet, the scroll (Item 5) contains the array formula {=ScrollArea}. The scroll is formatted using patterns and borders. The scrollbar is linked to cell A41 (Item 6) on Workarea, completing the connection.

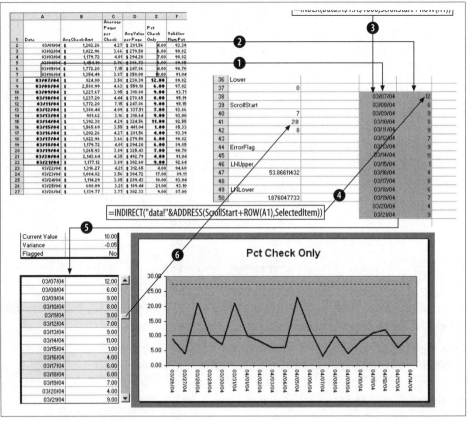

Figure 5-13. Building the scroll

Other parts of the Display sheet

The chart area is completed using named values shown in Figure 5-14.

	A	B	C	D	E	F	G	H
1	LastRow		Date	Avg Check A	Upper Limit	Lower Limit	Mean	
2	46		3/26/2004	1139.77074	1977.10237	359.91091	1168.507	
3		=Upper	3/27/2004	1542.01601	1977.10237	359.91091	1168.507	
4	FirstRow		3/28/2004	766.962692	1977.10237	359.91091	1168.507	
5	26	=Lower	3/29/2004	1189.98927	1977.10237	359.91091	1168.507	
6			3/30/2004	1538.54947	1977.10237	359.91091	1168.507	
7	SelectedItem		3/31/2004	1167.22405	1977.10237	359.91091	1168.507	
8	2	=Average	4/1/2004	1389.86021	1977.10237	359.91091	1168.507	
9	1		4/2/2004	1635.21	1977.10237	359.91091	1168.507	
10			4/3/2004	974.15	1977.10237	359.91091	1168.507	
11	StandardDevaition		4/4/2004	1074.40555	1977.10237	359.91091	1168.507	
12	269.5319095		4/5/2004	846.448136	1977.10237	359.91091	1168.507	
13			4/6/2004	1086.4613	1977.10237	359.91091	1168.507	
14	Average		4/7/2004	942.854054	1977.10237	359.91091	1168.507	
15	1168.506638		4/8/2004	1623.15036	1977.10237	359.91091	1168.507	
16			4/9/2004	931.036291	1977.10237	359.91091	1168.507	
17	Sigma		4/10/2004	1225.00457	1977.10237	359.91091	1168.507	
18	3		4/11/2004	1061.86085	1977.10237	359.91091	1168.507	
19	6		4/12/2004	1238.54507	1977.10237	359.91091	1168.507	
20			4/13/2004	810.4275	1977.10237	359.91091	1168.507	
21	NameofItem		4/14/2004	583.623333	1977.10237	359.91091	1168.507	
22	Avg Check Amt							

Figure 5-14. Completing the chart area

Columns E, F, and G are used to draw lines on the chart showing the control limits and the mean. Using this range, a line chart is inserted on Display. The other piece of the Display sheet is the area shown in Figure 5-15.

	A	B	C	D
2				
3		Date	14-Apr-04	
4		Item Name	Avg Check Amt	
5		Upper Limit	1,977.10	
6		Lower Limit	359.91	
7		Mean	1,168.51	
8		Current Value	583.62	
9		Variance	-584.88	
10		Flagged	No	
11				

Figure 5-15. Data display area

This links to the named range DisplayData on the Workarea sheet. Displayarea, C25: D32, uses named values to arrange the data for Display. The array formula for Display is {=DisplayData}.

Customizing the Application

The design of the application makes it easy to change. Using separate worksheets to isolate the data, the logic, and the display means that they can be modified without disturbing each other. First we will rearrange the Display sheet.

Changing the Display Sheet

Rearranging the elements on the Display sheet is just a matter of dragging the controls and chart to new locations. The areas that reference named ranges can be cut and pasted without interfering with their formulas. By using these techniques and changing patterns and borders, the Display sheet can be rearranged to look like Figure 5-16 in a couple of minutes.

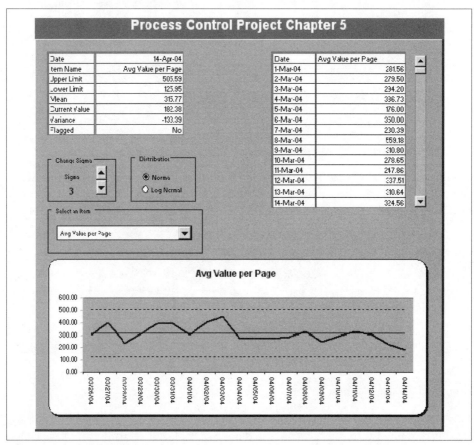

Figure 5-16. A new Display sheet

Adding Logic

In Statistical Process Control, it is considered significant if the metric being measured has been on the same side of the average for three consecutive days. This could mean that a trend has started. A serious problem can start slowly. So, we want to be alerted if the last three days were higher or lower than average even if we are still within the control limits.

We start on the Workarea sheet, as in Figure 5-17.

	B	C	D	E	F	G	H	I
1		Date	StDev Amt Lengt	Upper Limit	Lower Limit	Mean		
2		3/26/2004	0.816524804	1.5414116	0.5556754	1.048543		
3		3/27/2004	1.255764102	1.5414116	0.5556754	1.048543		
4		3/28/2004	1.273045338	1.5414116	0.5556754	1.048543		
5		3/29/2004	0.899924766	1.5414116	0.5556754	1.048543		
6		3/30/2004	0.85212688	1.5414116	0.5556754	1.048543		
7		3/31/2004	1.042416619	1.5414116	0.5556754	1.048543		
8		4/1/2004	0.943276842	1.5414116	0.5556754	1.048543		
9		4/2/2004	0.980861739	1.5414116	0.5556754	1.048543		
10		4/3/2004	1.098135433	1.5414116	0.5556754	1.048543		
11		4/4/2004	1.117089004	1.5414116	0.5556754	1.048543		
12		4/5/2004	0.967438944	1.5414116	0.5556754	1.048543	=IF(D19>G19,1,(IF(D19<G19,-1,0)))	
13		4/6/2004	0.944202502	1.5414116	0.5556754	1.048543		
14		4/7/2004	1.206437829	1.5414116	0.5556754	1.048543		
15		4/8/2004	1.078912032	1.5414116	0.5556754	1.048543		
16		4/9/2004	1.094058312	1.5414116	0.5556754	1.048543		
17		4/10/2004	0.790343854	1.5414116	0.5556754	1.048543		
18		4/11/2004	1.02557981	1.5414116	0.5556754	1.048543		
19		4/12/2004	1.116187441	1.5414116	0.5556754	1.048543	1	
20		4/13/2004	1.42	1.5414116	0.5556754	1.048543	1	
21		4/14/2004	1.63	1.5414116	0.5556754	1.048543	1	
22								
58								
59		Alert						
60		High Alert						
61								
62		=IF(SUM(H19:H21)=3,"High Alert",(IF(SUM(H19:H21)=-3,"Low Alert","")))						
63								
64								

Figure 5-17. Adding new Logic to Workarea

The last three days are in rows 19 through 21 in column D. In cell H19 we enter =IF(D19>G19,1,(IF(D19<G19,-1,0))). This is a nested IF function that returns 1 if the metric is above average, -1 if it is below, or 0 if it is equal to the average. The formula is filled down to cell H21. If the sum of H19:H21 is 3 or -3, the metric has been on the same side of the average for three days in a row. In cell A60 another nested IF function builds the alert. A result of blank is returned if there is no alert. This cell is named Alert.

On the Display sheet in M8, just above the upper-right corner of the chart, the formula =Alert is entered. The cell is formatted bold and red. If there is no alert, the value is blank so the user sees nothing.

Adding a Macro

The way the application works, the user selects and checks each metric separately. It would be better if the application cycled through all of the metrics and only stopped on ones that are flagged as out of limits. The following VBA code will do the job.

```
Sub FindProblem( )
'****************************
' Macro to cycle through all
' of the metrics stopping
' if any are out of limits.
```

```
' The macro starts at the
' current position in the
' list of metrics.

' If no out of limits
' condition is found
' the macro returns to
' the first metric
' and diplays a message.
'*****************************

' Range A9 is linked to the combo box on
' the display sheet. We start by adding
' one to this cell to advance one metric
' in the list.
Range("Workarea!A9").Value = Range("Workarea!A9").Value + 1

' We now setup a loop to continue checking
' metrics until a flagged item is found or
' all of the metrics have been checked.

' NameofItem contains the name of the metric being
' checked. If it is equal to zero the end of
' the list has been reached
While Range("Flagged").Value = 0 And Range("NameofItem").Value <> 0
    ' In the loop one is added to the
    ' value in A9 advancing through the list.
    Range("Workarea!A9").Value = Range("Workarea!A9").Value + 1
Wend

' The loop has ended so we have either found
' a flagged item or we are at the end.
' If we are at the end we need to take action
' so we check.

' If NameofItem is zero we are at the end.
If Range("NameofItem").Value = 0 Then
    ' Return to the first item in the list.
    Range("Workarea!A9").Value = 1
    ' Put up a message box.
    MsgBox ("No alerts found.")
End If

End Sub
```

To add the code to the application, select Tools → Macro → Macros. You can also get to this dialog by pressing Alt-F8. Type in the macro name FindProblem and click the Create button.

Next, type or paste in the code. After the code has been entered go back to the Macros dialog box and with FindProblem highlighted, click on Options... This will bring up a dialog box allowing you select a short cut key to run the macro. Enter a lowercase "e" as the shortcut key.

The macro can now be run by pressing Ctrl-e.

CHAPTER 6

Monitoring Complex Systems

Chapter 5 looked at Statistical Process Control. These techniques were developed before modern computers, so limiting the complexity of the calculations was an important consideration. This, however, imposes limits on power and flexibility. Business processes are often dependent on the day of the week and the traditional Statistical Process Control approach ignores this, reducing the accuracy and sensitivity of the process.

Business processes interrelate in complex ways, and these relationships need to be monitored along with the metrics themselves. If a day has an unusual amount of activity, it is important to know if the relationships in the data are normal. If you have a large amount of activity because a competitor has a problem, you don't want all your metrics to flag because they are high. But you do need to know if the product mix is normal or the percentage of items returned has changed.

Today we are not restricted to simple calculations that can be done by hand. Excel allows us to take on all the complexity and monitor the whole process. In this chapter we look at ways to monitor a complex business process using Excel. We also build a reusable application based on these techniques.

For each item to be monitored, we build a regression model using the last week's value for the item and current values for three other principal data items. The model will be built using enough history to give a good estimate of its accuracy. The current value of each item will be predicted and the accuracy of the prediction will be used to calculate the probability that the item is an anomaly. The basic approach is like the one used in Chapter 5, in which the average served as the prediction. Here we use a more complex and accurate prediction method, explained in the Workarea section.

The application discussed in this chapter uses no other files or components. You can replace the data used in the example without changing the application. It uses the Excel functions and features listed in Tables 6-1 and 6-2, respectively.

Table 6-1. Excel functions used in this chapter's application

INDEX( )	MAX( )	AVERAGE( )
INDIRECT( )	COL( )	STDEV( )
ADDRESS( )	SUM( )	NORMDIST( )
NORMINV ( )	LINEST( ) ( )	LEN( )
ROW( )	IF( )	ABS( )

Table 6-2. Excel features used in this chapter's application

Formatting	Named Ranges	Charting
Named Cells	Array Formulas	VBA
		Form controls

The Application

The application follows the same design principles we have been using. The sample data is based on a transportation operation. It includes 40 daily metrics looking at both operations and billing, with 242 days of data. The main display is shown in Figure 6-1.

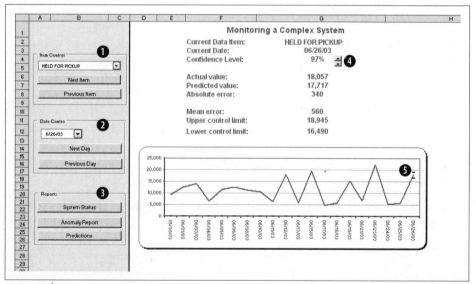

Figure 6-1. The application's main display

This display shows the monitoring status for the current item and allows the user to control the data item being monitored, the date, and the confidence level. It also allows the user to view three reports.

Item 1 contains a combo box that lets the user select an item to be monitored. There are also buttons allowing the user to cycle through the items one by one. Item 2 provides the same functions for date. In Item 3 there are buttons to view reports on three other displays. The spinner control in Item 4 allows the user to change the confidence level. This level sets the sensitivity of the application; in Figure 6-1 it is set to 97%. This means that items will flag if the difference between the prediction and the actual value is so great that it would only occur by chance 4% of the time.

The actual values for the last 20 days are shown in the chart along with the control limits in Item 5. If the current value is between the control limit markers, it is inside the confidence level.

The System Status button (Item 3) brings up the sheet shown in Figure 6-2.

	A	B	C	D	E	F	G	H	
1									
2				System Status				Back	
3			Earliest date:	06/13/03					
4			Latest date:	03/30/04					
5									
6			Rows (days):	207					
7			Columns (items):	40					
8			Lag:	5					
9									
10			Independents:	HELD FOR PICKUP					
11				REGULAR STOP PICKUP					
12				TRANSPORTATION CHARGES - TOTAL					
13									
14			Alternate:	WEIGHT - TOTAL					
15									
16									

Figure 6-2. The system status sheet

The application is designed to be reusable. The Data sheet can be repopulated with different data as long as there are headings, there are dates in column A, and the values are numeric. The application uses up to 1,000 rows or days of information. The Settings sheet contains information about how the data is to be handled. The display in Figure 6-2 shows the dates and how many usable rows and columns there are. It takes 35 days of history for the application to work and the maximum lag is 7. It has a heading row, so the first 43 rows need to be there but are not usable.

This display also shows the lag and independent items for the regression calculations.

The Anomaly Report button checks all the items for the current day and builds a report with an entry for each item out of the control limits. An example of this report is in Figure 6-3.

	A	B	C	D	E	F
1	ANOMALY DETECTION REPORT	SENSITIVITY = 96%				05/23/03
2						
3	ITEM NAME	PREDICTED	ACTUAL	ERROR	SD	PROBABILITY
4	C.O.D. OUTBOUND	6,460	2,715	3,745	4.74	99.95%
5	CREDIT TO SHIPPER	754,244	637,508	116,736	5.05	100.00%
6	DOCUMENTS - TOTAL	933,674	833,931	99,743	4.75	99.99%
7	PICKED UP	344,316	261,041	83,275	3.25	98.14%
8	SHIPMENTS - TOTAL	949,966	869,227	80,739	4.09	99.89%
9	WEEKEND PICKUP	12,696	38,156	-25,460	-3.42	99.25%
10	ZONE 1	111,630	70,509	41,121	4.50	99.90%
11						
12						
13						
14						

Figure 6-3. The Anomaly Report

The sensitivity is set to 96%. So, seven items for this day have an error (difference between actual and predicted) so great that it would only occur by chance 4% of the time.

For each item the report presents the name, the predicted value, the actual value, the error amount, the error in standard deviations, and the probability. In the case of CREDIT TO SHIPPER, there is virtually no chance that an error of 116,736 could be caused by chance alone.

The Predictions button brings up a chart showing predictions and actual values for the last 20 days as in Figure 6-4.

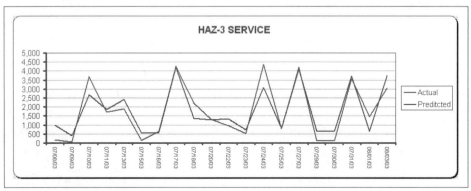

Figure 6-4. The Predictions chart

This chart shows the accuracy of the predictions. Most items are predictable and in general the accuracy is high. This technique's advantage is its accuracy. More accurate predictions allow more sensitive monitoring.

The Data

The data is on the Data sheet. As always, the sheet has no formulas. Its only job is to hold the data. The top left part of the sheet is shown in Figure 6-5.

	A	B	C	D	E	F	G	H
1	Date	C.O.D. OUTBOUND	CASH TRANSA(	CHANGEL	CREDIT TO PAYOR	CREDIT T(	DEFAULT	DELI
2	4/27/2003	19645	63550	10342	568025	2560748	1501737	168
3	4/29/2003	14777	16319	3364	297040	1718069	394251	45
4	4/30/2003	3037	28702	4274	187876	623772	719801	78
5	5/1/2003	25415	36247	5066	543802	2910304	691078	81
6	5/2/2003	17952	25754	3999	318558	1732205	469873	55
7	5/4/2003	19419	70289	10178	610775	2584557	1513641	169
8	5/6/2003	14131	27201	3639	354871	1856041	640629	69
9	5/7/2003	3576	22217	3300	156567	501016	567588	61
10	5/8/2003	27337	31731	6082	558029	2962330	736921	89
11	5/9/2003	17465	32988	5063	367200	1833883	762017	84
12	5/11/2003	18970	65705	10233	593129	2626122	1492419	170
13	5/13/2003	14812	25768	4340	303890	1839866	531880	58
14	5/14/2003	4058	24052	3658	148360	513816	530691	55

Figure 6-5. The Data sheet

This sheet uses 41 columns and 243 rows. If you want to put new data on this sheet, it is important not to delete any of the existing rows or columns. This would interfere with calculations elsewhere in the application. Just select the whole sheet and clear the contents. Then paste your new data on the Data sheet starting in cell A1.

Settings

The Settings sheet contains processing options for the application. If you are using new data, you will need to change the settings. The Settings sheet is shown in Figure 6-6.

Independent Columns

There are three independent columns, indicated by column labels in the range A2: A4. The regression model in the application uses these three columns from the Data sheet. It is important to select items that are central to the process being monitored but they must not be highly correlated with each other. In this case, I am using columns O, AC, and AF. These are CASH TRANSACTIONS, REGULAR STOP PICKUP, and TRANSPORTATION CHARGES – TOTAL. One deals with money, one with the operation, and one with billing. They are all high level metrics, but they come from different parts of the process. These cells on the Settings sheet are named ind1, ind2, and ind3.

The Alternate

But what happens when we predict one of the independent items? If we predict CASH TRANSACTIONS and it is in the model as an independent variable, our prediction will be as useless as it is accurate. This is where the alternate comes in.

When one of the independent variables is being predicted, the alternate takes its place in the model. The alternate item, WEIGHT – TOTAL, is in column AJ. This value is named Alt.

	A	B	C	D
1	Independent columns			
2	O			
3	AC			
4	AF			
5				
6	Current Column			
7	B	1	$B$1	
8				
9	Sensitivity			
10	0.96	96		
11				
12	Alternate			
13	AJ			
14				
15	Current Row			
16	36	1		
17				
18	OutMessage			
19	The current item outside the control range.			
20				
21	Lag			
22	5			
23				
24				
25				
26				

Figure 6-6. The Settings sheet

The Lag

The lag is the number of days in a week of data. In the example we are looking at a five days per week operation, so the lag is 5. The lag can be as high as 7, and naturally it is named Lag.

The Out of Limits Message

The named value outmessage is the message displayed when an item is out of the control limits. It appears on the main display under the chart.

The other values on the sheet should not be changed manually. They are set by controls or macros. They are the current sensitivity, and the row and columns settings.

The Current Column

The current column is calculated as in Figure 6-7.

The value in B7 is 1. It is set by a combo-box control on the main display and by the macros that run on the Next Item and Previous Item buttons. Here the 1 means the

6	Current Column			
7	B		1	$B$1
8	=MID(C7,2,LEN(C7)-3)			=ADDRESS(1,B7+1)

Figure 6-7. The current column calculation

first column is selected. But column A contains dates, so the first usable column is B. We want the letter B because we use it in the indirect functions on the Workarea sheet.

The address function in C7 adds 1 to skip the dates, then converts the number to an address. The MID function in A7 strips the letter B out of the address. This formula will work with two letter columns, like AB, as well. The final value in A7 is named CurCol and is used in other formulas.

The Current Row

The current row calculation is in Figure 6-8.

15	Current Row		
16		53	18
17	=B16+42		

Figure 6-8. The current row calculation

Here things are simpler because we want the row number, not a letter. The value in cell B16 is set by a combo box or a macro when the user changes the current date. The formula in A16 adjusts the value to skip the first 35 rows plus 7 additional rows to allow for the lag. This is the historical data the model needs to monitor the 43rd day. The value is named CurRow and is used in other formulas.

The Sensitivity

Figure 6-9 contains the calculation for sensitivity.

9	Sensitivity		
10		0.99	99
11	=B10/100		

Figure 6-9. Calculating the sensitivity

The spinner control on the Display sheet sets the value in cell B10. The control changes the value by 1 each time it is clicked, and is constrained to a maximum value of 99. The calculations need a number between 0 and 1, therefore the value is divided by 100 in cell A11.

Workarea

All the logic is on the Workarea sheet. It is organized into functional areas using the same conventions as the other applications in the book. The overall layout is shown in Figure 6-10.

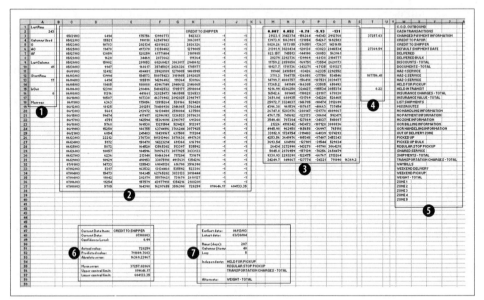

Figure 6-10. The organization of the Workarea sheet

Item 1 in Column A contains named values used in other formulas. The area in Item 2 is used to hold the needed values from the Data sheet, based on the current settings. These values change when either the selected item or date changes.

Item 3 contains the regression model. The coefficients and intercept are at the top and are recalculated every time the data in Item 2 changes.

Item 4 uses the results of the regression calculations to set the control limits.

The data in Item 5 is used to populate the combo box that allows the user to select an item. The combo-box control requires a column as its input range. These values are headings on the Data sheet and are in a row. This area transposes them into a column.

Item 6 is a display area. It is used for the main display sheet and contains general information about the current item and date.

Item 7 is also a display area and is used by the system status report.

The first area (Item 1), used for named values, is detailed in Figure 6-11.

	A	B
1	LastRow	
2	243	{=MAX((Data!A1:A1000<>")*ROW(Data!A1:A1000))}
3		
4	Columns Used	
5	O	=IF(Ind1=CurCol,Alt,Ind1)
6	AC	=IF(Ind2=CurCol,Alt,Ind2)
7	AF	=IF(Ind3=CurCol,Alt,Ind3)
8		
9	LastColumn	
10	41	{=MAX((Data!1:1<>")*COLUMN(Data!1:1))}
11		
12	StartRow	
13	17	=CurRow-36
14		
15	IsOut	
16	0	=IF(H37<J37,1,(IF(H37>I37,1,0)))
17		
18	Message	
19		=IF(IsOut=0,",OutMessage)
20		
21		

Figure 6-11. The section of Workarea indicated by Item 1

LastRow

The value in cell A2 is named `LastRow`. It keeps up with how many rows are used on the Data sheet. It is necessary to have a formula to calculate this because the number of rows could change if new data is put on the sheet. The formula is:

```
{=MAX((DATA!A1:A1000) * ROW(DATA!A1:A1000))}
```

This array formula is covered in Chapter 3. As written, it only considers rows 1-1000. Since each row contains one day's data, this means the application can hold over two years of information. The formula can be changed to look at 5,000 rows by changing A1000 to A5000 in the formula. It has to be changed in both places and reentered using Crtl-Shift-Enter.

Columns Used

These values tell the model which column to use as independent variables. These formulas are necessary because they decide if the alternate needs to be used. The basic formula is:

```
=IF(Ind1=CurCol,Alt,Ind1)
```

`CurCol` is a named value containing the column of the item being monitored. Here it is being tested against the first independent (`Ind1`). If they are equal the alternate value (`Alt`) is substituted. This formula is used for all three independents. The results in the range A5:A7 are named `UsedInd1`, `UsedInd2`, and `UsedInd3`.

LastColumn

The next value is LastColumn. It is the same as LastRow, except it looks at which columns are used.

StartRow

The model requires 35 days of data. Therefore, we need to pull data starting 36 days before the selected date, allowing one additional row for the headings. The named value StartRow in cell A13 keeps up with this value.

IsOut

The value IsOut in cell A16 is always 0 or 1. A 1 means the current item is out of the control limits. The formula is:

```
=IF(H37<J37,1,(IF(H37>I37,1,0)))
```

H37 is the current actual value. J37 is the lower control limit and I37 is the upper control limit. Message in A19 is used on the Display sheet as shown in Figure 6-12.

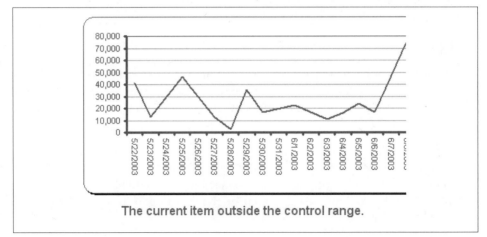

Figure 6-12. The message

On the Display sheet, cell E28 contains this formula:

```
=Message
```

The font for this cell is formatted red and bold. The message is blank if the item is inside the control limits and is set to outmessage if the item is outside the limits.

The Data Area

The next part of the Workarea sheet manages the link to the Data sheet, and is shown in Figure 6-13.

	C	D	E	F	G	H	I	J
1								
2						TRANSPORTATION CHARGES - TOTAL		
3	05/23/03	10783	202134	15615660	44465743	42818623	-1	-1
4	05/25/03	11478	417370	7363932	59700815	31350402	-1	-1
5	05/27/03	13059	128259	23655158	38170699	61771404	-1	-1
6	05/28/03	1620	34469	543434	13998773	2873662	-1	-1
7	05/29/03	15902	201053	22981977	62547903	60260421	-1	-1
8	05/30/03	9147	168617	13774814	42818623	35745031	-1	-1
9	06/01/03	12412	484481	8262150	31350402	35920189	-1	-1
10	06/03/03	13994	154573	22358723	61771404	58075423	-1	-1
11	06/04/03	6414	185519	3755611	2873662	14296482	-1	-1
12	06/05/03	11485	180088	17041170	60260421	43967149	-1	-1
13	06/06/03	12398	218406	19596768	35745031	54842532	-1	-1
14	06/08/03	11316	441661	7801142	35920189	32825473	-1	-1
15	06/10/03	10507	107338	19260409	58075423	46378902	-1	-1
16	06/11/03	6363	175056	3512471	14296482	13515264	-1	-1
17	06/12/03	18125	201251	30540035	43967149	78408930	-1	-1
18	06/13/03	5661	213972	3882648	54842532	16130480	-1	-1
19	06/15/03	19474	417417	29352521	32825473	82196193	-1	-1
20	06/17/03	4751	142594	4244688	46378902	15369010	-1	-1
21	06/18/03	5768	169538	3422356	13515264	13211504	-1	-1
22	06/19/03	15250	188755	24875655	78408930	63744116	-1	-1
23	06/21/03	6854	241483	4606205	16130480	18439167	-1	-1
24	06/23/03	22212	370738	38699184	82196193	101313966	-1	-1
25	06/24/03	5172	158478	3104808	15369010	14223214	-1	-1
26	06/25/03	5872	164520	3449106	13211504	13565302	-1	-1
27	06/26/03	18057	184596	31973757	63744116	78976273	-1	-1
28	06/27/03	6236	213140	4951272	18439167	18466364	-1	-1
29	06/29/03	10929	410953	7895102	101313966	33075110	-1	-1
30	07/01/03	14733	135543	28665096	14223214	69841138	-1	-1
31	07/02/03	5317	163532	3358344	13565302	13134468	-1	-1
32	07/04/03	15473	184345	24961188	78976273	62765202	-1	-1
33	07/04/03	11842	202179	20400871	18466364	55170621	-1	-1
34	07/06/03	11254	157579	16933460	33075110	43977918	-1	-1
35	07/08/03	5785	164398	4611017	69841138	16297655	-1	-1
36	07/09/03	3400	99227	2239081	13134468	7781384	-1	-1
37	07/10/03	13333	143010	20357721	62765202	51091338	53864570.04	49107427.92

Figure 6-13. The section of Workarea indicated by Item 2

This is a holding area for data. It uses the settings to determine what data is needed and builds an area for the regression model to use. The last two columns of this area are used by the chart on the Display sheet.

The formula in C3 is:

```
=TEXT(INDIRECT("Data!A"& ROW(A2)+StartRow),"mm/dd/yy")
```

Column A on the Data sheet contains the dates. The data starts in row two, as there are headings. The formula uses the named value StartRow to determine what row to start with. The formula fills down to C37. The dates are not used in the regression model, but they appear on the charts and in the displays. Excel's chart feature will fill in any skipped dates, and in this case we do not want that to happen. In the sample data we only have five days each week, so we don't need the other two days on the chart. The TEXT function is used to convert the date to a text string. This keeps Excel from seeing these as dates.

Columns D, E, and F are similar. They contain the independent variables. The basic formula in D3 is:

```
=INDIRECT("data!" & UsedInd1 & ROW(A2)+StartRow)
```

Here we do not know the column in advance. It is determined by the named value UsedInd1. Cells E3 and F3 are the same but reference UsedInd2 and UsedInd3. These also fill down to row 37.

Columns G and H both contain the current data item. Column G is offset by one lag and is used in the regression calculations. Column H is not offset and is the dependent or Y variable. The formulas for these rows are:

```
=INDIRECT("data!" & CurCol & StartRow+ROW(A2)-Lag)
=INDIRECT("data!" & CurCol & ROW(A2)+StartRow)
```

The heading in cell H2 uses the same formula except the heading is always in row 1. So, the formula is:

```
=INDIRECT("data!" & CurCol & ROW(A1))
```

Columns I and J are used to put the control limits on the chart. These appear as small tick marks at the right end of the plot area, as shown in Figure 6-14.

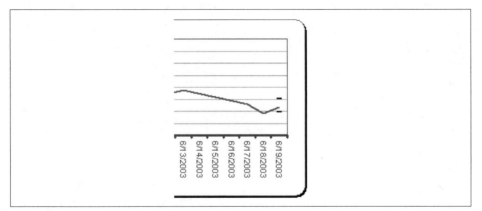

Figure 6-14. The chart shows the control limits

All the cells in these columns except the last row have a value of -1. The vertical axis of the chart is formatted with a minimum value of 0, as shown in Figure 6-15.

This keeps all the values except the last row off the chart. The values in row 37 are the control limits. Cell I37 has this formula:

```
=Q37+T12
```

Cell Q37 is the current prediction and T12 has the allowable error. So, this is the upper control limit. In cell J37 the formula is:

```
=MAX(Q37-T12,0)
```

This sets the lower limit. In some cases the limit would be a negative number, and for this kind of data that is not sensible. Therefore, we use a formula that will return a value of 0 if the limit comes out negative.

On the chart both of these items are formatted with no line, as shown in Figure 6-16.

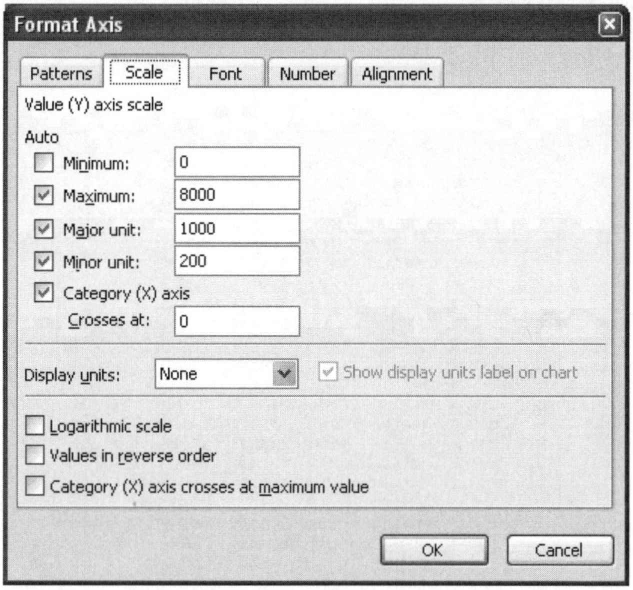

Figure 6-15. Formatting the vertical axis

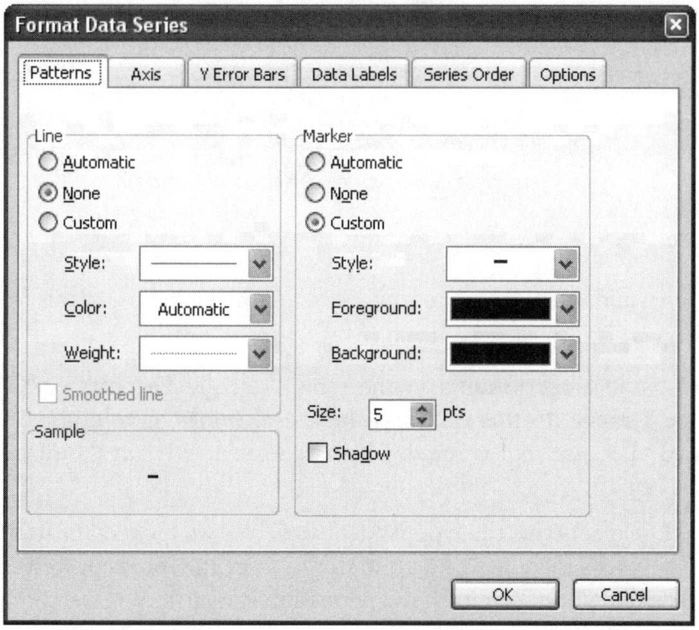

Figure 6-16. Formatting the control limits series on the chart

This makes the control limits appear as markers at the end of the chart.

The Regression Area

The regression area is shown in Figure 6-17.

	M	N	O	P	Q	R	S
1							
2	**0.48819**	**-0.0007**	**-0.0656**	**5.07329**	**4786.91**		
3	13727.06	-24038.15	-11065.58	46405.38	29815.62		
4	13287.68	-24155.94	-31794.32	62969.67	25094		
5	9989.44	-39055.09	-10143.93	70995.61	36572.93		
6	559.4711	-9614.229	-12174.78	32540.08	16097.45		
7	24620.15	-29567.43	-11818.37	58266.73	46287.98		
8	20821.99	-36881.01	-14333.01	62898.64	37293.53		
9	15271.22	-22074.78	-28984.23	57409.34	26408.46		
10	16649.39	-31189.31	-7044.112	53305.05	36507.93		
11	24308.19	-9088.869	-11488.14	32281.34	40799.43		
12	33419.37	-52729.16	-13207.2	91953.37	64223.29		
13	12175.58	-10847.57	-14042.02	28719.89	20792.78		
14	12958.15	-55276.05	-27393.21	98797.23	33873.04		
15	13658.71	-10335.49	-9357.805	24103.2	22855.52		
16	12710.15	-8884.593	-11126.02	29262.73	26749.18		
17	32921.41	-42867.23	-12387.14	77367.66	59821.61		
18	18627.56	-12400.14	-15847.45	34772.32	29939.2		
19	20204.43	-68132.55	-24329.87	112687.9	45216.82		
20	13590.85	-9564.957	-10400.2	26239.05	24651.66		
21	10649.97	-9122.519	-10796.71	29790.35	25308		
22	30478.48	-53110.69	-12114.21	91608.38	61648.88		
23	20476.35	-12418.43	-13987.42	31637.03	30494.44		
24	14588.72	-22242.65	-26969	55445.98	25609.95		
25	844.0886	-46967.41	-8895.079	74744.77	24513.28		
26	13171.49	-8832.788	-10731.87	26974.68	25368.42		
27	42994.33	-42208.92	-12097.74	78499	71973.59		
28	13529.83	-37101.65	-13268.1	60077.89	28024.88		
29	12220	-29574.67	-10341.2	57094.8	34185.83		
30	10695.86	-10960	-10788.7	29348.98	23083.04		
31	9289.369	-5232.896	-6511.823	17249.18	19580.74		
32	36771.8	-34358.37	-9385.105	67642.16	65457.4		
33	17569.64	-26477.75	-13528.44	48434.69	30785.06		
34	11218.71	-40902.3	-27536.27	78037.33	25604.39		
35	17620.41	-8837.263	-7107.243	22895.75	29358.57		
36	11942.71	-9636.617	-11521.54	30607.15	26178.61		
37	25325.1	-62231.75	-10584.15	95875.02	53171.13	7682.871	

Figure 6-17. The regression area

The coefficients and intercept are in row 2 and are calculated using this formula:

```
{=LINEST(H3:H36,D3:G36,TRUE,FALSE)}
```

It is entered as an array formula in the range M2:Q2. The first parameter is the dependent or Y range. In this case it is the actual values in column H. We do not include row 37 because that is the day being checked. We run the regression using only days in the past.

The range D3:G36 contains the independent variables we looked at earlier. The third parameter (TRUE) tells the LINEST function not to force the intercept to be 0. The final parameter tells LINEST not to return the regression statistics. We are not doing analysis here. We just want the answer.

In cell M3 the formula is:

```
=M$2*G3
```

This fills down but not to the right. Inconveniently, the LINEST function returns the coefficients in reverse order. So, the formulas have to be entered separately for each column. Column N has:

```
=N$2*F3
```

And so on. Finally in column Q we add the intercept with this formula:

```
=SUM(M3:P3,Q$2)
```

This is the predicted value.

The day being monitored is in row 37, and we need to know how accurate the prediction is. The formula in cell R37 is:

```
=ABS(Q37-H37)
```

We use the absolute value because we need to know how much error there is, not the error itself. This results in a one-tailed distribution, which is easy to handle with Excel's statistical functions.

The results of the regression are used to set the control limits. This is done in the area shown in Figure 6-18.

	T	U
1		
2		
3	334699.92	{=AVERAGE(ABS(H3:H36-Q3:Q36))}
4		
5		
6	306767.43	{=STDEV(ABS(H3:H36-Q3:Q36))}
7		
8		
9		
10		
11		
12	1048347.69	=NORMINV(Sen,T3,T6)
13		
14		
15	0.98	= NORMDIST(R37,T3,T6,TRUE)

Figure 6-18. The control limits

The actual values are in column H and the predictions are in Q. The array formula in cell T3 returns the average of the absolute values of the differences between the predicted and the actual. Once again, we do not use row 37 because it is the current day. We use an array formula for this because otherwise we would need another column with absolute error for the model.

In cell T6 we do the same thing in calculating the standard deviations of the errors.

These values are used in cell T12 to determine how much error is allowed for row 37. We know the mean and standard deviations of the errors, and we assume they are normally distributed. We know how much error we are willing to accept. Given these parameters, the NORMDIST function returns the value that is our limit. This is the amount of error that will cause an item to be flagged as an anomaly.

If an item is flagged, we need to know how far out it is. This is not just the size of the error. Very few predictions will be exactly right, and some error is expected. But relatively large errors should be rare. If we set the application's sensitivity to 0.99, we will be alerted when there is only a 1% chance that an item's error would occur as part of the past population of errors.

The formula in cell A15 calculates what percentage of errors is less than the error for the item being tested. If the formula returns a value of 0.98, then 98% of errors are less than the one for the item being tested.

The Combo Box Data Area

Column W of the Workarea sheet contains the names of the data items as shown in Figure 6-19.

	V	W	X	Y	Z
1		C.O.D. OUTBOUND			
2		CASH TRANSACTIONS			
3		CHANGED PAYMENT INFORMATION			
4		CREDIT TO PAYOR			
5		CREDIT TO SHIPPER			
6		DEFAULT SHIPMENT DATE			
7		DELIVERED			
8		DELIVERED BULK			
9		DISCOUNTS - TOTAL			
10		DOCUMENTS - TOTAL			
11		HAZ-1 SERVICE			
12		HAZ-2 SERVICE			
13		HAZ-3 SERVICE			
14		HELD FOR PICKUP			
15		HELD IN TRANSIT			
16		INSURANCE CHARGES - TOTAL			
17		INSURANCE VALUE - TOTAL			
18		LIST SHIPMENTS			
19		MISSROUTES			
20		NO HANDLING INFORMATION			
21		NO PAYMENT INFORMATION			

Figure 6-19. The item names

These are the headings from the Data sheet. The combo box control cannot use the headings directly because they are not in a column. The formula in cell W1 is:

```
=IF(INDEX(Data!B$1:IV$1,1,ROW(A1))=0,"",INDEX(Data!B$1:IV$1,1,ROW(A1)))
```

It fills down to cell W255. This formula contains an IF function because the index function returns a value of zero if the referenced cell is empty. This would cause the combo box to display a long list of zeros after the last item name. The IF function returns a blank (=" ") if the referenced cell is empty, causing the combo box to display a blank for the unused columns.

The Main Display Area

There are two display areas on the Workarea sheet. Figure 6-20 has the first.

	D	E	
47	Current Data Item:	HAZ-3 SERVICE	=H2
48	Current Date:	07/31/03	=C37
49	Confidence Level:	0.95	=Sen
50			=""
51	Actual value:	3573	=H37
52	Predicted value:	3802.365386	=Q37
53	Absolute error:	229.3653856	=R37
54			=""
55	Mean error:	404.0415683	=T3
56	Upper control limit:	4779.29	=I37
57	Lower control limit:	2825.44	=J37

Figure 6-20. The display area

This area is named Display. The main display uses it for the information above the chart. All the values come from the Workarea sheet itself. The references are shown in the figure. The Display sheet references this range with an array formula applied to an area with the same number of rows and columns, as demonstrated in Figure 6-21.

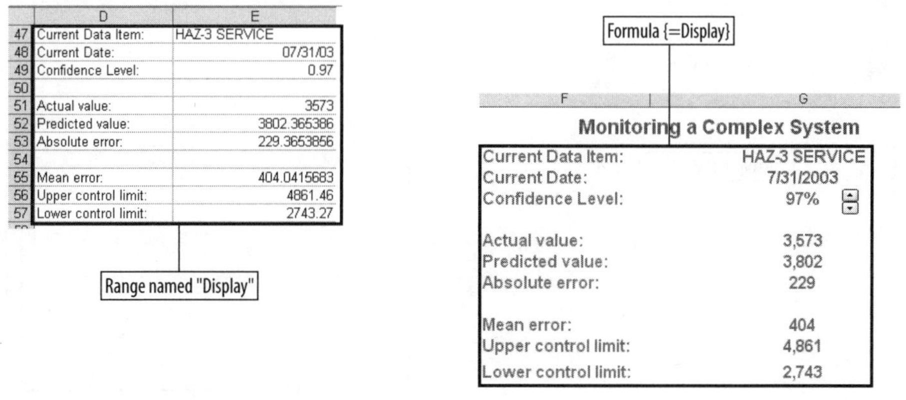

Figure 6-21. The display sheet references an area on the Workarea sheet

As in all the applications, this keeps the logic out of the display and allows the Display sheet to be concerned only with presentation issues.

The system status report is set up the same way, but some of its values come from the Data sheet. The formulas in its range on Workarea are shown in Figure 6-22.

	I	J	
47	Earliest date:	06/13/03	=Data!A44
48	Latest date:	03/30/04	=INDIRECT("data!a" & LastRow)
49			=""
50	Rows (days):	207	=LastRow-44
51	Columns (items):	40	=LastColumn-1
52	Lag:	5	=Lag
53			=""
54	Independants:	HELD FOR PICKUP	=INDIRECT("data!" & Ind1 & 1)
55		REGULAR STOP PICKUP	=INDIRECT("data!" & Ind2 & 1)
56		TRANSPORTATION CHARGES - TOTAL	=INDIRECT("data!" & Ind3 & 1)
57			=""
58	Alternate:	WEIGHT - TOTAL	=INDIRECT("data!" & Alt & 1)
59			

Figure 6-22. Building the system status report

The earliest date that the application can test is in the 44th row because the model requires 43 days of history. The latest date is the last used cell in column A on the Data sheet. Figure 6-23 shows the range named "Stats," which contains this information, and its relationship with the systems status report.

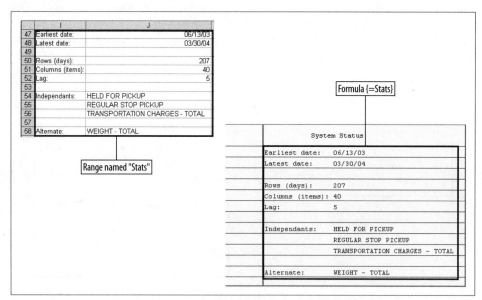

Figure 6-23. The relationship between the Workarea and the system status report

Again, the main point is keeping the logic and the presentation separate.

Macros

Visual Basic does not play a big part in this application. It is used for navigation, managing the item and date selections, and creating the anomaly report. All the code is in a code module and is run by buttons on various sheets.

These two macros control the items selection.

```
Sub NextItem( )
If Range("settings!b7").Value >= Range("LastColumn").Value - 1 Then
    Range("settings!b7").Value = 1
Else
    Range("settings!b7").Value = Range("settings!b7").Value + 1
End If
End Sub

Sub PreviousItem( )
If Range("settings!b7").Value <= 1 Then
    Range("settings!b7").Value = Range("LastColumn").Value - 1
Else
    Range("settings!b7").Value = Range("settings!b7").Value - 1
End If
End Sub
```

A number representing the current item selection is in cell settings!B7. If this number changes so does the selected item. The number can have any value from 1 to LastColumn - 1. Remember, the first column is used for the dates.

The NextItem subroutine checks to see if the current selection is the last column. If so, it sets the selection to the first column, otherwise it adds one to the number in B7 to select the next column.

The PreviousItem subroutine works the same way except it moves in the other direction.

A number representing the selected row/date is in cell settings!B16. There are two similar macros that control the date selection. This is the code:

```
Sub NextDay( )
If Range("settings!b16").Value >= Range("LastRow").Value - 25 Then
    Range("settings!b16").Value = 1
Else
    Range("settings!b16").Value = Range("settings!b16").Value + 1
End If
End Sub

Sub PreviousDay( )
If Range("settings!b16").Value <= 1 Then
    Range("settings!b16").Value = Range("LastRow").Value - 25
Else
    Range("settings!b16").Value = Range("settings!b16").Value - 1
End If
End Sub
```

The only difference is that we need to start with the date that is 35 days before the selected date to include the historical data the model needs.

These selections can also be changed using the combo box controls, so the macros are designed to match the results from the controls. The date selection macro changes the value in cell settings!B16. The combo box that allows the user to select a date is formatted as shown in Figure 6-24.

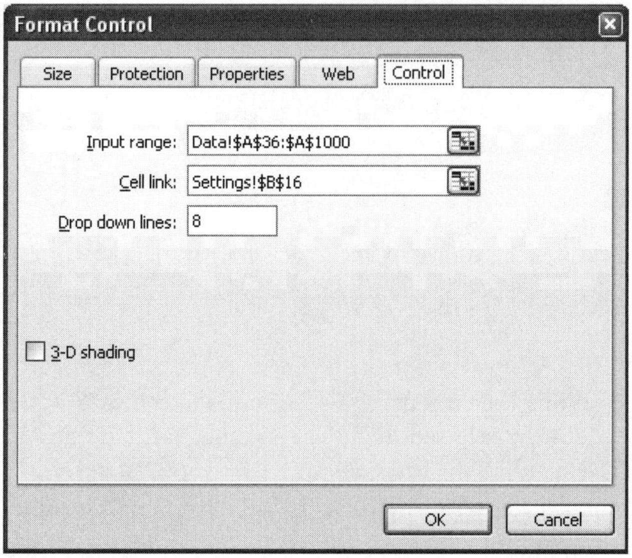

Figure 6-24. Formatting the combo box

The link cell is settings!B16. The combo boxes and the macros do the same thing but give the user different options.

This is the macro that produces the anomaly report:

```
Sub RunDay( )
Dim oldcol, Outline, x As Integer

' We are going to run through all the items. At the
' end we want to return to the item that was selected.
' So we need to save the current column number
oldcol = Range("settings!b7").Value

' The next step is to clear all information
' that is on the report sheet.
' Go to the Report sheet
Sheets("Report").Select

' Clear the data area. Rows above 4 are headings.
' There cannot be more than 255 items since there
' are only 255 columns in a worksheet.
```

```
' We clear rather than delete
' because this preserves all
' the formatting.
Range("a4:f259").ClearContents

' Put the sensitivity heading in cell B1
Range("B1").Value = "SENSITIVITY = " & Trim(Str((Range("sen").Value * 100))) & "%"

'Outline is a line counter. It starts at 3
' because we add 1 to it each time we
' add a line to the report and this
' way it will start with row 4.
Outline = 3

' Now we are ready to check each item for the
' current day. We change the item by changing the
' value in cell settings!B7.
' Here we set up a loop to check each item

For x = 1 To Range("LastColumn").Value - 1 ' Minus 1 because the first column
                                           ' has the dates
    ' Change the item setting
    Range("settings!b7").Value = x

    ' When B7 changes the entire application recalculates
    ' If the item is out of the control limits, the named value
    ' isout will be a 1.

    ' Test isout to see if it is 1
    If Range("isout").Value = 1 Then
        ' If it is add 1 to the line counter
        Outline = Outline + 1

        ' Now we fill in columns A-F on row Outline with
        ' the report information

        ' The name of the item
        Range("report!A" & Outline).Value = Range("workarea!h2").Value

        ' The predicted value
        Range("report!B" & Outline).Value = Range("workarea!q37").Value

        ' The actual value
        Range("report!C" & Outline).Value = Range("workarea!h37").Value

        ' The error (predicted - actual)
        Range("report!D" & Outline).Value = Range("workarea!q37").Value -
Range("workarea!h37").Value

        ' The number of standard deviations the error represents
        ' workarea!T6 is the standard deviation or errors
        Range("report!E" & Outline).Value = Range("report!D" & Outline).Value /
Range("workarea!t6").Value
```

```
            ' The percentage of error amount that would be less than the
            ' current error in a normal distribution. Effectively this is
            ' the probability that today's values for the item being tested
            ' is an anomaly
            Range("report!f" & Outline).Value = Range("workarea!t15").Value
        End If
    Next x   ' End the loop

    ' Select the top left cell of the report sheet
    Range("A1").Select

    ' Reselect the original item
    Range("settings!b7").Value = oldcol
    End Sub
```

This subroutine stays on the report sheet, so it is not necessary to turn off screen updating.

The rest of the code is pure navigation, like this macro:

```
Sub GoDisplay( )
Sheets("Display").Select
End Sub
```

This is run by all of the Back buttons and returns the user to the main display.

CHAPTER 7

Queuing

Work is frequently done in queues. Processes that were once based on paper are now handled as images with every step recorded. The flow of work from step to step is controlled by systems that establish priority and direct work to the appropriate area. Queuing applications accumulate large amounts of data that can be used to answer important questions about the operation.

This chapter is about organizing information. There aren't many calculations. This is not a statistical or forecasting problem. The challenge is extracting the important information and presenting it. We start with several thousand rows of data and a specific area of interest. Each row in the data contains information about an item in a work queue. The area of interest is the performance of the agents doing the work.

Our task is to build an application showing how the individual agents are performing. The emphasis is on extracting the right pieces of information and presenting them in a way that is easy to use and understand.

The application uses the Excel functions listed in Table 7-1.

Table 7-1. Excel functions used in this chapter's application

INDEX( )	MAX( )	ISERROR( )
INDIRECT( )	MIN( )	LOOKUP( )
ADDRESS( )	SUM( )	COUNTIF( )
MATCH( )	IF( )	HOUR( )
ROW( )	AVERAGE( )	VALUE( )
		INT( )

The INDEX, INDIRECT, and ADDRESS functions are vital to understanding the application, and they are explained in Chapter 1.

Table 7-2 lists the Excel features used in the application.

Table 7-2. The Excel features used in this chapter's application

Controls	Named Ranges	Charting
Named Cells	Array Formulas	Cell Formatting
		Visual Basic

The Data

The data for this chapter's example, shown in Figure 7-1, come from a typical work queue.

	A	B	C	D	E	F	G
1	agent	assigned_date	reference	completed_date	amount		
2	9321	2/19/2004 8:00		2/19/2004 8:00	$52.71		
3	9321	2/19/2004 8:00		2/19/2004 8:02	$1.35		
4	9321	2/19/2004 8:02		2/19/2004 8:03	$298.33		
5	9321	2/19/2004 8:03		2/19/2004 8:06	$1.35		
6	9321	2/19/2004 8:06		2/19/2004 8:07	$4.85		
7	9321	2/19/2004 8:07		2/19/2004 8:09	$73.62		
8	9321	2/19/2004 8:09		2/19/2004 8:11	$1.35		
9	9321	2/19/2004 8:11	15806	2/19/2004 8:12	$105.19		
10	9321	2/19/2004 8:12		2/19/2004 8:13	$355.47		
11	9321	2/19/2004 8:13		2/19/2004 8:13	$28.86		
12	9321	2/19/2004 8:13		2/19/2004 8:13	$13.43		
13	9321	2/19/2004 8:13		2/19/2004 8:14	$106.57		
14	9321	2/19/2004 8:14		2/19/2004 8:14	$130.18		
15	9321	2/19/2004 8:14		2/19/2004 8:15	$394.58		
16	9321	2/19/2004 8:15		2/19/2004 8:16	$102.00		
17	9321	2/19/2004 8:16		2/19/2004 8:17	$34.03		
18	9321	2/19/2004 8:17	2103447	2/19/2004 8:20	$1.35		
19	9321	2/19/2004 8:20		2/19/2004 8:21	$58.80		
20	9321	2/19/2004 8:21		2/19/2004 8:21	$10.00		
21	9321	2/19/2004 8:21		2/19/2004 8:22	$72.74		
22	9321	2/19/2004 8:22		2/19/2004 8:22	$63.80		
23	9321	2/19/2004 8:22		2/19/2004 8:23	$123.71		
24	9321	2/19/2004 8:23		2/19/2004 8:24	$183.04		
25	9321	2/19/2004 8:24		2/19/2004 8:25	$442.14		
26	9321	2/19/2004 8:25		2/19/2004 8:27	$191.47		
27	9321	2/19/2004 8:27	5163	2/19/2004 8:28	$463.57		

Figure 7-1. Sample queue data

This is the Data sheet from the application. Column A contains the employee number of the agent who processed the item. The date and time the work was assigned to the agent is in column B.

The reference in column C is optional. The agent can enter a reference number if they want to be able to retrieve their work later. We are tracking how often the number is entered to see how its use relates to productivity and accuracy.

Column D has the date and time the work was completed, and column E the value of the item.

The Data sheet contains no formulas or significant formatting. In production, it could be linked to a query and could be refreshed with a single command.

There are 4,457 rows of data, one for each item worked on 2/19/2004. The data is sorted by the agent and assigned_date columns, and contains a complete picture of the day's work. It tells how much work each agent did, how long it took, when they started and stopped, and how many breaks they took. But arranged as one big list it is hard to understand. It is our job to build a tool that extracts the meaning from the data and presents it in a way that is easy to understand.

The agent names are in a separate data source and will be matched to the agent employee numbers on the Data sheet. This data is on the Workarea sheet and is described in the section "The Logic."

The Application

There are three display sheets, a Data sheet, and a Workarea sheet. The application uses the Data sheet to build the displays. If the Data sheet is updated all of the other sheets will update automatically. The display sheets contain no logic. They link to the information on Workarea using named ranges. The look and feel is based on patterns and borders.

The main display is named Totals and is shown in Figure 7-2.

Figure 7-2. The Totals sheet

This sheet has the look and feel of a web page. Our users regularly work with web pages. So, we make our application easy to understand by using the web page metaphor.

Item 1 is a general heading and appears on all of the display sheets. Item 2 is a simple bitmap created with Paint. It is drawn and copied in Paint, then pasted on the sheet using Paste Special → Bitmap. It appears on all of the display screens, increasing their common appearance.

Item 3 is a list of the agents, showing their daily metrics. Average time per item is the average time it takes an agent to complete a work item in hours, minutes, seconds (hh:mm:ss). Item 4 gives the work group totals for the day. The headings in this area are also buttons that control the sort order. If the user clicks on the heading Items Worked, the area will sort by that item.

Item 5 contains navigation buttons. These buttons run simple macros that move the user between the display sheets. The sheet tabs do the same thing but there are a couple of reasons to include the buttons. First, there are sheets in the application that are not intended for display. The buttons keep users where they should be without actually hiding the data and Workarea sheets. Second, buttons are part of the web page metaphor. The user already knows what they do and how to use them.

Clicking the agent detail button causes the Detail sheet in Figure 7-3 to display.

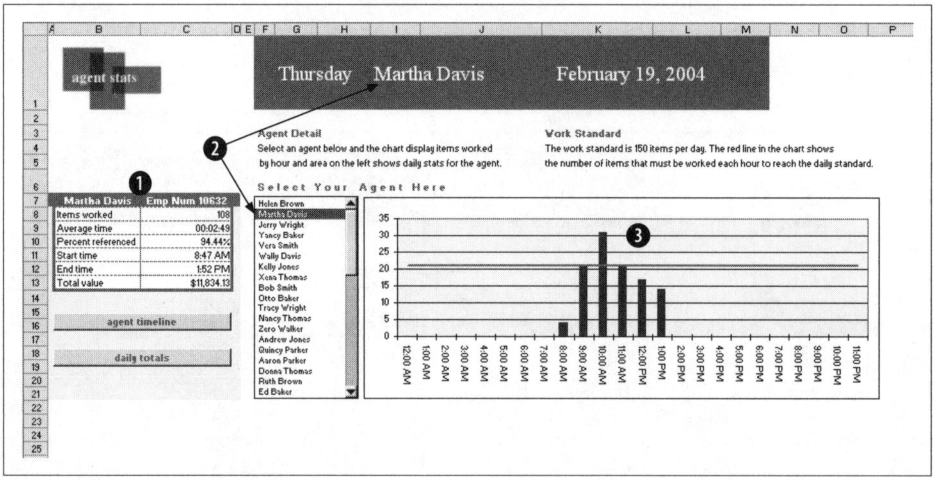

Figure 7-3. The agent detail sheet

The agent detail sheet follows the look and feel of the application and focuses on a single agent. Item 1 displays the daily totals for the agent. Item 2 is a listbox that allows the user to select an agent to view. As soon as a name is clicked, all headings and displays change to that agent. There is no macro; everything is based on Excel functions and controls.

Item 3 is a chart that shows how many items the agent worked during each hour of the day. Each agent is expected to complete 150 items per day. The workday has seven hours, so therefore the expected work rate is about 21 items per hour. The red line in the chart shows the hourly standard of 21 items.

This is an example of extracting information from the data. All of the times are on the Data sheet, but with this chart the manager can see what is going on without looking at thousands of rows.

Clicking the agent timeline button takes the user to the Timeline sheet in Figure 7-4.

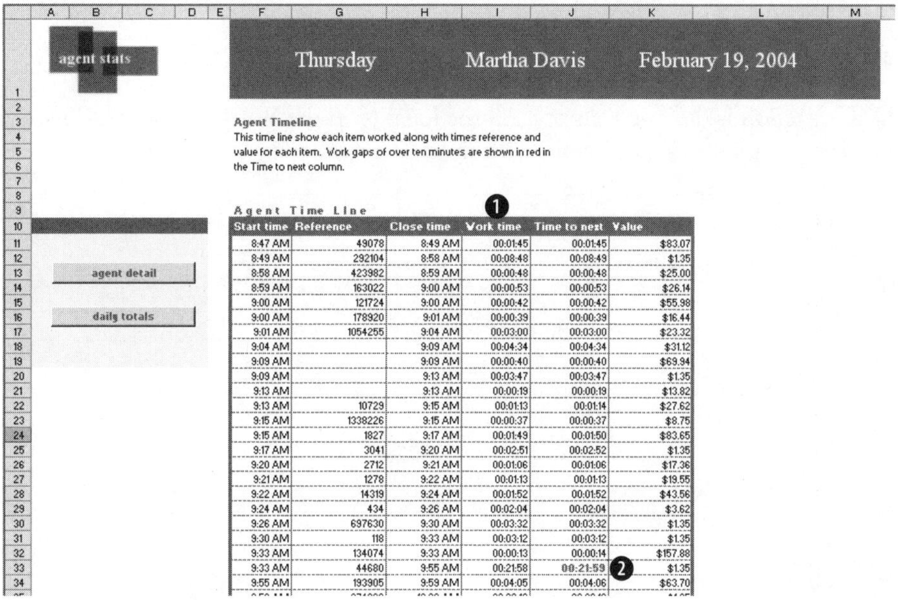

Figure 7-4. The Timeline sheet

The Timeline sheet shows each item the agent processed. Item 1 displays this information. The work time for each item is calculated along with the total time from one item to another.

The "Time to next" column shows the amount of time from the start of one item to the next. If this time is more than ten minutes, the row is flagged as in Item 2 using conditional formatting. With the "Time to next" area selected, we click Format → Conditional Formatting. The dialog is filled out as shown in Figure 7-5.

We want to change the format to bold red if the time from one item to the next is more than 10 minutes. In Excel a date and time is really a number. The integer part tells the date and the decimal part is the time. We are working with minutes and there are 60 minutes in each of the 24 hours in a day. That is 1440 minutes. That means that there are 144 ten-minute periods in a day. So, ten minutes is 1/144 or 0.006944 of a day. That is why we use 0.006944 in the dialog.

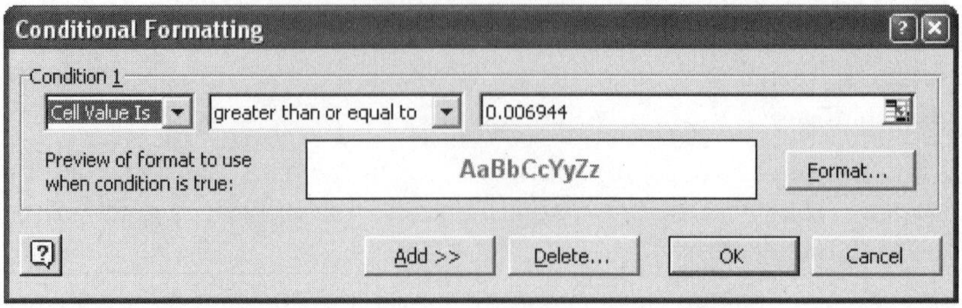

Figure 7-5. Adding a conditional format

The Logic

The application is designed simply. All the logic is on the Workarea sheet. It uses the usual conventions. The first section of this sheet is shown in Figure 7-6.

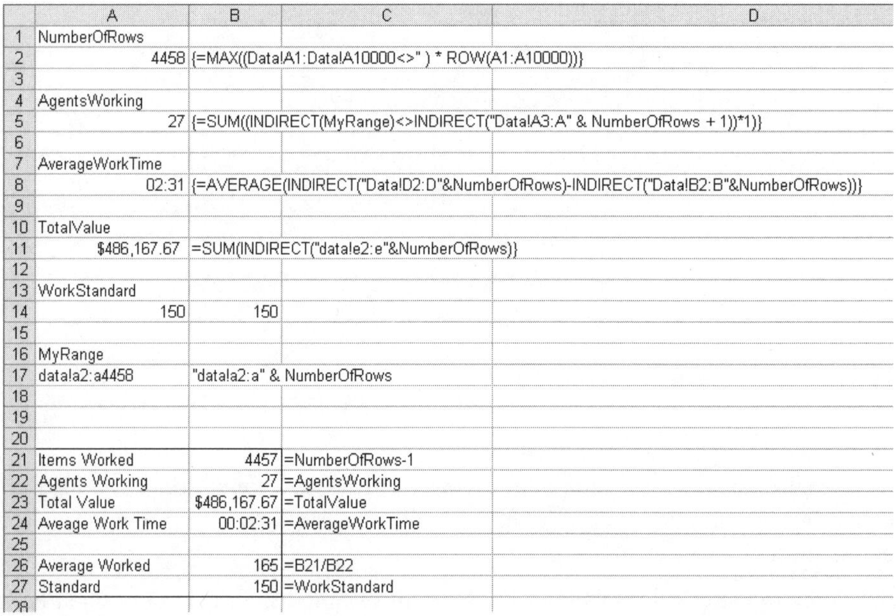

	A	B	C	D
1	NumberOfRows			
2	4458	{=MAX((Data!A1:Data!A10000<>") * ROW(A1:A10000))}		
3				
4	AgentsWorking			
5	27	{=SUM((INDIRECT(MyRange)<>INDIRECT("Data!A3:A" & NumberOfRows + 1))*1)}		
6				
7	AverageWorkTime			
8	02:31	{=AVERAGE(INDIRECT("Data!D2:D"&NumberOfRows)-INDIRECT("Data!B2:B"&NumberOfRows))}		
9				
10	TotalValue			
11	$486,167.67	=SUM(INDIRECT("data!e2:e"&NumberOfRows)}		
12				
13	WorkStandard			
14	150	150		
15				
16	MyRange			
17	data!a2:a4458	"data!a2:a" & NumberOfRows		
18				
19				
20				
21	Items Worked	4457	=NumberOfRows-1	
22	Agents Working	27	=AgentsWorking	
23	Total Value	$486,167.67	=TotalValue	
24	Aveage Work Time	00:02:31	=AverageWorkTime	
25				
26	Average Worked	165	=B21/B22	
27	Standard	150	=WorkStandard	
28				

Figure 7-6. The first section of the Workarea sheet

The application needs to be flexible. For 2/19/2004 we have 4457 rows, but the next day could be any number. So, we need to know how much data is on the Data sheet. To find the bottom row of the worksheet, we use this formula in cell A2:

```
{=MAX((Data!A1:Data!A10000<>"" ) * ROW(A1:A10000))}
```

There are other ways to do this, but this formula lets us work with the column we need and keeps the calculation on the worksheet. This is an array formula and is entered by pressing Ctrl-Shift-Enter simultaneously. It looks at the rows from 1 to 10,000 and works by building two lists of values. The first list (`Data!A1: Data!A10000<>""`) is just 10,000 zeros or ones. The value is 1 for cells in the range that contain data and 0 for those that are empty.

The second list (`ROW(A1:A10000)`) is the numbers from 1 to 10,000. The lists are multiplied together. Row numbers with data are multiplied by 1, while empty row numbers are multiplied by 0. The formula takes the maximum value from the products, which is the row number of the last row used.

The result of this formula is named `NumberOfRows`. This is a powerful formula and can be modified to find the last column used or the last row containing a specific value.

We will refer to column A (agent) on the Data sheet several times. To save keying, we build a reference to the range that contains the data. Cell A17, named `MyRange`, contains this formula:

```
="data!a2:a" & NumberOfRows
```

We can use `MyRange` in other formulas, such as the one in A5:

```
{=SUM((INDIRECT(MyRange)<>INDIRECT("Data!A3:A" & NumberOfRows + 1))*1)}
```

We need to know how many agents are working. This is not the same every day, so it needs to be calculated. Again we use an array formula. We know the Data sheet is sorted by agent, and we count the times the agent changes. The formula builds a list of zeros and ones. It is 1 only for cells that are not equal to the cell on the next row.

We use indirect functions because we do not know how many rows there will be. The second `INDIRECT` points to a range that is one row lower than `MyRange`.

The time it takes to work an item is the completed time minus the assigned time. In cell A8 the formula is:

```
{=AVERAGE(INDIRECT("Data!D2:D"&NumberOfRows)-INDIRECT("Data!B2:B"&NumberOfRows))}
```

The completed times are in column D of the Data sheet and the assigned times are in column B. This array formula takes the average of the work times. The result is named `AverageWorkTime`. We also want to know the total value of work done, so in cell A11 the formula is:

```
=SUM(INDIRECT("data!e2:e"&NumberOfRows))
```

The work standard in cell A14 is entered as a number and can be changed as needed.

The range A21:B27 is named `DailyTotals`. It is a display area and appears on the Totals sheet, Figure 7-2, as Item 4. It is referenced as an array formula. The range B8:C14 on the Totals sheet contains the formula:

```
{=DailyTotals}
```

The Data sheet only has employee numbers, and we want to display the names as well. The table of employee numbers and names is in columns E and F of Workarea, as shown in Figure 7-7.

E	F
agent	Name
9321	Helen Brown
10632	Martha Davis
11276	Jerry Wright
11287	Yancy Baker
15988	Vera Smith
16138	Wally Davis
25271	Kelly Jones
25811	Xena Thomas
26409	Bob Smith
27448	Robert Taylor
30443	Otto Baker
32852	Tracy Wright
36514	Nancy Thomas
62908	Zero Walker

Figure 7-7. Agent names

On the Totals sheet information is summarized by agent. The next part of Workarea contains the logic. The Data sheet is sorted by agent and assigned_date, making it easier to arrange the information by agent. This area is shown in Figure 7-8.

H	I	J	K	L	M	N	O	P
		Agent	Name	Items Worked	Start Time	End Time	Average Time per Item	Percent Referenced
2	221	9321	Helen Brown	220	8:00 AM	3:23 PM	00:02:01	7.73%
222	329	10632	Martha Davis	108	8:47 AM	1:35 PM	00:02:49	94.44%
330	449	11276	Jerry Wright	120	12:30 PM	3:21 PM	00:01:27	97.50%
450	495	11287	Yancy Baker	46	8:57 AM	11:40 AM	00:03:46	100.00%
496	649	15988	Vera Smith	154	8:12 AM	1:38 PM	00:02:07	0.00%
650	1012	16138	Wally Davis	363	7:36 AM	1:57 PM	00:01:00	4.13%
1013	1143	25271	Kelly Jones	131	8:12 AM	1:25 PM	00:02:25	94.66%
1144	1434	25811	Xena Thomas	291	8:03 AM	3:17 PM	00:01:31	0.00%
1435	1436	26409	Bob Smith	2	8:57 AM	8:58 AM	00:04:06	100.00%
1437	1651	30443	Otto Baker	215	9:00 AM	3:36 PM	00:01:25	99.53%
1652	1744	32852	Tracy Wright	93	6:44 AM	12:42 PM	00:04:01	4.30%
1745	1757	36514	Nancy Thomas	13	7:25 AM	1:58 PM	03:01:55	76.92%
1758	1983	62908	Zero Walker	226	6:20 AM	2:18 PM	00:01:57	98.67%
1984	2139	66500	Andrew Jones	156	8:12 AM	2:54 PM	00:02:35	0.00%
2140	2303	74734	Quincy Parker	164	8:47 AM	3:36 PM	00:02:29	98.78%
2304	2504	75939	Aaron Parker	201	8:19 AM	2:50 PM	00:01:46	98.51%
2505	2819	78066	Donna Thomas	315	6:41 AM	2:20 PM	00:01:07	3.81%
2820	3176	84738	Ruth Brown	357	6:51 AM	3:20 PM	00:01:38	93.84%
3177	3523	113924	Ed Baker	347	6:49 AM	3:23 PM	00:01:29	98.85%
3524	3612	117527	Uma Jones	89	8:15 AM	2:01 PM	00:03:54	98.88%
3613	3767	130848	Larry Smith	155	8:12 AM	2:07 PM	00:02:18	81.94%

Figure 7-8. More Workarea

The first step is to determine the range of rows for each agent. This is done in columns H and I. The formula in column I finds the last row for each agent. It contains this formula:

```
=MATCH(J2,INDIRECT(MyRange),1)+1
```

Cell J2 contains the agent number. MyRange is a named value equal to data!a2:a4458. Option one in the match function returns the row with the largest value less than or equal to J2. We add 1 because MyRange starts in row two. This formula fills down for 50 rows. If more than 50 agents could be working, additional rows can be used.

Cell H2 contains the number 2. The first row number of the first agent is always 2. Cell H3 is set to one more than cell I2, since the first row for each agent is one more than the last row for the agent above. This formula also fills down.

The first cell in the agent column (J2) is set equal to cell data!a2, since that is the first agent number. The formula in cell J3 is:

```
=IF(ISERROR(INDEX(INDIRECT(MyRange),I2+1)),"",INDEX(INDIRECT(MyRange),I2+1))
```

This formula uses an INDEX function on MyRange. It points to the row after the last row for the agent above. The application will handle up to 50 agents but not all 50 are used in this example. After the last agent the INDEX function will generate an error. The IsError function is used to set the cells that are not used to blank.

Column K contains the agent name. The formula is:

```
=IF(J2="","",LOOKUP(J2,Agent,Name))
```

The IF function checks to be sure the current row is used. If it is, the LOOKUP function finds the value J2 in the range named Agent. It returns the value from the range Name.

The items worked in column L is based on the number of rows and is calculated with this formula:

```
=IF(J2="","",(I2-H2)+1)
```

The start and end times are on the first and last rows for the agent. For the start time we use the assigned_date (column B) since that is when the agents got their first piece of work for the day. For the end time we use completed_date (column D). The formulas are:

```
=IF(J2="","",INDIRECT("data!B" & Workarea!H2))
=IF(K2="","",INDIRECT("data!D" & Workarea!I2))
```

Average time per item is calculated using:

```
{=IF(J2="","",AVERAGE(INDIRECT("data!d" & H2 & ":d" & I2)-INDIRECT("data!b" & H2 & ":
b" & I2)))}
```

This takes the average of the difference between the completed and assigned times for the agent. It is an array formula. The values H2 and I2 in the INDIRECT functions are the starting and ending rows for the agent.

To get the percent of items referenced we count the number of cells in column C that are not empty and divide by the number of rows for the agent. The formula is:

```
=IF(J2="","",(COUNTIF(INDIRECT("data!c" & H2 & ":c" & I2),">0"))/L2)
```

This gives us a display area for the Totals sheet. But we are giving the user the ability to sort this information. This is complicated because all the information is linked and we cannot use Excel's sort tool directly.

Using a Tag Sort on Linked Information

We use a tag sort to get around this problem. A tag sort uses pointers to control the display order of the rows. We use the sort tool to sort the tags rather than the data. The tag sort area is shown in Figure 7-9.

R Row Number	S	T	U Agent	V Name	W Items Worked	X Start Time	Y End Time	Z Average Time per Item	AA Percent Referenced
1			9321	Helen Brown	220	8:00 AM	3:25 PM	00:02:01	7.73%
2			10632	Martha Davis	108	8:47 AM	1:52 PM	00:02:49	94.44%
3			11276	Jerry Wright	120	12:30 PM	3:24 PM	00:01:27	97.50%
4			11287	Yancy Baker	46	8:57 AM	11:50 AM	00:03:46	100.00%
5			15988	Vera Smith	154	8:12 AM	1:38 PM	00:02:07	0.00%
6			16138	Wally Davis	363	7:36 AM	1:59 PM	00:01:00	4.13%
7			25271	Kelly Jones	131	8:12 AM	1:30 PM	00:02:25	94.66%
8			25811	Xena Thomas	291	8:03 AM	3:27 PM	00:01:31	0.00%
9			26409	Bob Smith	2	8:57 AM	9:05 AM	00:04:06	100.00%
10			30443	Otto Baker	215	9:00 AM	3:36 PM	00:01:25	99.53%
11			32852	Tracy Wright	93	6:44 AM	12:58 PM	00:04:01	4.30%
12			36514	Nancy Thomas	13	7:25 AM	2:48 PM	03:01:55	76.92%
13			62908	Zero Walker	226	6:20 AM	2:18 PM	00:01:57	98.67%
14			66500	Andrew Jones	156	8:12 AM	2:56 PM	00:02:35	0.00%
15			74734	Quincy Parker	164	8:47 AM	3:36 PM	00:02:29	98.78%
16			75939	Aaron Parker	201	8:19 AM	2:51 PM	00:01:46	98.51%
17			78066	Donna Thomas	315	6:41 AM	2:20 PM	00:01:07	3.81%
18			84738	Ruth Brown	357	6:51 AM	3:20 PM	00:01:38	93.84%
19			113924	Ed Baker	347	6:49 AM	3:27 PM	00:01:29	98.85%
20			117527	Uma Jones	89	8:15 AM	2:02 PM	00:03:54	98.88%
21			130848	Larry Smith	155	8:12 AM	2:10 PM	00:02:18	81.94%
22			148475	Ginger Parker	120	9:24 AM	2:53 PM	00:02:44	99.17%
23			280407	Pam Walker	189	8:43 AM	3:35 PM	00:02:10	99.47%
24			285000	Ira Logan	103	7:41 AM	2:18 PM	00:03:51	0.00%

Figure 7-9. The tag sort area of the Workarea sheet

Column R contains row numbers. These are just the numbers from 1 to 50 and correspond to the row numbers in the range J2:P51. These row numbers control the order of the same information in the range U2:AA51.

The formula in cell U2 is:

```
=INDEX(J$2:J$51,$R2)
```

This formula points to column J. The rows in the range are locked with $. The index is in R2 and its column is locked. This formula is filled right and down for the whole range U2:AA51.

As a result, columns U:AA look exactly like columns J:P. But if the order of the numbers in column R changes, the order of the rows in U:AA will also change. The range U1:AA51 is named AgentList and is displayed on the Totals sheet using the array formula:

```
{=AgentList}
```

When the user clicks on one of the headings, the tag sort is performed. It is a two step procedure. Sorting by Items Worked, the tag sort area is shown in Figure 7-10.

J	K	L	M
Agent	Name	Items Worked	Start Time
9321	Helen Brown	220	8:0
10632	Martha Davis	108	8:4
11276	Jerry Wright	120	12:3
11287	Yancy Baker	46	8:5
15988	Vera Smith	154	8:1
16138	Wally Davis	363	7:3
25271	Kelly Jones	131	8:1
25811	Xena Thomas	291	8:0
26409	Bob Smith	2	8:5
30443	Otto Baker	215	9:0
32852	Tracy Wright	93	6:4
36514	Nancy Thomas	13	7:2
62908	Zero Walker	226	6:2
66500	Andrew Jones	156	8:1
74734	Quincy Parker	164	8:4
75939	Aaron Parker	201	8:1
78066	Donna Thomas	315	6:4
84738	Ruth Brown	357	6:5
113924	Ed Baker	347	6:4
117527	Uma Jones	89	8:1
130848	Larry Smith	155	8:1
148475	Ginger Parker	120	9:2
280407	Pam Walker	189	8:4
285000	Ira Logan	103	7:4

R	S	T	U	V	W	X
Row Number	Items Worked		Agent	Name	Items Worked	Start Time
9	2		26409	Bob Smith	2	8:57
12	13		36514	Nancy Thomas	13	7:25
4	46		11287	Yancy Baker	46	8:57
27	61		335112	Fred Walker	61	8:44
26	84		325936	Sam Logan	84	8:28
20	89		117527	Uma Jones	89	8:15
11	93		32852	Tracy Wright	93	6:44
24	103		285000	Ira Logan	103	7:41
2	108		10632	Martha Davis	108	8:47
3	120		11276	Jerry Wright	120	12:30
22	120		148475	Ginger Parker	120	9:24
7	131		25271	Kelly Jones	131	8:12
25	134		306235	Carl Davis	134	8:44
5	154		15988	Vera Smith	154	8:12
21	155		130848	Larry Smith	155	8:12
14	156		66500	Andrew Jones	156	8:12
15	164		74734	Quincy Parker	164	8:47
23	189		280407	Pam Walker	189	8:43
16	201		75939	Aaron Parker	201	8:19
10	215		30443	Otto Baker	215	9:00
1	220		9321	Helen Brown	220	8:00
13	226		62908	Zero Walker	226	6:20
8	291		25811	Xena Thomas	291	8:03
17	315		78066	Donna Thomas	315	6:41

Figure 7-10. Tag sort on Items Worked

In Item 1 the information in column W (Items Worked) is copied and pasted (Paste Special → Values) into column S.

Next, in Item 2, columns R and S are sorted ascending on column S.

Item 3 shows the result, in which the first agent (Helen Brown) is now on the 22nd row of the AgentList range. The Totals sheet only sees this range, so the display is now sorted.

This is done with two macros. The first contains only one line. If the user clicks on Items Worked, the sort needs to be on column W. A macro named Sortw runs, passing the value w to a function named Sortit. Here is the code:

```
Sub Sortw()
R_code = Sortit("w")
End Sub
```

Sortit is a custom function written for this application. It can sort AgentList for any column. It gets the column as a passed value. This is the Sortit macro:

```
Function Sortit(MyCol As String)

    Dim ToSort As String

    'Turn off screen updating so the user will not
    'see all of the steps
    Application.ScreenUpdating = False

    'MyCol contains the column to be sorted. It is a value from U to AA
    'depending on which column the user selected.
    'MyRange holds the range of cells to be sorted. Agentsworking
    'is a named value on workarea and contains the number of
```

```
'agents working. We add one to include the heading.
MyRange = MyCol & "1:" & MyCol & Range("agentsworking").Value + 1

'The sort is performed on the workarea sheet
Sheets("Workarea").Select

'Copy the cell range to be sorted
Range(MyRange).Copy

'Move to the S column
Range("S1").Select

'Perform a PasteSpecial Values
Selection.PasteSpecial Paste:=xlPasteValues, Operation:=xlNone, SkipBlanks _
    :=False, Transpose:=False

'ToSort holds the range to be sorted.
ToSort = "r1:s" & Range("agentsworking").Value + 1

'Select the sort range
Range(ToSort).Select

'Perform the sort
Selection.Sort Key1:=Range("S2"), Order1:=xlAscending, Header:=xlGuess, _
OrderCustom:=1, MatchCase:=False, Orientation:=xlTopToBottom, _
DataOption1:=xlSortNormal

'Return to the Totals sheet
Sheets("Totals").Select

'Turn screen updating back on
Application.ScreenUpdating = True
End Function
```

The Sortw macro runs when the user clicks on the Items Worked heading on the Totals sheet.

Invisible Rectangles

This happens because there is a rectangle object over the heading. The setup is shown in Figure 7-11.

If the drawing toolbar is not visible, you need to go to the View → Toolbars menu and check Drawing. A rectangle is drawn over the heading. Then right-click on the rectangle and select Format AutoShape. The dialog in Figure 7-12 will display.

The rectangle has no fill and no line making it invisible. Next we assign the Sortw macro to the rectangle. We right-click again and select Assign Macro. This brings up the dialog in Figure 7-13.

The rectangle is invisible but still responds to the click event.

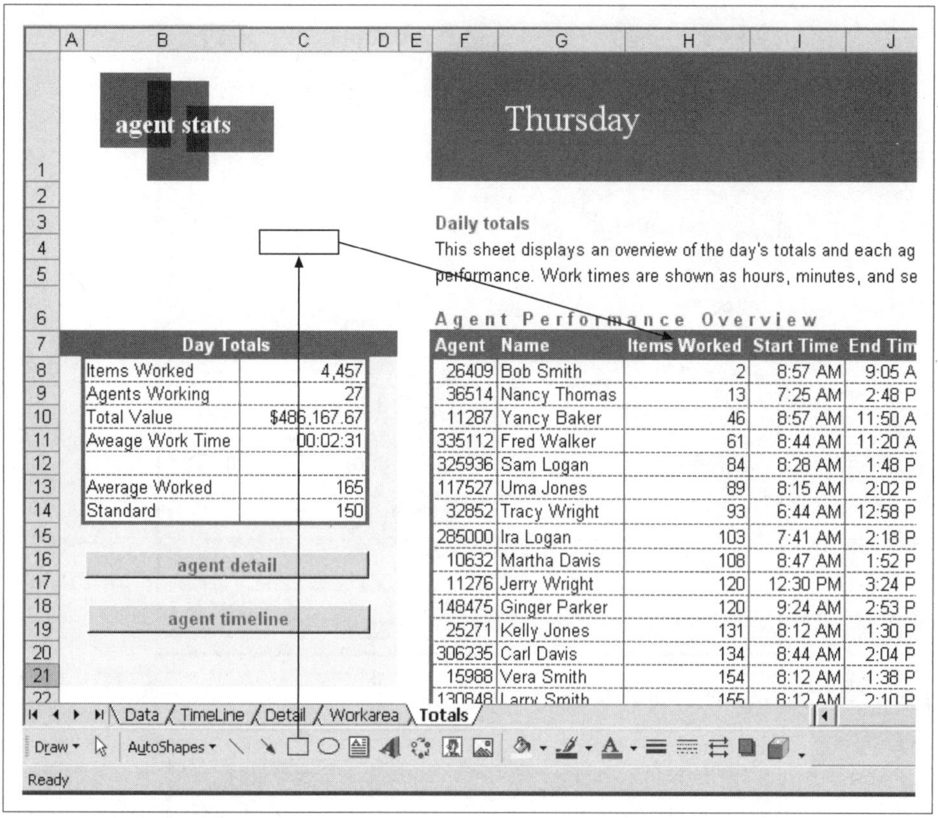

Figure 7-11. Adding a rectangle

There is a separate macro (Sortu, Sortv, ... etc) for each column and a separate rectangle for each heading.

The Agent Detail Area

On the Detail sheet the user can select an agent. When this happens, Workarea needs to calculate metrics for the agent, populate the chart, and build the timeline.

Totals for the selected agent are calculated in the range shown in Figure 7-14.

Cell A40, named AgentRow, is linked to the listbox on the Detail sheet. The value tells which agent the user selected. The value in cell A42 gives the starting row for the agent. This is the row on the Data sheet that starts this agent's information. This value is in the H column at the row given by AgentRow. The cell is named AgentStartRow and the formula is:

```
=INDEX(H2:H51,AgentRow)
```

AgentEndRow works the same, getting its value from column I with the formula:

```
=INDEX(I2:I51,AgentRow)
```

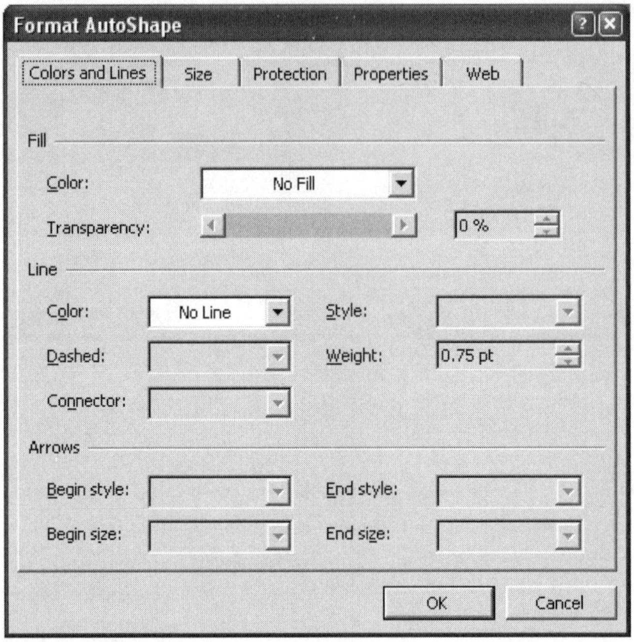

Figure 7-12. Making the rectangle invisible

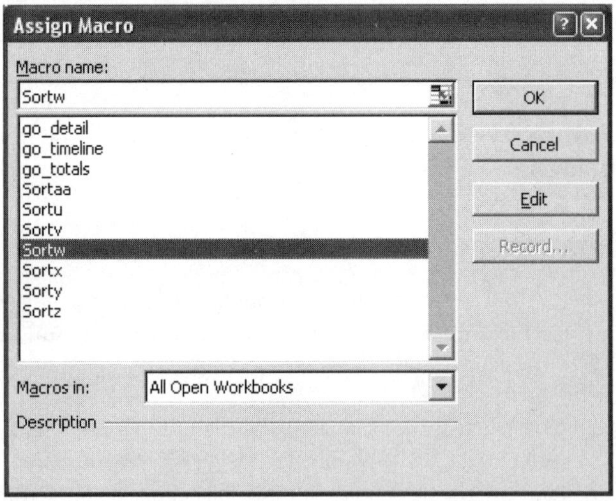

Figure 7-13. Assigning the macro

The number of items worked is the number of rows. The formula in cell A46 is:

```
=AgentEndRow-AgentStartRow
```

	A	B	C	D	E	F
32						
33						
34						
35						
36						
37						
38				Ed Baker	Emp Num 113924	
39	AgentRow			Items worked	347	
40	19			Average time	00:01:29	
41	AgentStartRow			Percent referenced	98.85%	
42	3177			Start time	6:49 AM	
43	AgentEndRow			End time	3:27 PM	
44	3523			Total value	$37,245.31	
45	AgentItemsWorked					
46	346					
47	AgentAssignedRange					
48	c59:c405					
49	AgentClosedRange					
50	e59:e405					
51	AgentName					
52	Ed Baker					
53	ChartHeading					
54	Hourly items worked for Ed Baker					
55	AgentEmpNumber					
56	113924					
57						

Figure 7-14. Agent totals on the Workarea sheet

This returns a value one less that the number of rows because the first row is not zero. This situation comes up all the time when working with cell ranges. We need this value for more than one thing. For building ranges this is fine, but when we display the number of items worked we will add 1 to the value.

The ranges for the assigned_date and completed_date are used in other calculations. So, to simplify things we will build the ranges and name them. The formulas are:

```
="c59:c" & 59+AgentItemsWorked
="e59:e" & 59+AgentItemsWorked
```

AgentName, cell A52, is from column K and uses this formula:

```
=INDEX(K2:K51,AgentRow)
```

The chart heading is just text and uses AgentName. The cell (A54) is not named because names cannot be used in chart headings. The formula is:

```
="Hourly items worked for " & AgentName
```

AgentEmpNumber is extracted from the J column with this formula:

```
=INDEX(J2:J51,AgentRow)
```

The range D38:E44 is named AgentDetail. It is displayed on the Detail sheet as an array. The relationship is shown in Figure 7-15.

Using this technique keeps the display and the logic separate.

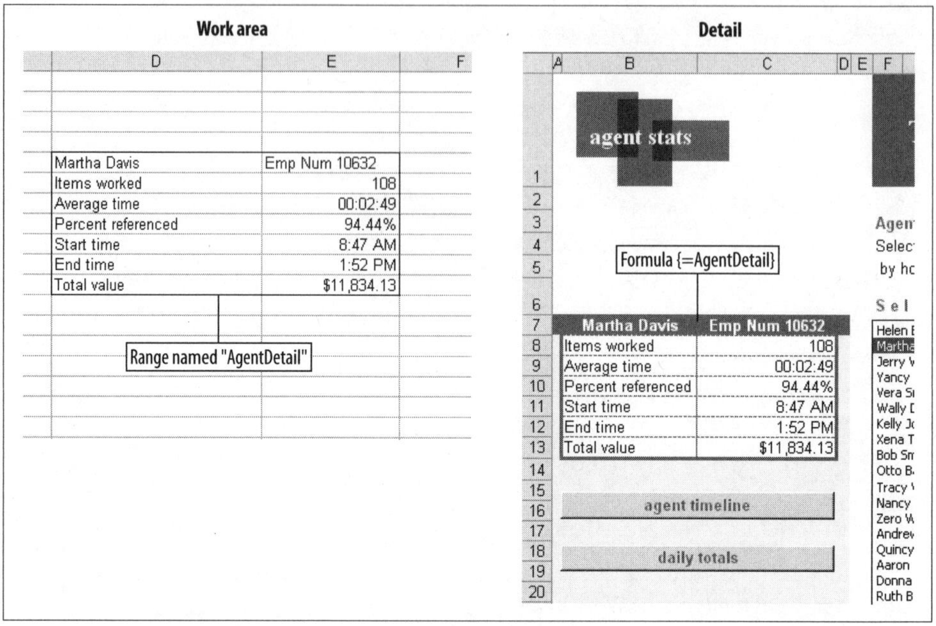

Figure 7-15. Using an array formula to display a named range

The Chart Area

The chart on the Detail sheet is populated using the range J58:M82. This range is not named, and is shown in Figure 7-16.

The numbers in column J are the hours of the day. The same hours are displayed using a time format in column K. The numbers in column J are used by the array formula in column L:

```
{=SUM((HOUR(INDIRECT(AgentAssignedRange))=J59)*1)}
```

The formula checks the range containing the assigned dates and counts the number that are in each hour. It fills down for all the hours.

Column M is the standard. Each day an agent is expected to work 150 items. This is in the cell named WorkStandard (A14). A workday has seven hours. So, column M contains the integer value of 150/7. It is the number of items an agent must work each hour to meet the goal.

The range K58:M82 is selected and the chart is added by selecting Insert → Chart from the menu. This is a Line – Column chart found on the Custom Types list, as shown in Figure 7-17.

The chart is placed on the Detail sheet using the dialog in Figure 7-18.

J	K	L	M
	Hour	Count	Standard
0	12:00 AM	0	21
1	1:00 AM	0	21
2	2:00 AM	0	21
3	3:00 AM	0	21
4	4:00 AM	0	21
5	5:00 AM	0	21
6	6:00 AM	0	21
7	7:00 AM	0	21
8	8:00 AM	4	21
9	9:00 AM	21	21
10	10:00 AM	31	21
11	11:00 AM	21	21
12	12:00 PM	17	21
13	1:00 PM	14	21
14	2:00 PM	0	21
15	3:00 PM	0	21
16	4:00 PM	0	21
17	5:00 PM	0	21
18	6:00 PM	0	21
19	7:00 PM	0	21
20	8:00 PM	0	21
21	9:00 PM	0	21
22	10:00 PM	0	21
23	11:00 PM	0	21

Figure 7-16. The chart on the Detail sheet uses this area

It results in the chart shown in Figure 7-19. This is the basic chart for the application. It can be positioned and sized by dragging. It will be further customized on the Detail sheet.

The first step is to remove the markers on the standard line and change the color and weight of the line. We start by right-clicking on the standard line (Item 1 in Figure 7-19). We select Format Data Series and the dialog in Figure 7-20 displays.

We click on the Patterns tab and set the options as shown in Figure 7-20. The bars showing the hourly counts need to be changed to blue. The process is the same as for the standard line. We right-click on the count bar (Item 2 in Figure 7-19) and change the Patterns tab.

Next, we change the alignment on the X axis. The times are displayed diagonally and are hard to read. So, right-click on the axis (Item 3 in Figure 7-19) and select the Alignment tab. The orientation is set as shown in Figure 7-21.

Finally we link the chart title to cell A54 on Workarea, but the chart tool won't let us do this directly. So, we start by adding a simple title that can be edited. With the

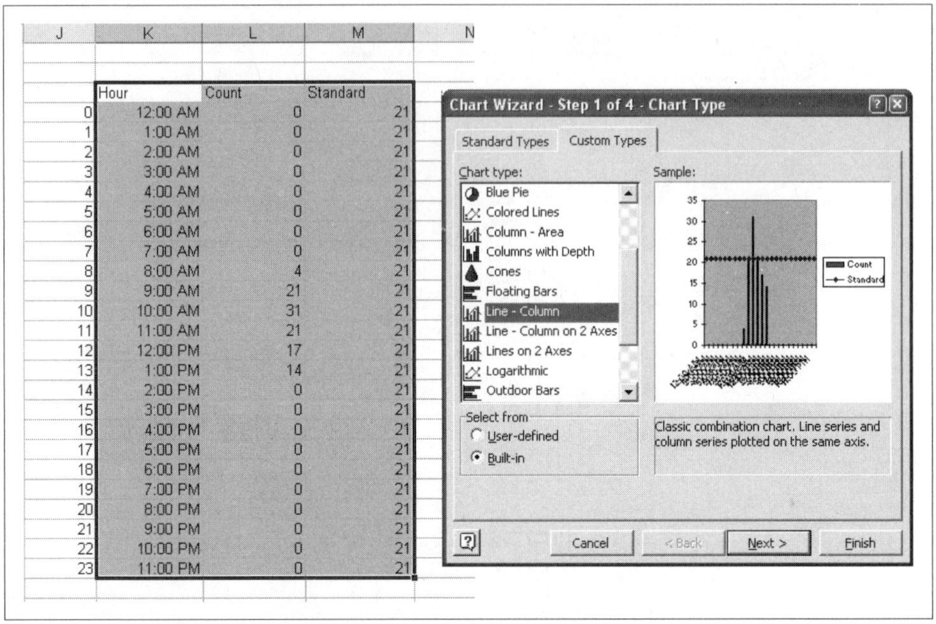

Figure 7-17. Inserting the chart

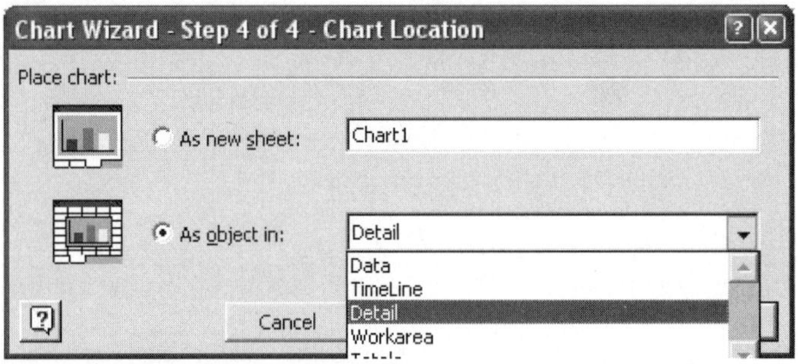

Figure 7-18. Putting the chart on the Detail sheet

chart selected, we select Chart → Chart Options from the menu. This displays the dialog shown in Figure 7-22.

We enter a title of *XXX* to make it easy to edit. After the title is on the chart, we right-click on it. Then the formula is entered in the formula bar, as shown in Figure 7-23.

This links the title to the Workarea sheet and when the user selects a new agent the title will change along with the chart.

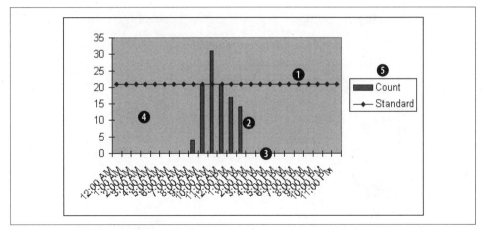

Figure 7-19. The basic chart ready to be customized

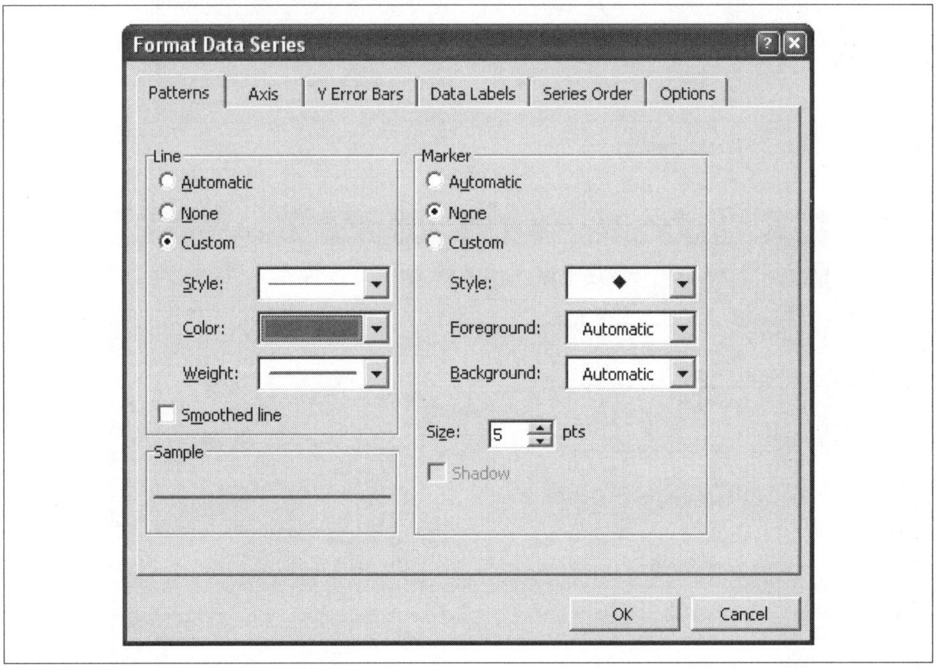

Figure 7-20. Formatting the standard line

The Timeline

The last area in the Workarea sheet is the display range for the timeline. We are allowing for 500 items for an agent in one day. In this application that will be enough, but if more are needed it is simple to fill the formulas down further and increase the size of the named range. Figure 7-24 shows the range.

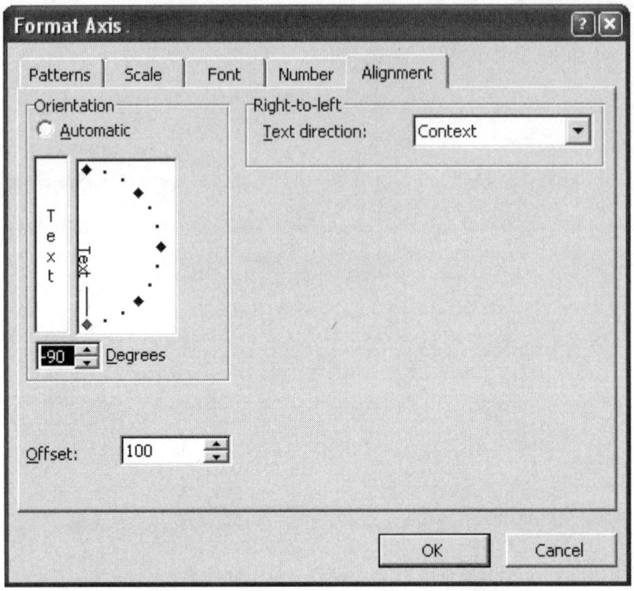

Figure 7-21. Setting the alignment

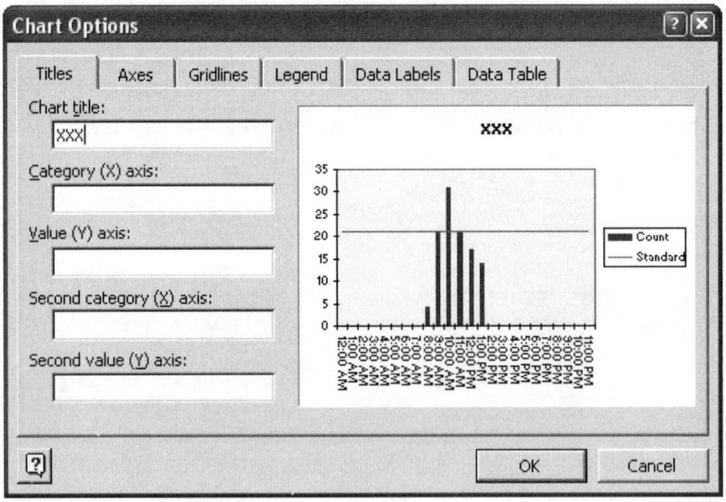

Figure 7-22. Adding a chart title

Column A contains row numbers on the Data sheet. They give the location of the agent's data. It is not part of the display and is used to map the agent's rows on the Data sheet to this part of the Workarea sheet. The first cell (A59) is set equal to the named value AgentStartRow. Cell A60 contains this formula:

```
=IF(A59<AgentEndRow,A59+1,"")
```

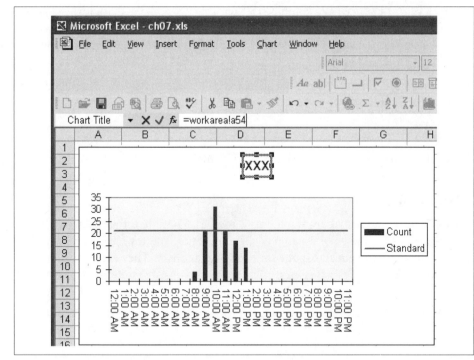

Figure 7-23. Customizing the chart title

	A	B	C	D	E	F	G	H
58			Start time	Reference	Close time	Work time	Time to next	Value
59	222		2/19/04 8:47 AM	49078	2/19/04 8:49 AM	00:01:45	00:01:45	$83.07
60	223		2/19/04 8:49 AM	292104	2/19/04 8:58 AM	00:08:48	00:08:49	$1.35
61	224		2/19/04 8:58 AM	423982	2/19/04 8:59 AM	00:00:48	00:00:48	$25.00
62	225		2/19/04 8:59 AM	163022	2/19/04 9:00 AM	00:00:53	00:00:53	$26.14
63	226		2/19/04 9:00 AM	121724	2/19/04 9:00 AM	00:00:42	00:00:42	$55.98
64	227		2/19/04 9:00 AM	178920	2/19/04 9:01 AM	00:00:39	00:00:39	$16.44
65	228		2/19/04 9:01 AM	1054255	2/19/04 9:04 AM	00:03:00	00:03:00	$23.32
66	229		2/19/04 9:04 AM		2/19/04 9:09 AM	00:04:34	00:04:34	$31.12
67	230		2/19/04 9:09 AM		2/19/04 9:09 AM	00:00:40	00:00:40	$69.94
68	231		2/19/04 9:09 AM		2/19/04 9:13 AM	00:03:47	00:03:47	$1.35
69	232		2/19/04 9:13 AM		2/19/04 9:13 AM	00:00:19	00:00:19	$13.82
70	233		2/19/04 9:13 AM	10729	2/19/04 9:15 AM	00:01:13	00:01:14	$27.62
71	234		2/19/04 9:15 AM	1338226	2/19/04 9:15 AM	00:00:37	00:00:37	$8.75
72	235		2/19/04 9:15 AM	1827	2/19/04 9:17 AM	00:01:49	00:01:50	$83.65
73	236		2/19/04 9:17 AM	3041	2/19/04 9:20 AM	00:02:51	00:02:52	$1.35
74	237		2/19/04 9:20 AM	2712	2/19/04 9:21 AM	00:01:06	00:01:06	$17.36

Figure 7-24. The display area for the Timeline sheet

This formula fills down and gives us the row numbers of the data we need.

Columns C, D, E, and H all use the same basic formula. Cell C59 contains:

```
=IF($A59="","",INDIRECT("data!" & ADDRESS($A59,COLUMN(B1))))
```

The IF function checks to see if we have reached the end of the agent's data, and if so it returns a blank. The ADDRESS function takes a row and column and returns an address. In this case ADDRESS($A59,COLUMN(B1)) is equivalent to ADDRESS(222,2) and returns a value of $B$222. We combine this with the sheet name (Data is the sheet we are referencing) and use the resulting reference in an INDIRECT function. This returns the first assigned_date for the agent. This formula fills down and across, covering columns C, D, E, and H.

Work time and "Time to next" are calculated as in other parts of the application by using these formulas:

```
=IF(A59="","",E59-C59)
=IF(A60="","",C60-C59)
```

On the Timeline sheet this area is referenced by the name TimeLine.

Navigation

The navigation buttons are from the Forms toolbar. They are formatted to use a font color that matches the color scheme of the application and they are each assigned a macro. There are three macros, one for each display sheet. They each have only one line, and this is the code:

```
Sub go_detail()
Sheets("detail").Select
End Sub

Sub go_totals()
Sheets("totals").Select
End Sub

Sub go_timeline()
Sheets("timeline").Select
End Sub
```

This code provides simple navigation. The user clicks the button and the destination sheet is selected.

CHAPTER 8

Custom Queuing Presentation

The data in a queuing system can be used for many purposes. In the last chapter we used the data to manage employees. In this chapter we use the same kind of data to monitor the amount and status of work in the queue. Once again, this is mainly a presentation problem. There are not a lot of statistics or calculations. We simply use formatting and charts to tell managers how the work is progressing.

The application in this chapter uses metaphors and some VBA to create an easily understood interactive view of the work process.

The Application

The application in this chapter provides an example, not an easily reusable application. Much of the design depends on the data, and an application like this is easier to build from scratch than to customize. The design and concepts, however, are reusable and the application can serve as a starting point for custom development.

The application operates on data from a workflow with five queues. The work arrives as images. They could be incoming faxes or scanned paper documents. The first queue feeds a fully automated process that attempts to handle the work via optical character recognition (OCR).

The work starts in a queue named OCR, and if the OCR process is successful then the work is complete and leaves the system. If the OCR process it is unsuccessful, the document is routed to a manual queue named MAN. Any document that can only be partially processed and requires research is routed to the partially processed queue named PAR.

For documents that require extensive research there is a separate queue named EXT. Finally, in some cases the work results in a refund. Refunds also have their own queue named REF.

Documents are in one of three statuses:

- Documents in status 1 have not been processed in their current queue and are ready to be assigned to an agent.

- Documents in status 2 are being worked now. Sometimes a document cannot be completed without additional information. The customer may need to be contacted, or a document obtained from another department. An agent can put a document on hold in these cases.

- Documents in status 3 are on hold.

Once a document is complete it leaves the queuing system, and might be used by an application like the one in Chapter 7.

The main display in Figure 8-1 shows these queues as one continuous workflow.

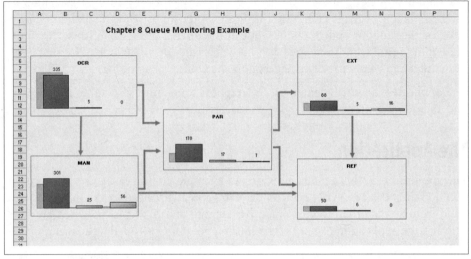

Figure 8-1. The application's main display

The display is basically a flow diagram of the operation. The design elements are charts containing information about each queue, and the flow is represented by arrows. This metaphor is easily understood and can be used for almost any multi-step process.

Figure 8-2 shows one of the charts in detail.

This is a standard bar chart created with Excel's chart tool. It shows the EXT queue, and there are 88 unprocessed documents represented by the red bar, Item 1.

Item 2 is the smaller green bar and it represents documents currently being worked on. The yellow bar, Item 3, is the documents on hold. These have been assigned to an agent but cannot be completed without additional information. The chart's information is updated periodically and it is helpful to know how things are changing.

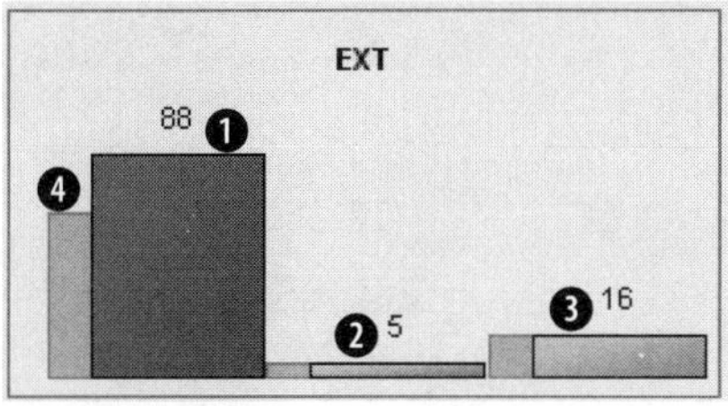

Figure 8-2. Chart detail

The gray bars behind the colored bars, Item 4, show where each bar was at the previous update.

So, we can see there are now 88 items in the queue and that the queue has grown since the previous update.

The colored bars were formatted separately using the Format Data Point dialog box. The color of the red bar is set as shown in Figure 8-3.

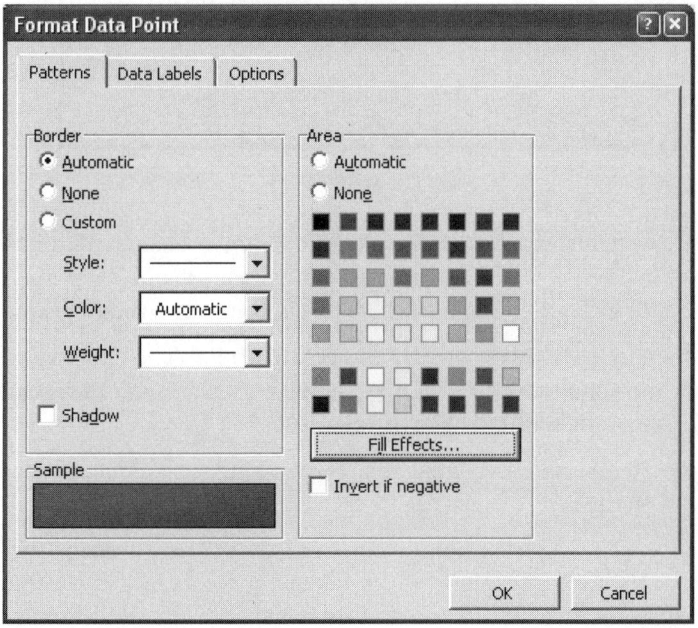

Figure 8-3. Setting the color of the red bar

I selected red for the area and black for a thin border. The shadowing effect was created using the Fill Effects button, which brings up the dialog shown in Figure 8-4.

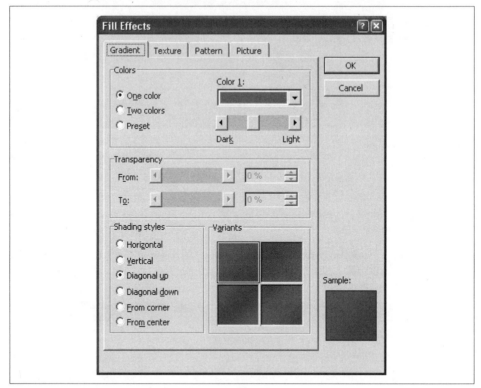

Figure 8-4. Add a fill effect

The gray bars were formatted together using the Format Data Series dialog box. The color is set to light gray with a darker gray border. This dialog's Options tab, shown in Figure 8-5, allowed me to offset the bars by choosing an Overlap setting of 75%.

This puts the gray bars partly behind the colored ones. The chart was finished by deleting the horizontal and vertical axis, removing grid lines, and filling the chart area with the same background color as the sheet.

There is a macro associated with each chart, allowing the charts to function as buttons. Clicking on the PAR queue chart brings up the display in Figure 8-6.

This is a report showing each item in the partially processed queue with summary information at the top. This report is rebuilt each time a chart is clicked. The original work document is an image file and its name is in the file column. If the user selects a row by clicking on a row number, the document on that row is displayed.

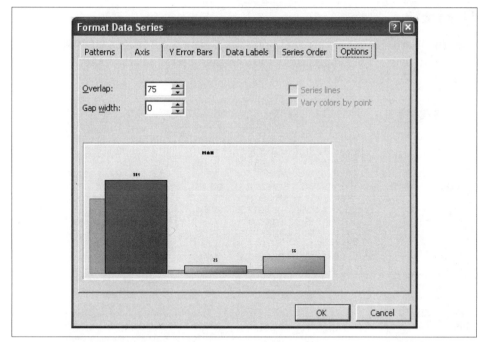

Figure 8-5. Offsetting the gray bars

	A	B	C	D	E	F	G	H	I
1				PAR Queue		8-Jun-2005			
2			Type	Count	Oldest	Value		Go Back	
3			New	178	5/31/05 12:45	$18,003.64			
4			Working	17	5/31/05 11:46	$1,856.46			
5			On Hold	7	5/30/05 7:48	$407.29			
6									
7	Queue	Status	Create Date/Time	Assign Date/Time	Value		Agent	File	
8	PAR	3	5/29/05 18:28	5/30/05 8:15	$9.46		15988	Figure7-30.TXT	
9	PAR	3	5/30/05 3:50	5/30/05 7:48	$20.14		74734	Figure7-30.TIF	
10	PAR	3	5/30/05 4:26	5/30/05 22:21	$1.35		66500	Figure7-30.TIF	
11	PAR	3	5/30/05 20:33	5/31/05 14:42	$11.70		26409	Figure7-30.BMP	
12	PAR	3	5/31/05 6:18	5/31/05 20:05	$35.67		30443	Figure7-30.TXT	
13	PAR	3	5/31/05 8:42	6/1/05 7:31	$144.63		36514	Figure7-30.TIF	
14	PAR	2	5/31/05 3:51	5/31/05 15:45	$184.34		11276	Figure7-30.BMP	
15	PAR	2	5/31/05 2:44	6/2/05 15:41	$154.26		10632	Figure7-30.TXT	
16	PAR	2	5/31/05 12:40	6/2/05 15:37	$12.84		25271	Figure7-30.TIF	
17	PAR	2	5/31/05 12:40	6/2/05 15:36	$31.24		27448	Figure7-30.TIF	
18	PAR	2	5/31/05 12:38	6/2/05 15:39	$58.70		15988	Figure7-30.BMP	
19	PAR	2	5/31/05 12:37	6/2/05 15:40	$30.00		25271	Figure7-30.TXT	
20	PAR	2	5/31/05 12:31	6/2/05 15:44	$55.94		16138	Figure7-30.TIF	
21	PAR	2	5/31/05 12:26	6/2/05 15:40	$22.82		84738	Figure7-30.BMP	
22	PAR	2	5/31/05 12:23	6/2/05 15:43	$88.03		95489	Figure7-30.TXT	
23	PAR	2	5/31/05 12:16	6/2/05 15:35	$355.92		66500	Figure7-30.TIF	

Click here

Figure 8-6. Detail report for the partially processed documents queue

The Data

As with all applications in this book, the data is on a worksheet named Data. There are no formulas or meaningful formatting on this sheet. The Data sheet is shown in Figure 8-7.

	A	B	C	D	E	F	G	H
1	EXT	3	5/29/05 15:55	5/30/05 6:30	$137.64	9321	ImageExample.TIF	
2	EXT	3	5/30/05 5:17	5/30/05 8:23	$165.57	16138	ImageExample.BMP	
3	EXT	3	5/30/05 7:51	5/30/05 15:23	$38.51	16138	ImageExample.TXT	
4	EXT	3	5/30/05 18:18	5/31/05 6:58	$13.62	62908	ImageExample.TIF	
5	EXT	3	5/30/05 23:59	5/31/05 6:26	$27.11	16138	ImageExample.BMP	
6	EXT	3	5/31/05 0:31	5/31/05 18:38	$453.83	148475	ImageExample.TXT	
7	EXT	3	5/31/05 7:12	5/31/05 19:16	$13.62	25271	ImageExample.TIF	
8	EXT	3	5/31/05 12:00	6/1/05 7:38	$96.41	62908	ImageExample.TIF	
9	EXT	3	5/31/05 13:55	6/1/05 11:16	$480.63	11276	ImageExample.BMP	
10	EXT	3	5/31/05 16:59	6/1/05 13:55	$41.04	117527	ImageExample.TXT	
11	EXT	3	5/31/05 17:11	6/1/05 0:25	$73.57	62908	ImageExample.TIF	
12	EXT	3	5/31/05 19:18	6/1/05 10:41	$47.68	16138	ImageExample.BMP	
13	EXT	3	5/31/05 22:00	6/1/05 2:25	$109.03	27448	ImageExample.TXT	
14	EXT	3	5/31/05 22:52	6/1/05 10:16	$127.00	117527	ImageExample.TIF	
15	EXT	3	6/1/05 5:00	6/1/05 21:08	$1.35	75939	ImageExample.TIF	
16	EXT	3	6/1/05 11:33	6/1/05 14:29	$1.35	27448	ImageExample.BMP	
17	EXT	2	6/2/05 13:53	6/2/05 15:42	$445.88	16138	ImageExample.TXT	
18	EXT	2	6/2/05 13:47	6/2/05 15:41	$18.72	30443	ImageExample.TIF	
19	EXT	2	6/2/05 13:39	6/2/05 15:36	$1.35	16138	ImageExample.BMP	
20	EXT	2	6/2/05 13:30	6/2/05 15:35	$119.34	130848	ImageExample.TXT	
21	EXT	2	6/2/05 13:52	6/2/05 15:40	$62.32	25271	ImageExample.TIF	
22	EXT	1	6/2/05 13:57		$137.62		ImageExample.TIF	
23	EXT	1	6/2/05 13:58		$59.04		ImageExample.BMP	
24	EXT	1	6/2/05 13:58		$29.46		ImageExample.TXT	
25	EXT	1	6/2/05 13:59		$159.06		ImageExample.TIF	

Figure 8-7. The Data sheet

Column A contains the queue name. Here we see part of the extended research queue (EXT). Column B has the status. The date and time that the document entered the queue are in column C. The date and time the document was assigned to an agent are in column D. Column E has the value of the item being worked on. The employee number of the agent assigned to the document is in Column F. The name of the file containing the document image is in column G.

This application is only an example. It is not connected to a data source and cannot update. In a production situation the Data sheet would be re-populated frequently, perhaps once an hour. Each time the update runs, the entire data sheet is copied to a sheet named OldData, which is used to draw the gray bars on the charts.

The Logic

All of the calculations are done on the Workarea sheet shown in Figure 8-8.

	A	B	C	D	E	F	G	H
1	**LastRow**							
2	209		OCR	PAR	MAN	EXT	REF	
3	**BRange**	1	335	178	406	88	50	
4	Report!b8:b209	2	5	17	25	5	6	
5	**BHeadingRange**	3	0	7	56	16	0	
6	Report!b7:d209							
7	**Erange**							
8	Report!e8:e209							
9	**Criteria1**							
10	Status							
11	=1							
12	**Criteria2**		OCR	PAR	MAN	EXT	REF	
13	Status	1	471	90	239	65	48	
14	=2	2	5	3	9	5	6	
15	**Criteria3**	3	0	7	13	16	0	
16	Status							
17	=3							
18								
19								
20								
21								
22			PAR Queu		6/8/05 17:20			
23		Type	Count	Oldest	Value			
24		New	178	5/31/05 12:45	18,003.64			
25		Working	17	5/31/05 11:46	1,856.46			
26		On Hold	7	5/30/05 7:48	407.29			
27								

Figure 8-8. Workarea

The values in column A are used in other calculations and are named. The names are in bold font and are above the value. The summary area in cells B22:E26 is built using the Report sheet. This makes the calculations simpler because the Report sheet only contains one queue at a time. Cell A2 is named LastRow and contains the array formula:

```
{=MAX((Report!A1:A5000<>"")*ROW(Report!A1:A5000))}
```

This keeps up with the row number of the last row used on the Report sheet. It is only looking at the first 5,000 rows of the Report sheet, but that is enough for this application. We are going to build references to some of the columns on Report and this lets us set the range correctly.

The formula in A4 is:

```
="Report!b8:b" & LastRow
```

It returns the range of cells in column B, containing status, on the Report sheet. It starts at row 8 because that is where the data starts. Cells A6 and A8 are similar but reference different ranges on the Report sheet.

There are two calculation areas that populate the charts, and one named display area for the summary at the top of the detail report (Figure 8-6).

The calculation areas for the charts are in Figure 8-9.

	A	B	C	D	E	F	G	H	I	J	K
1											
2			OCR	PAR	MAN	EXT	REF ←		Queue Name		
3		1	335	178	406	88	50				
4		2	5	17	25	5	6				
5		3	0	7	56	16	0				
6											
7			Status	{=SUM((OldData!$A$1:$A$4103=C$12)*(OldData!$B$1:$B$4103=$B13)*1)}							
8											
9											

Figure 8-9. Building the chart area

The names of the queues are in row 2 and the statuses are in column B. They are just typed in, but in a production application they could link to a settings sheet allowing the user to change the queue names and status numbers without modifying Workarea.

We need the counts for each queue and status. If we had only one criterion, queue or status, we would use the COUNTIF function. But here we have two logical tests to perform, so we use the array formula in cell C3:

```
{=SUM((Data!$A$1:$A$5000=C$2)*(Data!$B$1:$B$5000=$B3)*1)}
```

The first part builds a list of zeros and ones, testing the values in column A of the Data sheet against the value in cell C2 (which is OCR). So this value will be 1 for rows containing items in the OCR queue. The second test checks column B on the Data sheet against the value in B3. It looks for items with a status of 1.

These lists are multiplied together and by 1, because we count one for each row that has the right queue and status. The whole thing is inside a sum function that adds up the ones, giving us the value we need.

The formula is built to be filled across and down to cell G5. In the lower area (B12:G15) we do the same thing for the OldData sheet with this formula:

```
=SUM((OldData!$A$1:$A$5000=C$12)*(OldData!$B$1:$B$5000=$B13)*1)
```

The logic is the same. Only the sheet name and row numbers for the criteria values are different.

If more queues or statuses are required, these areas could become bigger. Each new queue would add a column and a new chart on the display sheet. Each new status adds a row and a new bar on the charts. The charts would have to be added and the display adjusted manually.

The area at the bottom of Workarea is shown in Figure 8-10. It uses the named values in column A to calculate summary totals for the report.

Cell C24 contains this formula:

```
=COUNTIF(INDIRECT(BRange),A11)
```

	A	B	C	D	E
22			PAR Queue		6/9/05 13:57
23		Type	Count	Oldest	Value
24		New	178	5/31/05 12:45	18,003.64
25		Working	17	5/31/05 11:46	1,856.46
26		On Hold	7	5/30/05 7:48	407.29

Figure 8-10. The Summary calculation area

This formula counts the number of rows on the Report sheet that have a 1 (status 1) in column B. It uses the name value BRange in cell A3 for its range and the value in cell A11, which is =1, for its criteria.

This formula fills down to C26, but the criteria references have to be changed to A14 and A17 in cells C25 and C26.

The formula in cell D24 finds the oldest date/time for status 1 in the report. The formula is:

```
=DMIN(INDIRECT(BHeadingRange),Report!C7,Criteria1)
```

We use the named value BHeadingRange because the DMIN function requires the heading. This range starts one row higher than BRange in order to include headings.

Report!C7 contains "Create Date/Time". The data for an application like this comes from a computer. If there is a change in the column heading our application will fail if we hardcode the column name in the formula. Putting the name here and using it later as a reference makes the application more stable.

This function uses the named range Criteria1 for its criteria and fills down, but the Criteria references need to be changed to Critieria2 and Criteria3.

The formula in E24 returns the total value of all items in this queue and status. The formula is:

```
=SUMIF(INDIRECT(BRange),A11,INDIRECT(ERange))
```

This is similar to the formula in C24 but uses SUMIF and the ERange, since column E contains the value.

This area is named ReportTotals and is referenced by an array formula on the Report sheet, thus keeping all calculations on the Workarea sheet.

VBA

Formatting is the most important feature of this application but it also uses VBA to interact with the user. When the user clicks on one of the charts, a small macro assigned to the chart runs. This is the code assigned to the OCR chart:

```
Public Sub OCR_click()
Call GetData("OCR")
End Sub
```

To add this code to the project, click on Tools → Macro → Visual Basic Editor or press Alt-F11 to launch the editor. Use the Insert → Module menu to insert a module to hold the code. The code for each chart and the GetData macro can then be entered.

All this first macro does is run another macro named GetData, passing in the name of the queue associated with this chart. Using a separate macro to do the work eliminates the need to duplicate the code for all the charts. There is a separate macro for each chart and they all consist of one line of code passing the name of the selected queue to the GetData macro. Here is the GetData macro:

```
Public Sub GetData(MyType as String)

Dim WritePoint As Integer
Dim ReadPoint As Integer
Dim ToGet As String

' This macro reads all the rows on the data sheet and copies the
' ones with the selected queue type to the Report sheet.
' The selected queue type is in MyType which is passed by the
' calling code.

' Turn off screen updating - This keeps the user from seeing all of the
' screen changes.
Application.ScreenUpdating = False

' Excel will try to recalculate every time we change value. We will be
' moving a large number of rows and this will cause a lot of unnecessary
' recalculation and will slow down the process. Turning calculations off will
' speed things up.
Application.Calculation = xlManual

' First we need to get rid of any old data on the Report sheet.

Sheets("Report").Select    ' Select the Report sheet
Range("A8:J5000").ClearContents    ' Clear the cells that might contain old data

WritePoint = 7 ' WritePoint is the next row to be used on the Report
               ' We need to skip the first seven rows because of the
               ' summary and headings

ReadNext:      ' This is a named location in the program and lets
               ' us set up a loop to check all of the rows on
               ' the Data sheet

ReadPoint = ReadPoint + 1 ' ReadPoint is the row number of the next row to
                          ' check on the Date sheet. The value starts
                          ' at zero by default so each time we go
                          ' through the loop we add one.

If Range("data!a" & ReadPoint).Value <> "" Then ' If column A of the current row is
                                                ' empty we are at the end of the data.
```

```
        If Range("data!a" & ReadPoint).Value = MyType Then ' Check to see if the
                                                            ' current row is in the
                                                            ' selected queue.

            ' At this point we know the current row has data we want
            ' on the Report sheet.
            WritePoint = WritePoint + 1             ' Add one to the WritePoint

            ToGet = ReadPoint & ":" & ReadPoint     ' Build a reference to the
                                                    ' entire row

            Sheets("Data").Select   ' Go to the data sheet

            Rows(ToGet).Copy     ' Copy the current row - toget contains
                                 ' the reference

            Sheets("Report").Select   ' Go back to the Report sheet

            toput = "A" & WritePoint ' Build a reference to the A column of
                                     ' the current row

            Range(toput).Select      ' Select the cell

            ' Paste the row onto the Report sheet
            Selection.PasteSpecial Paste:=xlPasteValues, Operation:=xlNone, SkipBlanks _
                :=False, Transpose:=False
        End If

        GoTo ReadNext ' Go back and check the next row on the data sheet

    End If

    ' At this point the macro is done
    Application.ScreenUpdating = True   ' Turn screen updating back on
    Application.Calculation = xlAutomatic ' Set calculations back to automatic
    Range("A1").Select ' select the upper left cell
    End Sub
```

We want to let the user see the source documents for the work. There are two problems with this. First, there is nothing to click on, no button or chart. So, we have to make the sheet respond to a click on itself. Second, we don't know what kind of document we will be working with. In this case it is an image, perhaps a TIFF or BMP. But, in a real world situation it could be a text file, a WAV file, or even an Excel workbook. We need a way to show it to the user without even knowing what it is.

Making that work requires some code. The report worksheet is an object, and like any object it has events. We need to assign a macro to an event on the Report sheet so that when the user selects a row we can show them the document. We start in the Visual Basic editor, but instead of working in a code module, we click on the Report sheet as shown in Figure 8-11.

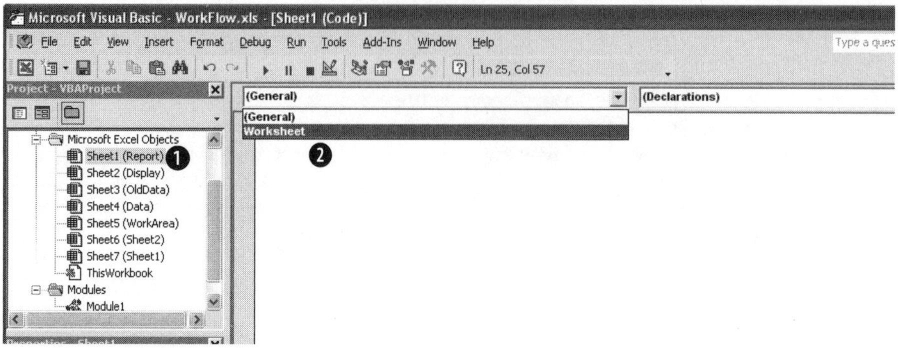

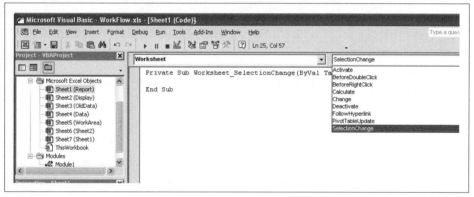

Figure 8-11. Adding code to a worksheet

Clicking on the sheet (Item 1) brings up the code window for the sheet. By default we are in Declarations. We need to access the worksheet's events, so we select Worksheet from the drop-down box indicated in Item 2. This displays the code window in Figure 8-12.

Figure 8-12. Inside the worksheet's code

The worksheet's events are now available in the box in the upper-right part of the window. We can launch code with any of them. For this application we are interested in the Worksheet_SelectionChange event. This event fires every time the user selects a cell, range, row, or column on the sheet. Select SelectionChange in the box to create an empty macro in the code window and enter the following code in it:

```
Private Sub Worksheet_SelectionChange(ByVal Target As Range)

Dim MyPath As String
Dim MyFile As String
Dim q As Double

' The user has selected something on the Report sheet. We need to know
' if the selection is a row containing data. If the selection is an
```

```vba
' entire row the count of cells selected will be 256 and the column
' selected will be one.

' We know that rows 1-7 contain the summary and heading. If the user
' selected one of those rows we do nothing.

' This if statement checks to be sure that 256 cells were selected, that
' the selection is column one, and that the row selected is greater
' than seven.
If Target.Count = 256 And Target.Column = 1 And Target.Row > 7 Then

    ' We still need to be sure that the row selected
    ' contains data.
    If Range("a" & Target.Row).Value <> "" Then

        ' This is not how it would be done in production.
        ' In this example the files are in the same folder
        ' as the worksheet. So, we use the same path. But
        ' in the real world this would probably be a path
        ' on a local network or perhaps a path contained
        ' in the data.
        MyPath = ActiveWorkbook.Path & "/"

        ' This is the file name from the data.
        MyFile = Range("g" & Target.Row).Value

        ' Here we create a batch file that can be run by MS-DOS.
        Open MyPath & "ExampleShell.bat" For Output As 1

        ' The start command will associate the file type
        ' with the appropriate application.
        Print #1, "Start " & MyPath & MyFile

        Close 1

        ' The shell command executes the batch file.
        q = Shell(MyPath & "ExampleShell.bat", 1)
    End If
End If
End Sub
```

This code displays a file, but the file can only be viewed using a program. The registry knows what program to use based on the file type, as indicated by the extension at the end of the file name. For example if you open a file with a *.xls* extension it will be displayed using Excel.

The start command in MS-DOS associates a file with the correct program and brings it up in a new window. We can execute a start command by putting it in a batch file, a file with a *.bat* extension. The shell command executes the batch file and the desired file is displayed.

If you are working with several users they may not all use the same program to view a TIFF. Different systems use different viewers. This technique eliminates the need for the application to know what program to run and where to find it.

Extending the Application

This is a simple version of an application that I have used in several projects. It is most likely to be part of a larger effort including the application in Chapter 7. The data on completed items is the input to the Chapter 7 application. Keeping the data available after an item is complete also allows you to add more functions to this chapter's application.

Sometimes it is helpful to make the arrows on the Display sheet clickable (like the charts). A report and chart can be displayed showing how many work items have moved through that arrow during a given period of time, giving a more complete picture of the operation. It is also possible to change the thickness of the arrows to indicate the relative amount of work moving in different parts of the workflow.

The data from finished work items could also be used to populate an application like the one in Chapter 6. This could let managers know if there is a change in the work process.

The important point is that the same data can be used to answer different questions.

CHAPTER 9

Optimizing

You make decisions all the time. You decide where to go for lunch or what kind of car to buy, and you hope for the best possible outcome. In these situations defining "best possible outcome" can be difficult, and there is no way to be sure things will work out for the best. In business there are times when the best possible outcome can be defined and measured. If we know the costs and potential gain and we know what outcome we want, Excel has tools that can find the best decision.

Sometimes you are only deciding one thing. You may be setting the price of a product or deciding how many employees will be needed to do a job. In cases where only one value is being set, Excel's Goal Seek tool can find the value that gives the desired outcome. In order to use Goal Seek you have to model the situation, building in the costs and benefits. You also have to define the desired outcome. In this chapter, we learn to use Goal Seek both as a one-time problem solver and as a way to add power to a macro.

Not all problems can be solved with one value. Excel's Solver tool is designed to handle problems with multiple variables. As with Goal Seek, you must first model the problem. Solver problems are more complex, since they involve more options. This chapter demonstrates ways to build Solver solutions. At the end of the chapter we build a macro that uses the Solver to handle a typical business problem.

Goal Seek

I need $100,000. The bad news is that I only have $65,000. The good news is that I don't need the $100,000 until 60 months from now. So, I will put the $65,000 in the bank at 3.5% interest, and each month I will pay an amount into the account that will make it worth $100,000 after 60 months.

How much do I have to put in each month? The money in the account is earning interest, so the solution is not obvious. First, I build the worksheet in Figure 9-1.

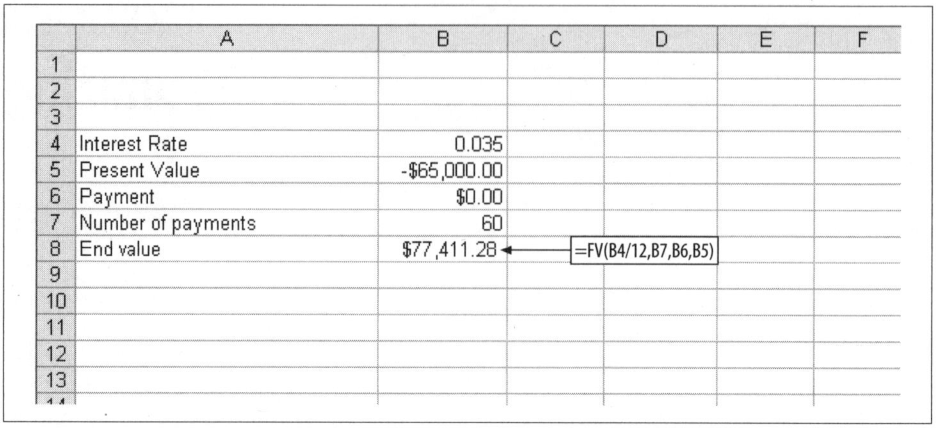

Figure 9-1. Future value worksheet

This models the problem. The interest rate is 3.5%. Present value is the amount I put in the account to start. It is negative because I am putting money in. The payment is zero for now. The number of monthly payments is 60.

The formula in cell B8 calculates the future value of the account. The formula is:

```
=FV(B4/12,B7,B6,B5)
```

The 3.5% interest rate is per year. The FV function requires the interest per payment period (month in this case), therefore we divide by 12. The rest of the parameters, number of payments, payment amount, and starting value are values on the sheet.

This function returns a value of $77,411.28. This is how much the account will be worth if I make no monthly payment and rely totally on interest.

With the model built, we go to Tools → Goal Seek and fill out the dialog as shown in Figure 9-2.

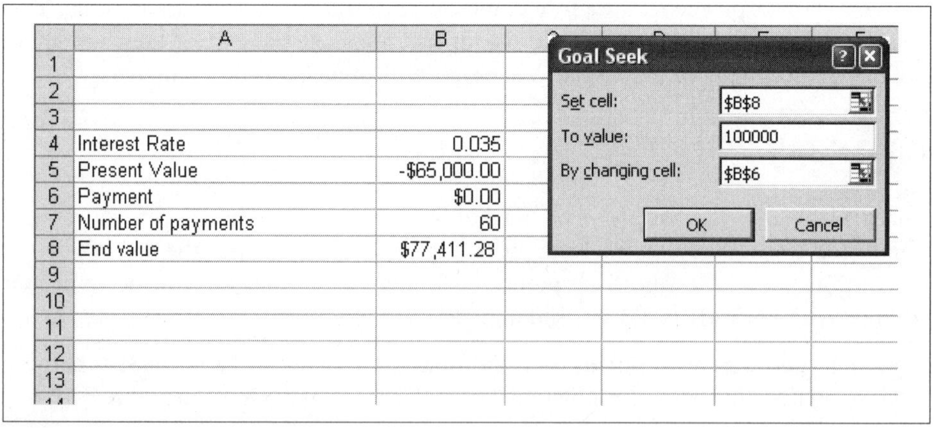

Figure 9-2. Using the Goal Seek tool

"Set cell" is the target cell. I want this cell to have a value of 100,000, so that's what I enter in the "To value" text box. "By changing cell" is the cell Goal Seek is allowed to change in order to reach the target value.

Click OK and Goal Seek finds the answer shown in Figure 9-3.

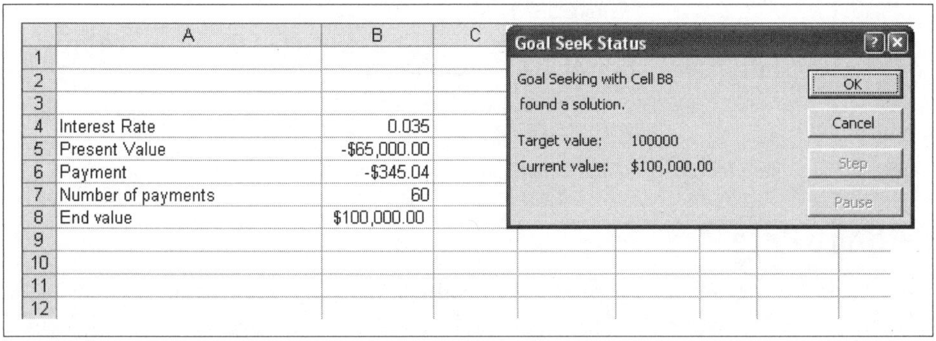

	A	B	C
1			
2			
3			
4	Interest Rate	0.035	
5	Present Value	-$65,000.00	
6	Payment	-$345.04	
7	Number of payments	60	
8	End value	$100,000.00	
9			
10			
11			
12			

Goal Seek Status

Goal Seeking with Cell B8 found a solution.

Target value: 100000
Current value: $100,000.00

OK Cancel Step Pause

Figure 9-3. Goal Seek finds the payment amount

The payment in B6 is now -$345.04 and the End value is $100,000. So, it is going to cost me $345.04 for 60 months.

Goal Seek makes it easy to try different scenarios. If I can only afford a monthly payment of $275 how many more months will it take to get to $100,000?

The problem is set up in Figure 9-4.

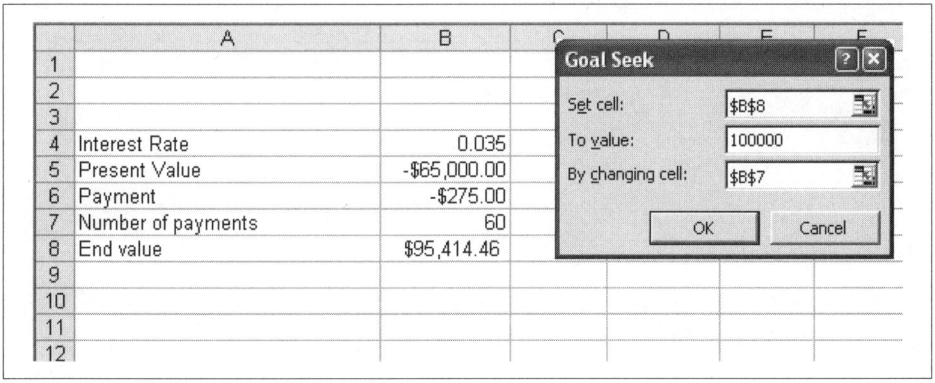

	A	B	C	D	E	F
1						
2						
3						
4	Interest Rate	0.035				
5	Present Value	-$65,000.00				
6	Payment	-$275.00				
7	Number of payments	60				
8	End value	$95,414.46				
9						
10						
11						
12						

Goal Seek

Set cell: $B$8
To value: 100000
By changing cell: $B$7

OK Cancel

Figure 9-4. Changing the problem

Here the payment is set at $275. Goal Seek has the same target cell and value, but is now allowed to change the number of payments in cell B7.

The result is in Figure 9-5.

It will take 68 months to reach the Goal with a $275 payment. (Actually, I will still be a few dollars short since it takes a little over 68 payments.)

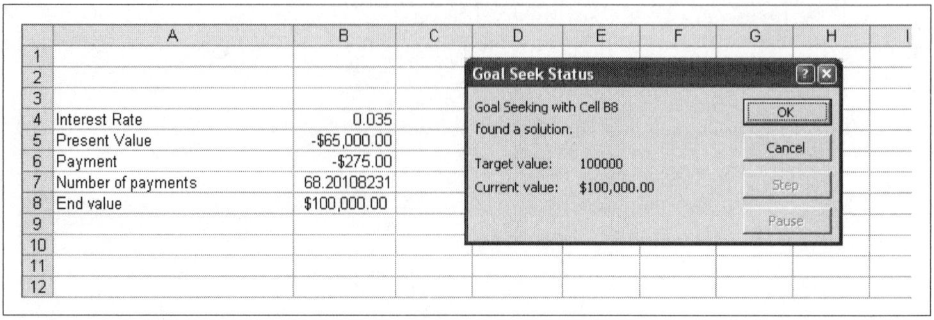

Figure 9-5. The months needed to reach the Goal

Setting a Price

Goal Seek can set the selling price of a product. Our customer wants to buy 1,200 units of a product we make. If we get the order, our fixed cost will be $1,500. Our variable cost is $52 per item. We want to set a price that gives a 20% profit.

We start by building the model in Figure 9-6.

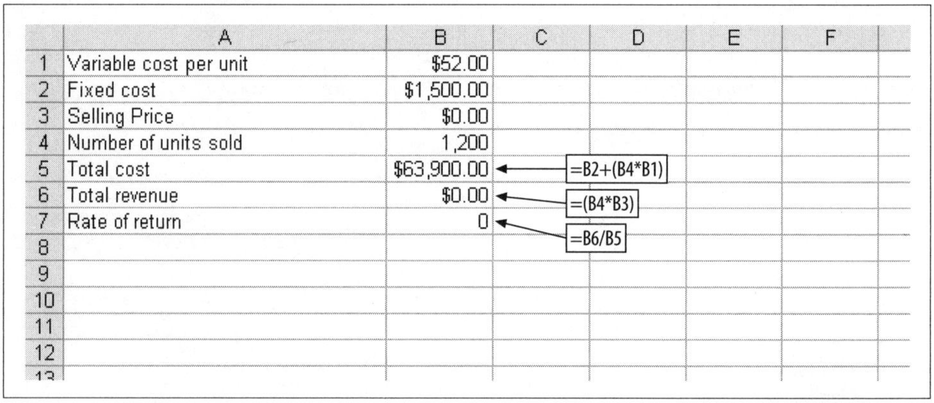

Figure 9-6. The pricing model

The selling price is zero for now, since Goal Seek will set it later. Total cost is the fixed cost plus the number of units multiplied by the variable cost.

Goal Seek is used as in Figure 9-7.

Our desired rate of return is fixed at 20% profit, so cell B7 is set to the target value of 1.2. Goal Seek is allowed to change the selling price in cell B3. The results are in Figure 9-8.

Our selling price is $63.90.

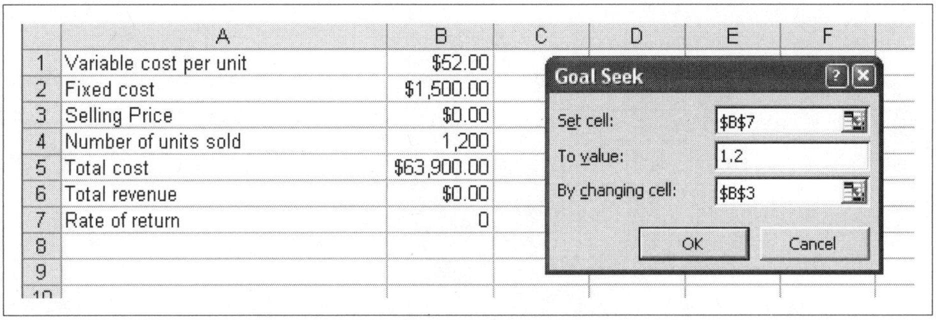

Figure 9-7. Goal Seek and the pricing model

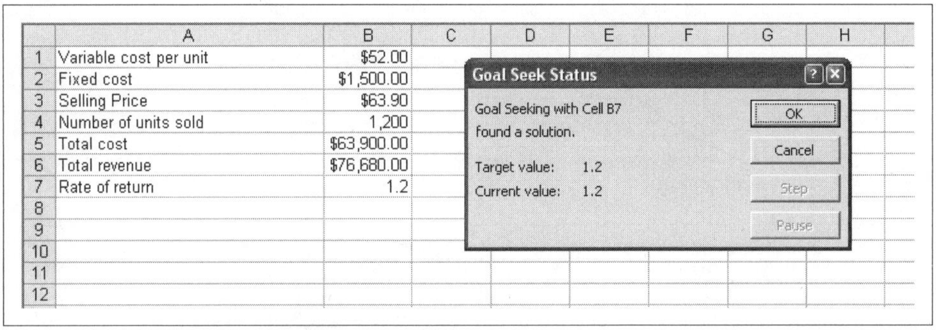

Figure 9-8. Results for the pricing model

A Quadratic Equation

We can see a couple of Goal Seek's weaknesses when we use it to solve this quadratic equation:

$$Y = X^2 - .5X - 3$$

The problem is modeled in Figure 9-9.

The formula in cell B2 is the Excel equivalent of the equations, and it fills down to cell B8. The chart shows the relationship between X and Y. There are two solutions. They are the points where Y is zero. In the chart they are represented by the points where the Y plot crosses the x-axis. Figure 9-10 shows how the problem is set up.

The formula in column B is copied and pasted into cell B10. Cell A10 starts at 0. Goal Seek sets B10 to 0 by changing A10. The result is in Figure 9-11.

Goal Seek is not a perfectionist. It gets close and then quits. The real solution is, of course, -1.5. And there are two solutions to this equation. What about the other one? Goal Seek just finds *a* solution. If there are two or more possibilities it will not let you know.

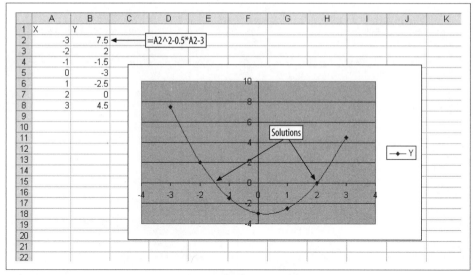

Figure 9-9. A quadratic equation

	A	B	C	D	E	F	G
1	X	Y					
2	-3	7.5					
3	-2	2					
4	-1	-1.5					
5	0	-3					
6	1	-2.5					
7	2	0					
8	3	4.5					
9							
10	0	-3					
11							
12							
13							
14							

Goal Seek

Set cell: $B$10

To value: 0

By changing cell: $A$10

OK   Cancel

Figure 9-10. Setting up the quadratic problem

Which solution you get depends on what value you start with. In this case we started with 0 and -1.5 was the closest. If we had started with a value of 5, Goal Seek would have found the other solution, which is 2.

A Matrix Problem

The previous examples were simple, but Goal Seek can solve complex problems as well.

Suppose we work for a pharmaceutical company that makes a medication used by 1,000,000 people. We have a competitor that makes a similar medicine, and we each

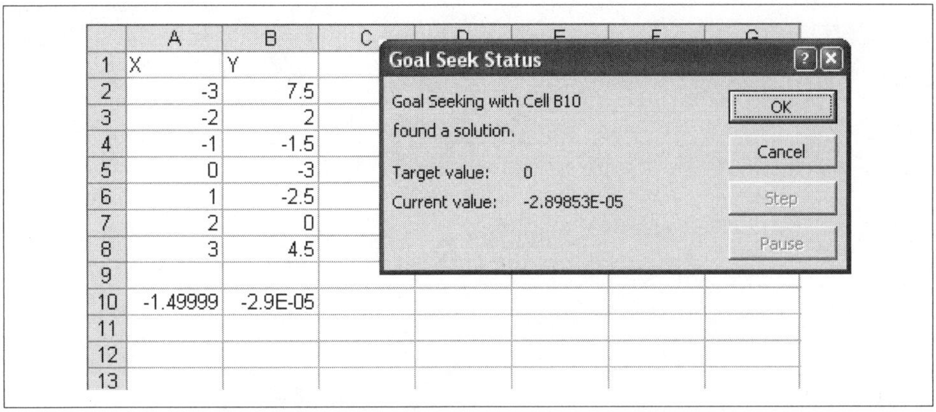

	A	B	C	D	E	F	G
1	X	Y					
2	-3	7.5					
3	-2	2					
4	-1	-1.5					
5	0	-3					
6	1	-2.5					
7	2	0					
8	3	4.5					
9							
10	-1.49999	-2.9E-05					
11							
12							
13							

Goal Seek Status

Goal Seeking with Cell B10 found a solution.

Target value: 0
Current value: -2.89853E-05

OK   Cancel   Step   Pause

Figure 9-11. Goal Seek has found a solution

have half the market. It is easy for a customer to change medicines, and each month we keep 96% of our customers. The other 4% change to our competitor. But our competitor has the same problem, and each month they only keep 89% of their customers. We get the other 11%.

Today we have 50% of the market. If this situation continues for several months, our market share will stabilize at a new level. We need to figure out what our new market share will be.

Again we start by building a model, as shown in Figure 9-12.

Cells B2 and B3 contain the customer retention rates for our company and the competition. The matrix in Item 1 is based on these rates. In B5 and B6 are retention and loss rates or our company. In C5 and C6 are the same for the competition, but the order is reversed.

The vector in Item 2 represents the final market share. We start this at 1 to 1, as we do not know the ratio yet. This is the problem that Goal Seek will solve.

The matrix and vector are multiplied together using the MMULT function, which is an array formula that returns the product.

The ending ratio is a vector that does not change when multiplied by the matrix. So if the vector (cells B8 and C9) is equal to the product of the matrix and the vector (cells B11 and B12), then we have solved the problem. The test value is 0 when the problem is solved.

The rest of the sheet breaks down the customer population and calculates our ending market share.

We are not going to cover the theory behind the matrix calculation in this example. It uses an *eigenvector*, which is a value encountered in linear equations.

	A	B	C	D	E	F	G
1	Customers we keep	0.96					
2	Customers they keep	0.89					
3							
4							
5	Matrix	0.96	0.11 ← ❶				
6		0.04	0.89				
7							
8	Vector	1 ← ❷					
9		1					
10							
11	Matirx times Vector	1.07 ← {=MMULT(B5:C6,B8:B9)}					
12		0.93					
13							
14	Test value	0.14 ← =SUM(ABS(B8-B11),ABS(B9-B12))					
15							
16							
17	Ending Ratio	1.0 to 1					
18							
19	Total customers	1,000,000					
20	Ours	500,000 ← =(B19/SUM(B8:B9))*B8					
21	Theirs	500,000					
22							
23	Our market share	50.00% ← =B20/B19					
24							
25							

Figure 9-12. Modeling the problem

With the model built, we use Goal Seek to solve the problem as shown in Figure 9-13.

Here we want Goal Seek to set the test value in cell B14 to zero by changing B8. Only the top cell in the vector needs to change since we are looking for a ratio. Any ratio can be expressed as X/1.

The solution is in Figure 9-14.

The ending ratio will be 2.75 to 1, and our market share will increase from 50% to 73.33%.

Using Goal Seek in a Macro

Goal Seek can become part of an application. Suppose we need to calculate market share at different retention rates. We can add a macro to the worksheet that runs Goal Seek automatically.

When Goal Seek runs from a macro it does not display the ending dialog, so it requires no user interaction.

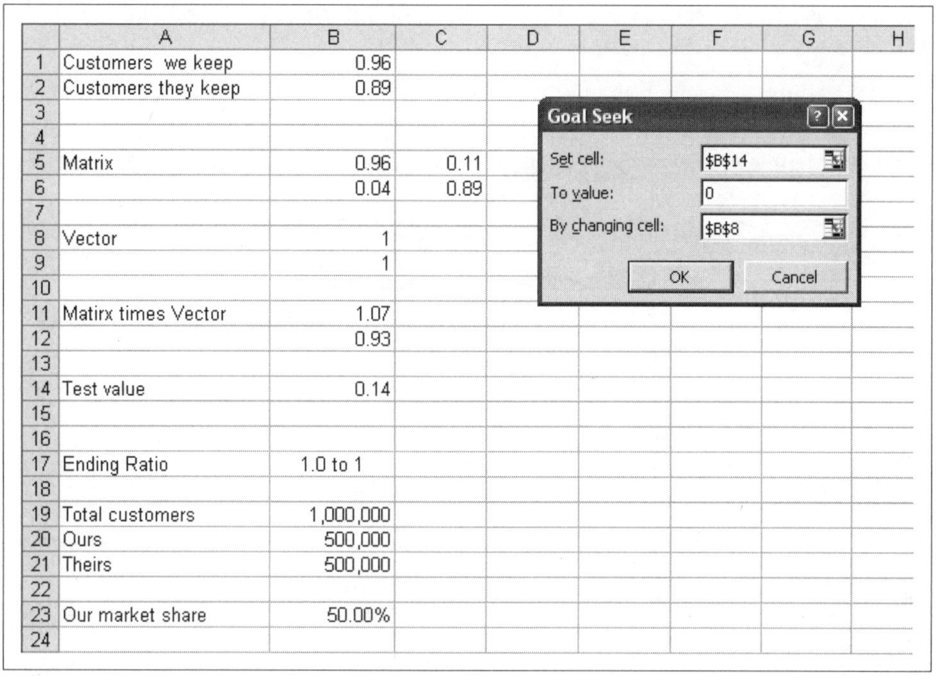

	A	B	C	D	E	F	G	H
1	Customers we keep	0.96						
2	Customers they keep	0.89						
3								
4								
5	Matrix	0.96	0.11					
6		0.04	0.89					
7								
8	Vector	1						
9		1						
10								
11	Matirx times Vector	1.07						
12		0.93						
13								
14	Test value	0.14						
15								
16								
17	Ending Ratio	1.0 to 1						
18								
19	Total customers	1,000,000						
20	Ours	500,000						
21	Theirs	500,000						
22								
23	Our market share	50.00%						
24								

Goal Seek dialog box:
- Set cell: $B$14
- To value: 0
- By changing cell: $B$8
- [OK] [Cancel]

Figure 9-13. Using Goal Seek to solve the market share problem

	A	B	C	D	E	F	G	H
1	Customers we keep	0.96						
2	Customers they keep	0.89						
3								
4								
5	Matrix	0.96	0.11					
6		0.04	0.89					
7								
8	Vector	2.75						
9		1						
10								
11	Matirx times Vector	2.75						
12		1						
13								
14	Test value	4.44089E-16						
15								
16								
17	Ending Ratio	2.75 to 1						
18								
19	Total customers	1,000,000						
20	Ours	733,333						
21	Theirs	266,667						
22								
23	Our market share	73.33%						
24								

Goal Seek Status dialog box:
- Goal Seeking with Cell B14 found a solution.
- Target value: 0
- Current value: 4.44089E-16
- [OK] [Cancel] [Step] [Pause]

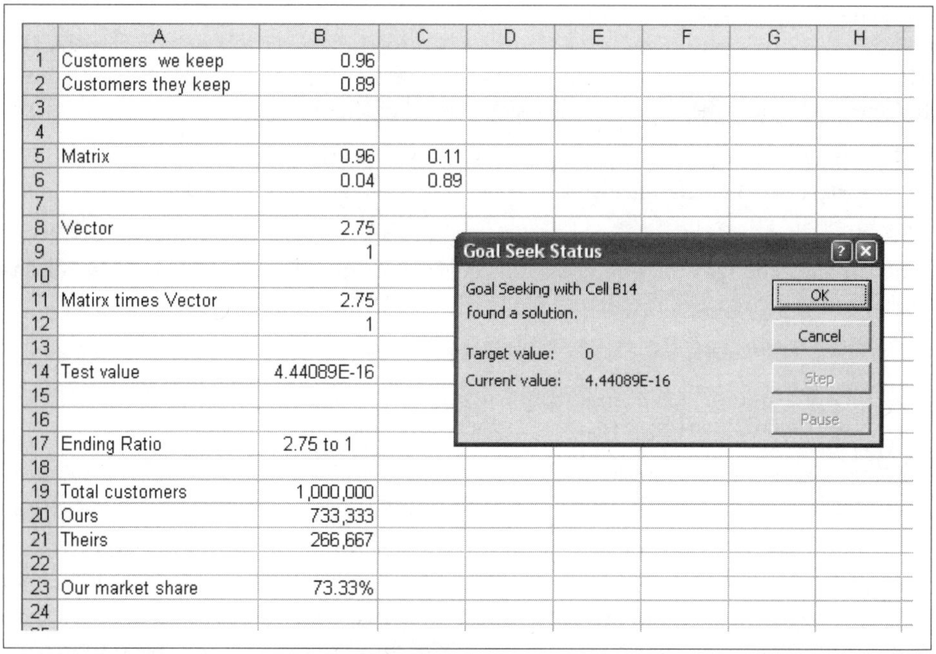

Figure 9-14. The solution to the market share problem

To add code to the sheet we go the Visual Basic Editor either by clicking Tools →
Macro → Visual Basic Editor or by pressing Alt-F11.

Once the editor is running, the options shown in Figure 9-15 are selected.

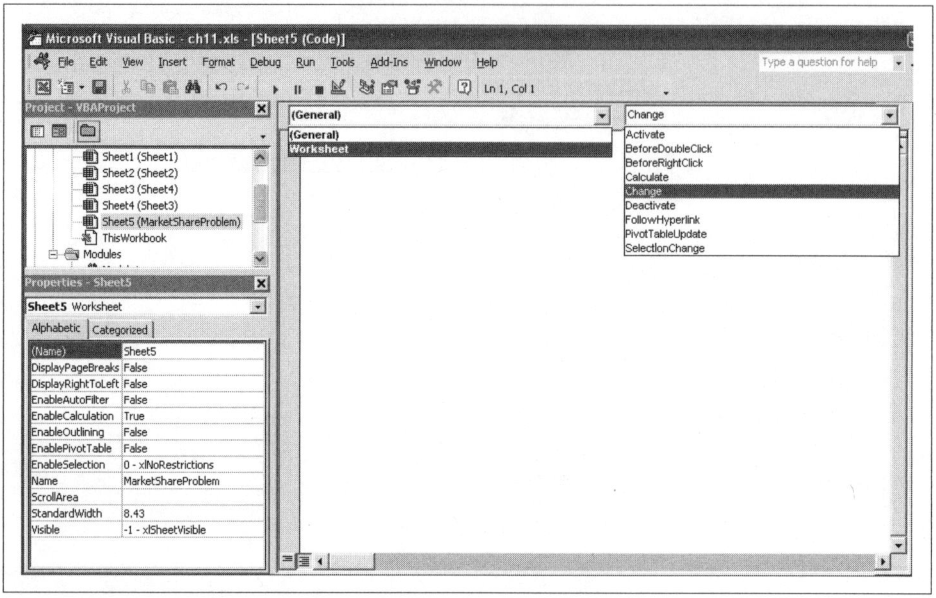

Figure 9-15. Adding code to a worksheet

Most VB code is in a module, but in this case we put the code inside the worksheet.
In Item 1 we select the sheet containing the market share problem.

In Item 2 we select the worksheet itself. This exposes the worksheet's events, and in
Item 3 we select the Change event.

This puts an empty change event macro in the worksheet. A change event fires every
time the user changes the contents of a cell on the worksheet. The following code is
added to the change event macro:

```
Private Sub Worksheet_Change(ByVal Target As Range)

If Target.Column = 2 And Target.Row < 3 Then
    Range("B14").GoalSeek Goal:=0, ChangingCell:=Range("B8")
End If

End Sub
```

Excel passes a range object called Target to the macro. It contains information about
the changed cell including column and row properties. The range object has an
Address property, but since we are interested in two cells we use Column and Row to
decide if the changed cell is B1 or B2. If it is, we run Goal Seek. If not, we don't.

The statement that runs Goal Seek answers the questions the Goal Seek dialog asks. We are still asking for cell B14 to be changed to zero by changing B8.

With this code in place the worksheet will update every time either retention rate changes.

The Solver

Goal Seek has some limitations. It does not have a way to keep results reasonable. You could get a solution that includes spending a negative amount of time on a project or sending half a person to St Louis. And sometimes one value is not enough.

For more complicated problems we use the Solver. The Solver is on the Tools menu. If it is not there, go to Add-Ins (also on the Tools menu) and be sure it is checked.

The biggest difference from Goal Seek is the Solver's ability to find more than one value.

Finding Two Values at Once

I can buy three apples and two oranges for $2.75. I can buy one apple and four oranges for $2.50. What are the unit prices of apples and oranges?

The model for this problem is in Figure 9-16.

	A	B	C	D	E	F	G	H	I	J
1										
2										
3	Price of apples	0.00								
4	Price of Oranges	0.00								
5				Total Spent	Apples	Oranges				
6				2.75	3	2				
7				2.5	1	4				
8										
9	Test Value	5.25	◄——	=SUM(ABS(D6-((E6*B$3)+(F6*B$4))),ABS(D7-((E7*B$3)+(F7*B$4))))						
10										
11										
12										
13										
14										
15										
16										
17										
18										
19										

Figure 9-16. The model for the two price problem

This sheet allows the costs and quantities to be changed. There is only one formula and it returns a zero when the prices of apples and oranges meet the requirements.

We now activate the Solver by selecting Tools → Solver, and set the problem up as in Figure 9-17.

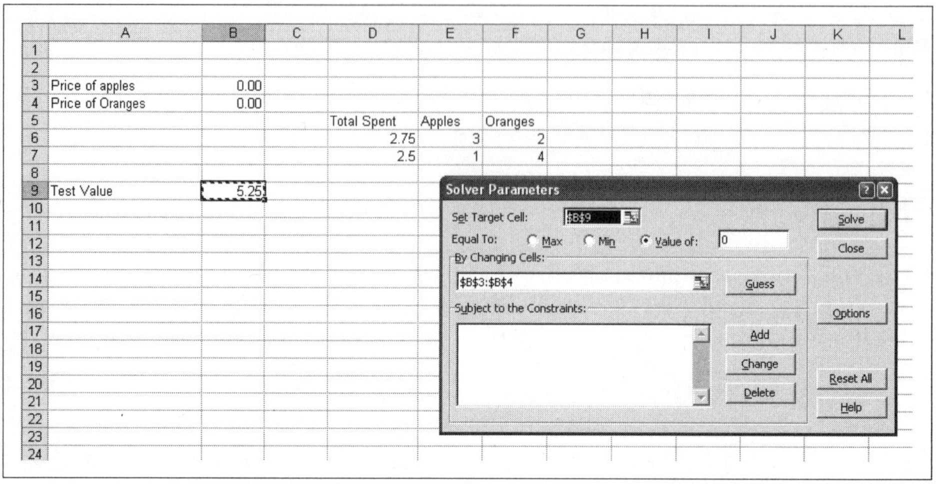

Figure 9-17. Using the Solver on the two price problem

This problem is solved similarly to using Goal Seek. We have a target cell and a target value. The difference is that we can tell Solver to change both prices at once. The result is shown in Figure 9-18.

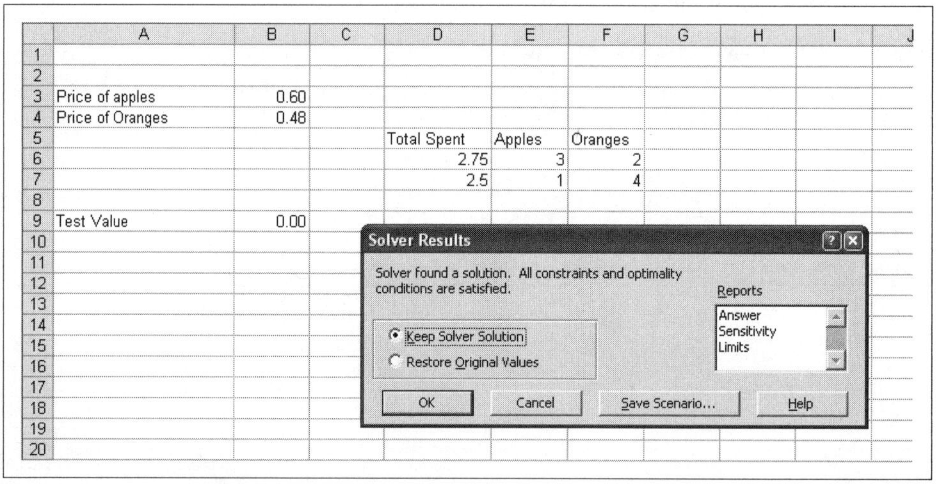

Figure 9-18. The solution to the two price problem

Apples cost $0.60 and oranges $0.48.

Regression with the Solver

The Solver also lets you try different combinations easily. Suppose we need to build a model that predicts billable minutes on a network. We have several metrics that could be used to predict this value, but we don't know which ones give the best results. We could handle this as a typical regression problem, but we can also use the Solver to quickly try different combinations.

The data available is shown in Figure 9-19.

	A	B	C	D	E	F
1	Billable Minutes	Europe	Shared service	Total Calls	Out of area	Asia
2	3130714	5709	19903	1361889	24426	10352
3	2022682	554	8881	548686	40610	3377
4	811543	2131	4817	530219	34554	4266
5	3451629	2887	9141	938707	67398	5087
6	2045521	2656	6474	621616	16143	4000
7	3181913	5540	25716	1380989	32915	10157
8	2202584	380	8007	684278	29062	3638
9	658091	2394	640	418576	12994	3289
10	3528201	3304	9268	1009265	60204	6092
11	2194440	2714	14200	776173	38415	5051
12	3218996	6048	21763	1376413	33844	10238
13	2142903	756	7752	629825	19565	4351
14	664238	2673	8247	403404	19443	3658
15	3282940	2999	7505	869150	38423	4944
16	2472109	2737	10075	900932	45217	6449
17	3238235	5726	23222	1438053	37048	11233
18	2194924	458	9867	672203	21510	3705
19	702782	2356	1388	472784	23244	4748
20	3564162	2961	14659	946506	58447	4628
21	2407282	2596	7859	789488	28133	4483
22	1643953	5503	14830	1098882	27199	9853

Figure 9-19. The data for the billable minutes problem

Column A contains the value we want to predict. We can use any combination of the other data items. There are 242 rows of data on the sheet.

A calculation area is in columns G-M of the same sheet. It is set up as in Figure 9-20.

G	H	I	J	K	L	M	N
1	1	1	1	1	1	Average Error	
5709	19903	1361889	24426	10352	1422280	1528354.455	
554	8881	548686	40610	3377	602109		
2131	4817	530219	34554	4266	575988		
28 =B2*G$1	41	938707	67398	=SUM(G2:K2,L$1)	1023	{=AVERAGE(ABS(A2:A243-L2:L243))}	
2656	6474	621616	16143	4000	650890		
5540	25716	1380989	32915	10157	1455318		
380	8007	684278	29062	3638	725366		
2394	640	418576	12994	3289	437894		
3304	9268	1009265	60204	6092	1088134		
2714	14200	776173	38415	5051	836554		
6048	21763	1376413	33844	10238	1448307		
756	7752	629825	19565	4351	662250		
2673	8247	403404	19443	3658	437426		
2999	7505	869150	38423	4944	923022		

Figure 9-20. The calculation area for the billable minutes problem

We are going to predict billable minutes by multiplying some or all of the metrics by a weight. Then we sum the products along with an intercept value, just like a normal regression problem.

The formula in G2 multiplies the first value in column B (Europe) by the weight in G1. This formula fills across to column K and down to row 243.

In L2 the products on row two are summed with the value in L1. This gives the prediction for the row. This is an estimate of the value in A2. This formula fills down to row 243.

The array formula in cell M2 is the objective function. It is the average difference between the predictions in column L and the actual values in column A. We use the ABS (absolute value) function because all error is equally bad, high or low.

With the calculation area built, we use the Solver to set the weights as in Figure 9-21.

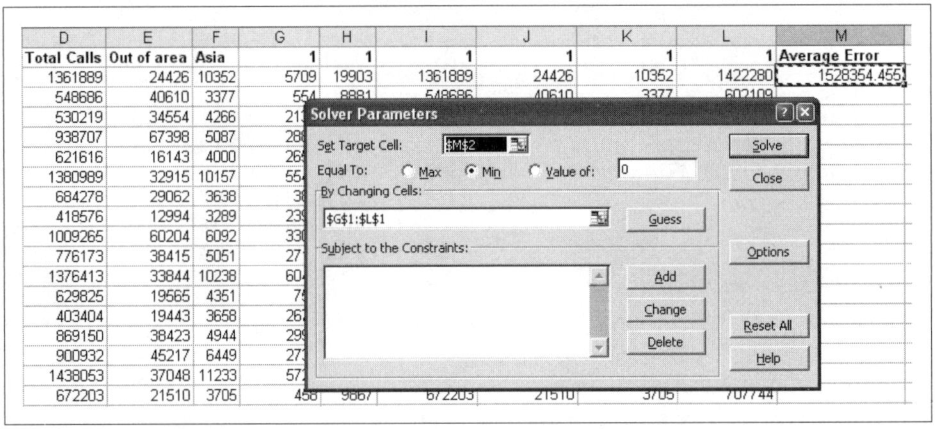

Figure 9-21. Using the Solver on the billable minutes problem

The target cell is M2, our objective function. In this case we are not setting the target sell to a specific value. We just want the average error as low as possible, so we select minimum instead of specifying a value.

The Solver is allowed to change the weights and the intercept in the range G1:L1. The Solver comes up with the results shown in Figure 9-22.

The weights and intercept are set and the average error is 313,573. The weights in G1 and K1 are high. This means the model is depending heavily on these values. The weight in H1, in contrast, is low, so low that it is probably doing nothing useful. The Solver lets us test this premise easily. I set the weight in H1 to zero and re-run the Solver with the settings shown in Figure 9-23.

Everything is the same except the By Changing Cells box now contains G1,I1:L1. It skips cell H1. We re-run the Solver and get the result in Figure 9-24.

G	H	I	J	K	L	M
-290.61423	-0.552	5.75922264	2.808411277	-321.5189333	0.414343934	Average Error
-1659116.6	-10987	7843421.962	68598.25386	-3328363.997	2913552.511	313573.0938
-161000.28	-490					
-619298.93	-26					
-839003.29	-50					
-771871.4	-35					
-1610002.8	-1419					
-110433.41	-44					
-695730.47	-353					
-960189.42	-51					
-788727.02	-78					
-1757634.9	-120					
-219704.36	-4280	3627302.399	54946.56664	-1398928.879	2059336.642	

Solver Results

Solver found a solution. All constraints and optimality conditions are satisfied.

Reports

Answer
Sensitivity
Limits

○ Keep Solver Solution
○ Restore Original Values

[OK] [Cancel] [Save Scenario...] [Help]

Figure 9-22. The results for the billable minutes problem

F	G	H	I	J	K	L	M
Asia	-290.61423	0	5.759226868	2.808411462	-321.5189332	0.414343935	Average Error
10352	-1659116.6	0	7843427.72	68598.25838	-3328363.997	2924545.749	313783.143
3377	-161000.28	0	3160007.153	114049.5895	-1085769.438	2027287.435	
4266							079
508							206
400							038
10152							584
3638							424
3289							172
6092							361
505							781
10238							313
435							809
3658							158
494							355
644							384
11233							652
3705							957
4748	-684687.13	0	2722870.315	65278.71603	-1526571.895	576890.422	

Solver Parameters

Set Target Cell: $M$2

Equal To: ○ Max ● Min ○ Value of: 0

By Changing Cells:
$G$1,$I$1:$L$1

Subject to the Constraints:

[Solve] [Close] [Guess] [Options] [Add] [Change] [Reset All] [Delete] [Help]

Figure 9-23. Eliminating one of the metrics

	D	E	F	G	H	I	J	K	L	M
1	Total Calls	Out of area	Asia	-291.24897	0	5.763821288	2.783221715	-323.1573188	0.207961619	Average Error
2	1361889	24426	10352	-1662740.3	0	7849684.809	67982.97361	-3345324.564	2909603.08	313566.2696
3	548686	40610	3377						00.696	
4	530219	34554	4266						18.542	
5	938707	67398	5087						86.129	
6	621616	16143	4000						26.761	
7	1380989	32915	10157						55.588	
8	684278	29062	3638						21.368	
9	418576	12994	3289						8.2039	
10	1009265	60204	6092						823.41	
11	776173	38415	5051						22.819	
12	1376413	33844	10238						35.737	
13	629825	19565	4351	-220184.22	0	3630198.742	54453.73285	-1406057.494	2058410.971	

Solver Results

Solver has converged to the current solution. All constraints are satisfied.

Reports

Answer
Sensitivity
Limits

○ Keep Solver Solution
○ Restore Original Values

[OK] [Cancel] [Save Scenario...] [Help]

Figure 9-24. The new results

Column H and its supporting data in column C are no longer part of the model. Setting their weight to zero eliminates them. With less information, however, the model is doing a slightly better job. The average error is now 313,566. Using this technique we can quickly test any combination of metrics. You get the best results in this kind of problem if you can eliminate unnecessary metrics. They confuse the process and tend to make predictions less accurate.

A Problem with Constraints

Constraints are rules. They let you set conditions the Solver has to meet while finding a solution. They are common in business situations that have several possible courses of action.

A mixture problem is a classic example. We make oat bread mix. Our main ingredients are flour, oars, and raisins. We have 150 lbs of flour, 80 lbs of raisins, and 90 lbs of oats. We make two varieties of mix. Our standard oat bread mix contains no more than 30% flour and at least 30% raisins, while oat bread lite mix has up to 50% flour and at least 20% raisins. We sell standard for $3.49 a pound and lite for $2.99 a pound. We can sell the flour for $1.50 a pound and the raisins for $1.75 a pound.

We want to make as much money as possible. How much of each product should we make? Or should we sell some of the ingredients?

The model for this problem is shown in Figure 9-25.

	A	B	C	D	E	F	G	H	I
1		Sell the ingredients		Oat bread lite mix			Oat bread standard mix		
2		Flour	Raisins	Flour	Raisins	Oats	Flour	Raisins	Oats
3	Selling prices per Lb	$ 1.50	$ 1.75	$ 2.99	$ 2.99	$ 2.99	$ 3.49	$ 3.49	$ 3.49
4	Lbs to be used	0.00	0.00	0.00	0.00	0.00	0.00	0.00	0.00
5									
6									
7	Total revenue	$ -		=SUMPRODUCT(B3:I3,B4:I4)					
8	Lbs of Oat bread lite mix	0.00		=SUM(D4:F4)					
9	Lbs of Oat bread standard mix	0.00		=SUM(G4:I4)					
10									
11									
12	Total flour used	0		=SUM(B4,D4,G4)					
13	Total raisins used	0		=SUM(C4,E4,H4)					
14	Total oats used	0		=SUM(F4,I4)					
15	Flour in lite - upper limit	0		=(-0.5*D4)+(0.5*E4)+(0.5*F4)					
16	Raisins in lite - lower limit	0		=(0.2*D4)-(0.8*E4)+(0.2*F4)					
17	Flour in standard - upper limit	0		=(0.7*G4)-(0.3*H4)-(0.3*I4)					
18	Raisins in standard - lower limit	0		=(0.3*G4)-(0.7*H4)+(0.3*I4)					
19									

Figure 9-25. The model for the mixture problem

For now all of the weights are zero. The Solver will adjust them later. In cell B7 the SUMPRODUCT function multiplies the selling prices times the pounds used for each possible use, and sums the products. This gives the total revenue and is the objective function.

Cells B8 and B9 simply add up the pounds of the ingredients in each selling possibility. Cells B12 to B14 contain total use constraints. The Solver needs to know how much of each ingredient is available. These cells keep up with the total flour, raisins, and oats used. Cells B15 to B18 contain rules. The upper limit for flour in the lite mix is 50%. So flour cannot be more than 50% of the weight of this product. The total weight is the sum of the weights of all three ingredients. This, then, is the rule:

```
Flour <= .5 x (Flour + Raisins + Oats)
```

This form will not work with the Solver. We have to express one side of the equation as a number. Therefore, multiply the .5 through the right side::

```
Flour <= .5Flour + .5Raisins + .5Oats)
```

Next we subtract Flour from both sides, resulting in:

```
0 <= -.5Flour + .5Raisins + .5Oats)
```

The weight of flour used in the lite mix is in cell D4, raisins in E4, and oats in F4. The Excel version of the equation is:

```
0 <= (-.5*D4) + (.5 * E4) + (.5 * F4)
```

The entry in cell B15 is:

```
=(-.5*D4) + (.5 * E4) + (.5 * F4)
```

We tell the Solver this value must be less than or equal to zero.

The other rules (in cells B16 – B18) work the same way.

There will also have to be a constraint on each cell in the range B4:I4. These are the pounds used and we need to tell the Solver that these values cannot be negative.

Now we are ready to use the Solver. We start as in Figure 9-26.

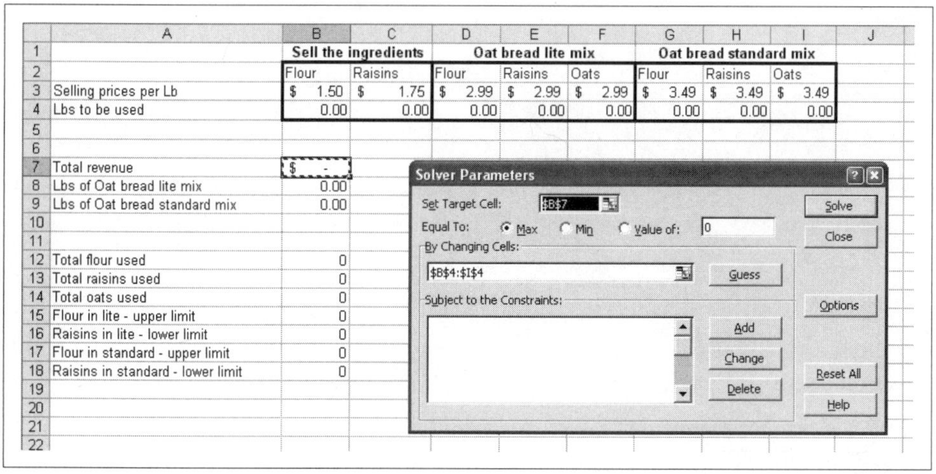

Figure 9-26. The Solver in the mixture problem

The setup starts like the other problems. The objective is to maximize the target cell (B7) by changing cells B4:I4. Next, we enter the constraints by clicking the Add button. This displays the dialog shown in Figure 9-27.

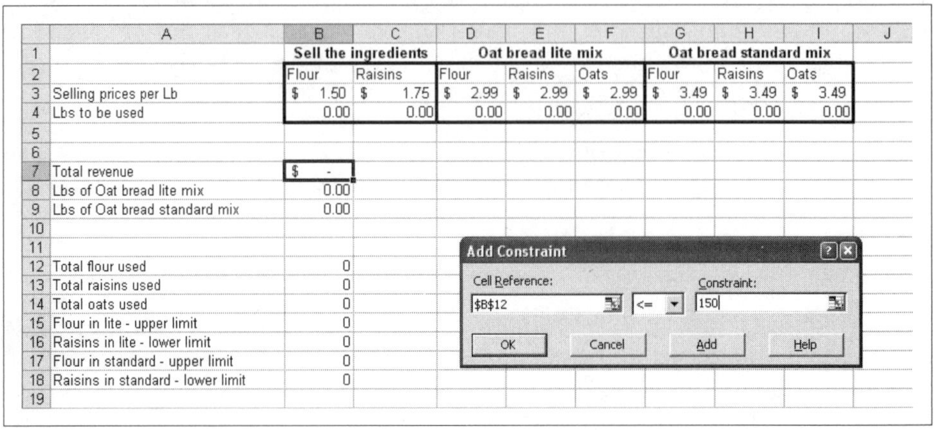

Figure 9-27. Adding the constraints

The first constraint is on the total pounds of flour used in cell B12. This must be less than or equal to 150 lbs, since that's all we have. We click the Add button rather than OK to go on to the next constraint and make all the entries in Table 9-1.

Table 9-1. Constraints for the mixture problem

B12	<=	150
B13	<=	80
B14	<=	90
B15	<=	0
B16	<=	0
B17	<=	0
B18	<=	0
B4	>=	0
C4	>=	0
D4	>=	0
E4	>=	0
F4	>=	0
G4	>=	0
H4	>=	0
I4	>=	0

When the last constraint is entered we press OK, bringing up the Solver display. Next we click the Options button, which displays the dialog in Figure 9-28.

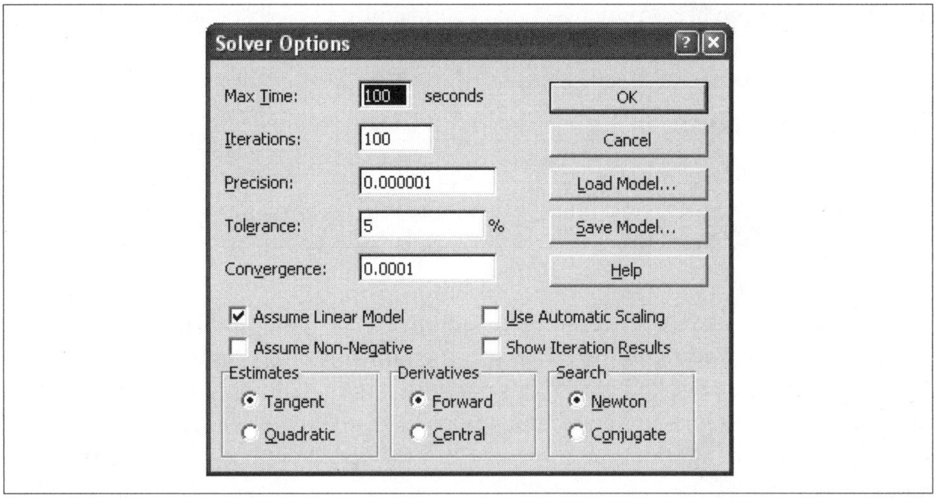

Figure 9-28. The options dialog

This is a linear problem. The objective function is the sum of products. Nothing is raised to a power, and there are no IF functions or other nonlinear calculations. So, we check Assume Linear Model. This lets the Solver run a little faster on this problem, but it is not required. If you are not sure about a model, it is best to leave this alone. We also click on Save Model. We entered a lot of constraints and we want them saved. The Save Model dialog will ask for a place to put the model. I entered K1 and then closed the Options dialog. This brings the main Solver dialog back. Then I clicked Solve, resulting in Figure 9-29.

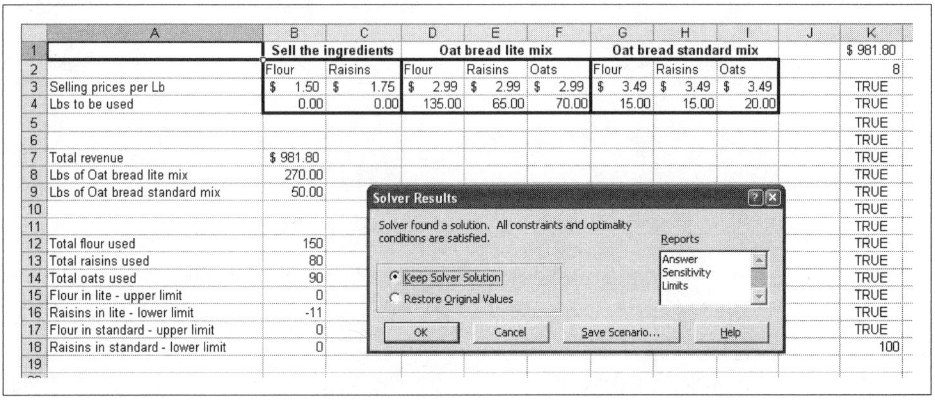

Figure 9-29. Solver results for the mixture problem

The model is in cells K1:K18, and I can reload it from the options dialog if I need to. The Solver has set the values in cells B4:I4 to a combination that results in revenue of $981.80. We will use all of the ingredients, making 270 pounds of lite mix and 50 pounds of standard.

The mixture for the lite product is: flour 135 lbs, raisins 65 lbs, and oats 70 lbs. The standard mixture is: flour 15 lbs, raisins 15 lbs, and oats 20 lbs.

Zero/One Problem

You can tell the Solver what kind of answer you want. Some problems can only be answered by an integer. You cannot schedule half of an airplane on a route, even if it would save money. Sometimes the answer needs to be yes or no, and this is called a zero/one problem.

We are making a weekly schedule for a salesman who has seven customers. All the sales calls require travel and the customers are different distances away. Travel costs $0.90 per mile. Travel speed is 50 miles per hour, and we can only schedule 40 hours of travel time per week. We know how much each customer will spend if the salesman calls on them. We need to come up with the schedule that will make the most money.

This is a zero/one problem because for each customer it is a yes or no question. We model the problem as in Figure 9-30.

	A	B	C	D	E	F	G	H	I	J	K
1			Potential sales calls						Calls scheduled		
2	Customer Number	Distance	Sales Potential	Hours	Call Cost	Yes/No		Sales	Costs	Hours	
3	1	435	$ 700.00	17.40	$ 391.50	0		$0.00	$0.00	0.00	
4	2	345	$ 1,400.00	13.80	$ 310.50	0		$0.00	0.00	0.00	
5	3	132	$ 2,100.00	5.28	$ 118.80	0		$0.00	0.00	0.00	
6	4	730	$ 2,500.00	29.20	$ 657.00	0		$0.00	0.00	0.00	
7	5	844	$ 1,900.00	33.76	$ 759.60	0		$0.00	0.00	0.00	
8	6	614	$ 2,300.00	24.56	$ 552.60	0		$0.00	0.00	0.00	
9	7	512	$ 1,100.00	20.48	$ 460.80	0		$0.00	0.00	0.00	
10						60					
11							Totals	$0.00	0.00	0.00	
12	Cost per mile	0.9	=B3/(B$13/2)		=B3*B$12			=C3*F$3			
13	Travel Speed	50					Profit	$0.00			
14											
15											

Figure 9-30. The model for the zero/one problem

The hours for the potential calls are calculated based on half the travel speed because it is a round trip. Call cost is just the miles multiplied by the cost per mile.

Cells F3:F9 are all 0. This means no sales calls are scheduled yet. When a call is scheduled, the 0 in that row is changed to 1. These are the cells the Solver will be allowed to change.

The values in the range H3:J9 are the sales potential, cost, and hours all multiplied by the yes/no value for the row. So, if the call is not scheduled they are 0. The profit is the sum of the sales minus the costs for the scheduled calls. This is the objective function for the problem. The Solver setup starts as shown in Figure 9-31.

The target cell H3 is to be set to a maximum value by changing the values in cells F3:F9.

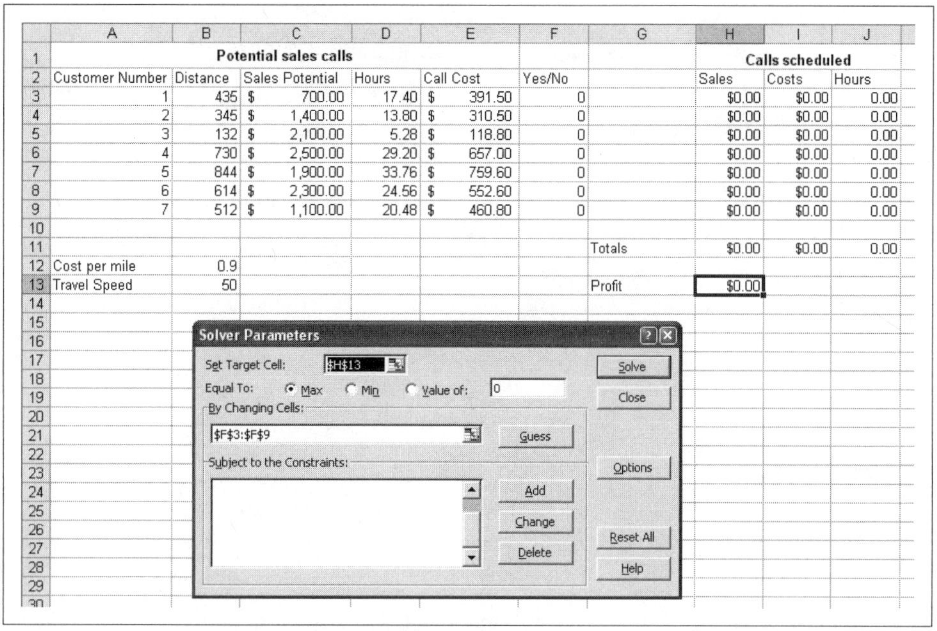

	Potential sales calls						Calls scheduled		
Customer Number	Distance	Sales Potential	Hours	Call Cost	Yes/No		Sales	Costs	Hours
1	435	$ 700.00	17.40	$ 391.50	0		$0.00	$0.00	0.00
2	345	$ 1,400.00	13.80	$ 310.50	0		$0.00	$0.00	0.00
3	132	$ 2,100.00	5.28	$ 118.80	0		$0.00	$0.00	0.00
4	730	$ 2,500.00	29.20	$ 657.00	0		$0.00	$0.00	0.00
5	844	$ 1,900.00	33.76	$ 759.60	0		$0.00	$0.00	0.00
6	614	$ 2,300.00	24.56	$ 552.60	0		$0.00	$0.00	0.00
7	512	$ 1,100.00	20.48	$ 460.80	0		$0.00	$0.00	0.00
						Totals	$0.00	$0.00	0.00
Cost per mile	0.9								
Travel Speed	50					Profit	$0.00		

Solver Parameters

Set Target Cell: $H$13

Equal To: ⊙ Max ○ Min ○ Value of: 0

By Changing Cells:

$F$3:$F$9

Subject to the Constraints:

[Solve] [Close] [Guess] [Options] [Add] [Change] [Delete] [Reset All] [Help]

Figure 9-31. The Solver setup for the salesman problem

Next we enter the constraints. There is only one rule. Hours cannot be more than 40. We click Add and enter the rule as in Figure 9-32.

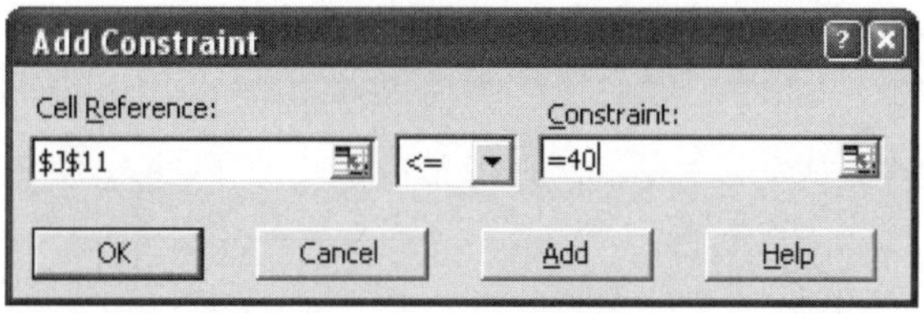

Add Constraint

Cell Reference:

$J$11   <=   =40

[OK] [Cancel] [Add] [Help]

Figure 9-32. Adding the hours rule

Cell J11 contains the total hours for the scheduled calls, and its value must be less than or equal to 40.

We also need to enter a constraint for each cell in the range F3:F9. These are yes/no values and can only be 0 or 1. These constraints are entered as shown in Figure 9-33.

When "bin" is selected in the drop-down list, the constraint is entered. If we wanted an integer value we would select "int."

After the constraints are added we save the model. We do this as before, by going to the Options dialog and clicking Save Model. The address for the model is N1.

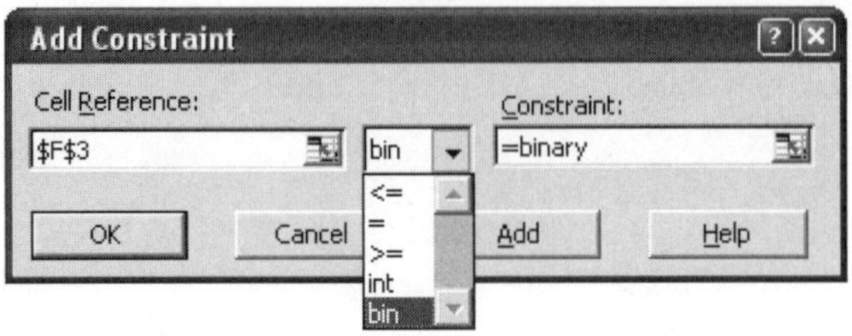

Figure 9-33. Adding a zero/one constraint

We return to the Solver dialog and click on Solve. The Solver returns results shown in Figure 9-34.

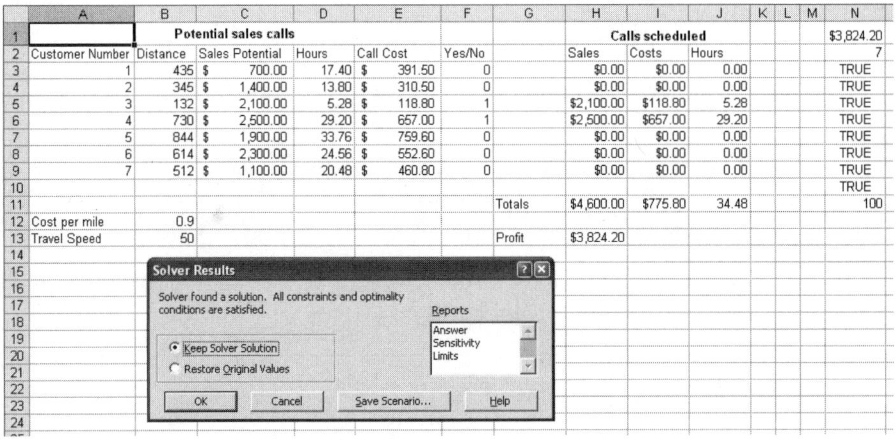

Figure 9-34. Solver results for the zero/one problem

Our most profitable schedule is to call on customers three and four. This results in a 34.48 hour travel week and a profit of $3824.20.

Running the Solver with a Macro

If this problem needs to be solved every week, it would be helpful to build a macro to run the Solver. Start by going to the Visual Basic Editor, either by way of the Tools → Macro → Visual Basic Editor menu or by pressing Alt-F11. Then enter the following code:

```
Sub RunTheSolver()
    SolverLoad LoadArea:="$N$1:$N$11"
    SolverSolve UserFinish:=True
End Sub
```

The macro is named RunTheSolver. We made things easy by saving the model on the worksheet. We don't have to tell the Solver what to do, just where the model is. The model is saved in the range N1:N11, which is the parameter for the SolverLoad statement.

The SolverSolve statement uses the UserFinish:=True option. This prevents the end dialog from displaying when the Solver finishes, making the process completely automatic.

We return to the worksheet, and add a button from the Forms toolbar as shown in Figure 9-35.

Figure 9-35. Adding a button

If this toolbar is not visible, go to the View → Toolbars and be sure the Forms toolbar is checked. Drag and draw a button and the Assign Macro dialog will display. Click on the RunTheSolver macro. The button will still be selected and you can highlight the button and change its caption to "Solve".

Suppose the assumptions have changed. With the rising price of gas we are now paying $1.75 per mile. To help offset this cost increase we are now assuming a travel speed of 60 miles per hour instead of 50.

We change the Cost per mile and Travel Speed in cells B12 and B13 and click our Solve button, resulting in the display in Figure 9-36.

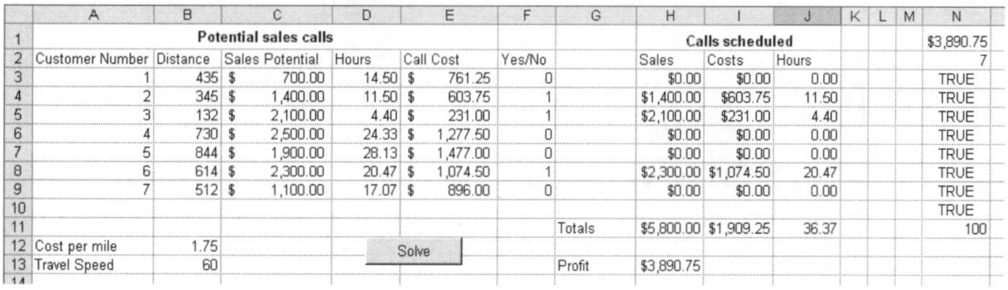

	A	B	C	D	E	F	G	H	I	J	K	L	M	N
1		Potential sales calls							Calls scheduled					$3,890.75
2	Customer Number	Distance	Sales Potential	Hours	Call Cost	Yes/No		Sales	Costs	Hours				7
3	1	435	$ 700.00	14.50	$ 761.25	0		$0.00	$0.00	0.00				TRUE
4	2	345	$ 1,400.00	11.50	$ 603.75	1		$1,400.00	$603.75	11.50				TRUE
5	3	132	$ 2,100.00	4.40	$ 231.00	1		$2,100.00	$231.00	4.40				TRUE
6	4	730	$ 2,500.00	24.33	$ 1,277.50	0		$0.00	$0.00	0.00				TRUE
7	5	844	$ 1,900.00	28.13	$ 1,477.00	0		$0.00	$0.00	0.00				TRUE
8	6	614	$ 2,300.00	20.47	$ 1,074.50	1		$2,300.00	$1,074.50	20.47				TRUE
9	7	512	$ 1,100.00	17.07	$ 896.00	0		$0.00	$0.00	0.00				TRUE
10														TRUE
11							Totals	$5,800.00	$1,909.25	36.37				100
12	Cost per mile	1.75			Solve									
13	Travel Speed	60					Profit	$3,890.75						
14														

Figure 9-36. Running the Solver with a macro

There are no dialogs. The new schedule just appears. With the new assumptions we now schedule three customers (numbers 2, 3 and 6) instead of two, and the profit goes up slightly.

Common Problems with the Solver

Solver problems are often complex and sometimes the Solver will fail. In most cases you can fix the problem if you understand what's wrong.

The Solver changes values on the sheet while trying to find the best solution. If these values can cause an error in a calculation anywhere on the sheet, you may get the message in Figure 9-37.

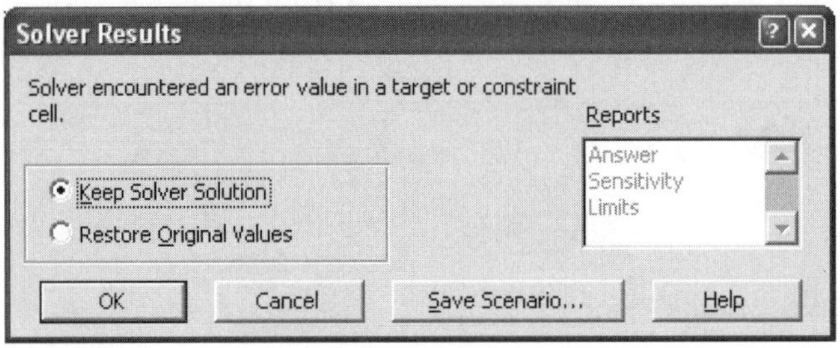

Figure 9-37. A calculation error with the Solver

This could mean the Solver has tried a value of zero that is used in a formula as a divisor. This will cause a divide by zero error. Another possibility is the Solver has tried a negative number for a value that cannot be negative.

If you get this error, review your calculations. It may be necessary to change the model or the Solver options.

Another possible problem is shown in Figure 9-38.

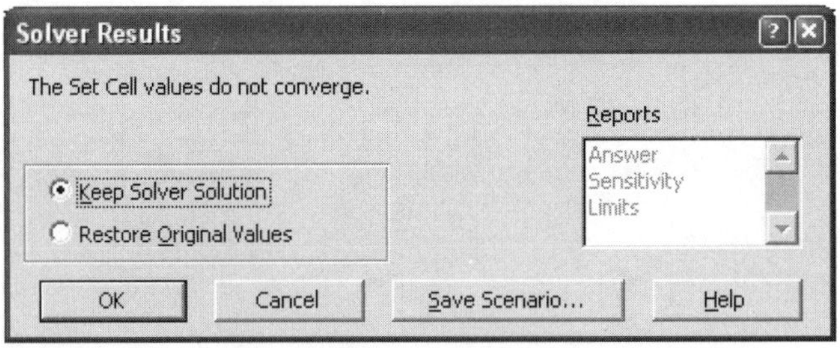

Figure 9-38. The Solver fails to find an answer

In this case the problem is just too hard and the Solver can't find the answer. If this happens rewrite the objective function. That lets the Solver try a different approach.

In a problem like the regression model in Figure 9-20, you may get this error if there are a large number of columns. The objective function in that problem is:

```
{=AVERAGE(ABS(A2:A243-L2:L243))}
```

This formula calculates the average error and is what we want to minimize. Another way of looking at the problem would be to maximize the correlation between the actuals and the predicted with this formula:

```
=CORREL(A2:A243,L2:L243)
```

If the first formula is in cell A1 and the second is in cell A2 you can combine these two approaches with this:

```
{=(1- A2) * A1
```

This is a more complicated function and it adds no value in theory. But it gives the Solver a different approach to the problem and often works in this situation.

Another error is shown in Figure 9-39.

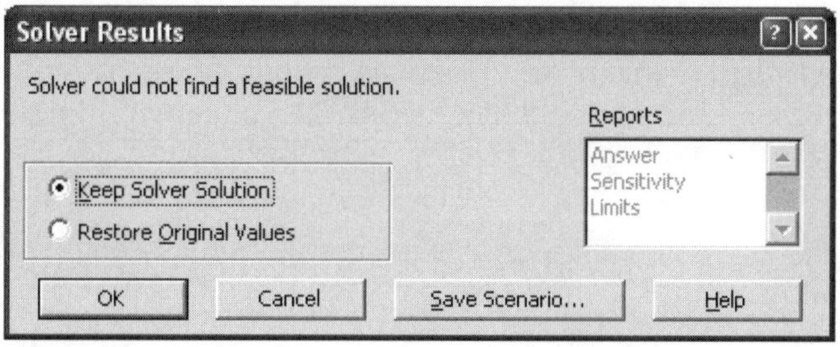

Figure 9-39. An impossible problem

Here we have mutually exclusive constraints. In the problem modeled in Figure 9-25, if I enter a new constraint telling the Solver that cell B4 must be greater than 200, I will get this error. This new constraint tells the Solver that the solution must include the sale of 200 lbs of flour while other constraints tell it that there are only 150 lbs of flour available.

This is impossible and there is no solution that meets all the constraints. If you get this error, go back and review the constraints. One has been entered wrong, the problem has not been modeled correctly, or it is just impossible to do what you are trying to do.

Another common, but less serious, situation occurs when the Solver reaches its time or iteration limit. The iteration limit dialog is shown in Figure 9-40.

The Solver looks for a solution by making small changes in the cells. If a change improves the solution, the Solver makes another small change in that direction. Each cycle of changes is called an iteration. The maximum number of iterations allowed is set on the Options dialog shown in Figure 9-28. If you get this error or the similar Max Time error dialog, it means the problem is difficult and it is taking the Solver a long time to find a solution. Usually you can just click continue, but if it keeps happening you may need to adjust the model.

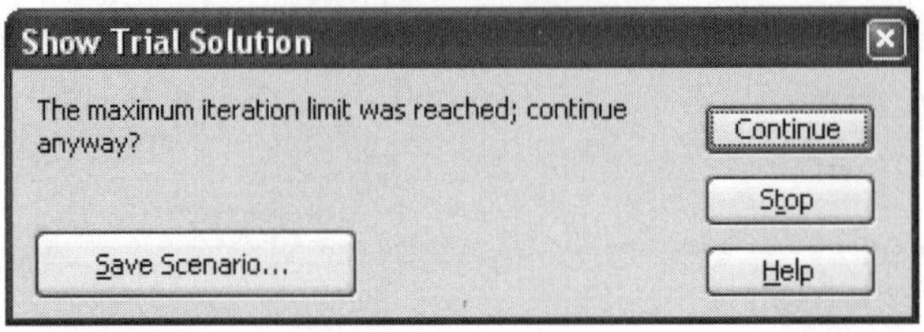

Figure 9-40. The iteration limit

Applications

The Solver and Goal Seek can be used in Excel applications. None of the applications in the book do this, but you can include either of these tools on a Workarea sheet. The macros in this chapter show how to run the tools. You would have to decide how and when to trigger the macros. They could be run from a button or tied to a change on a worksheet as we did in this chapter, or perhaps run when the workbook opens.

CHAPTER 10

Importing Data

Data is the raw material for everything Excel does, and the first step in any job is getting the data onto a worksheet. Excel can import data from almost any kind of data source, and in this chapter we look at the most common data import situations with Excel.

The applications in this book start with the data already on a worksheet called Data. This chapter will demonstrate ways to build a backend process to capture the data and update the Data sheet in the applications.

Text Files

Text files are the simplest kind of data to import. These files are common and can come from any kind of system. In some cases older mainframe systems have produced a file for years and an Excel application uses the file as input. When the time comes to rewrite the mainframe application it is not difficult for a modern server to create the same file. It is common to find an old data-sharing relationship based on text files even with today's technology. The advantages of this data-sharing scheme are simplicity, size, and stability. Excel understands two kinds of text files.

Fixed Length Files

In a fixed length file, every record or row has the same number of characters. Each data element, such as a name or phone number, has a fixed number of characters. If a name field is set up with a length of 25 characters and a name comes in that is too long, the extra characters are lost. If the name is less than 25 characters long, blanks are inserted to make up the difference. This kind of data storage is typical of older systems and dates from the era of punch cards and accounting machines. You are not likely to see a new process being built with this kind of file, but there are plenty of older systems that still use them.

In this chapter our sample data is stock prices. The data includes stock symbol, date, open, high, low, close, and volume. A fixed length version of this data is in a file named *ch10_FixedLen.txt* and is located on my *C* drive in the *My Documents* folder.

To import the file, I select Data → Import External Data → Import Data, then navigate to and select the file. If the filename does not show up in the dialog, I need to be sure the *.txt* file type is selected as shown in Figure 10-1.

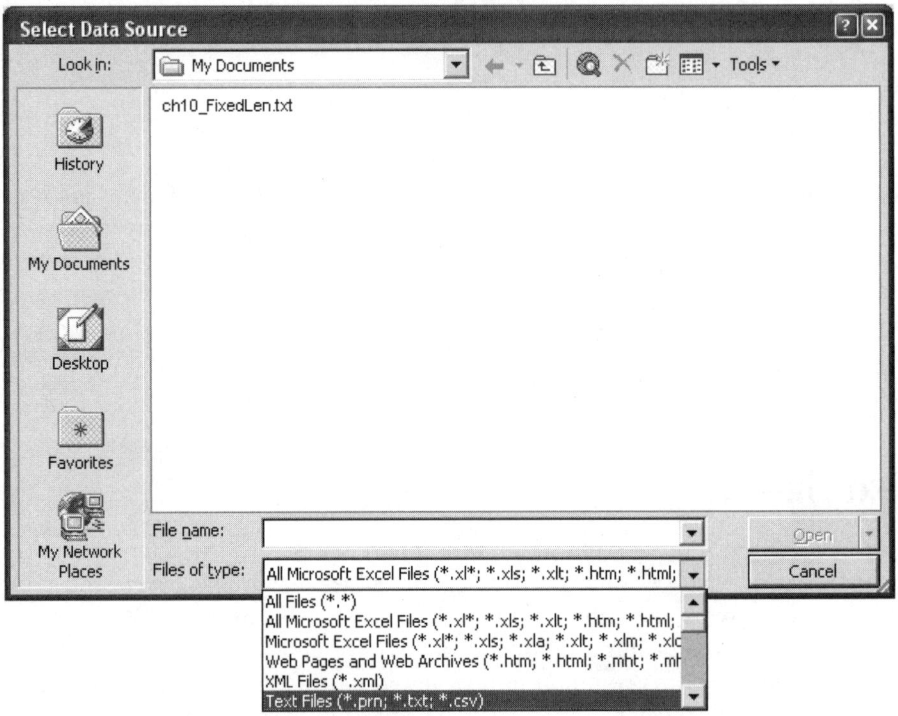

Figure 10-1. Selecting the text file type

Once the file is selected, the text import wizard starts and the dialog in Figure 10-2 is displayed.

This is a fixed length file and the Fixed Width option is selected. If I wanted to skip rows at the top of the file containing heading information, I could indicate the row number to start the import at. The display area at the bottom shows the contents of the file. It is easy to see that the file is fixed length. Clicking Next brings up the dialog in Figure 10-3.

In this step the data is mapped by position. Excel tries to map the file for you and in most cases it will be correct. The lines and arrows can be moved around and changed manually, allowing you to map the file anyway you like. Once the mappings are correct, clicking the Next button brings up Step 3 as in Figure 10-4.

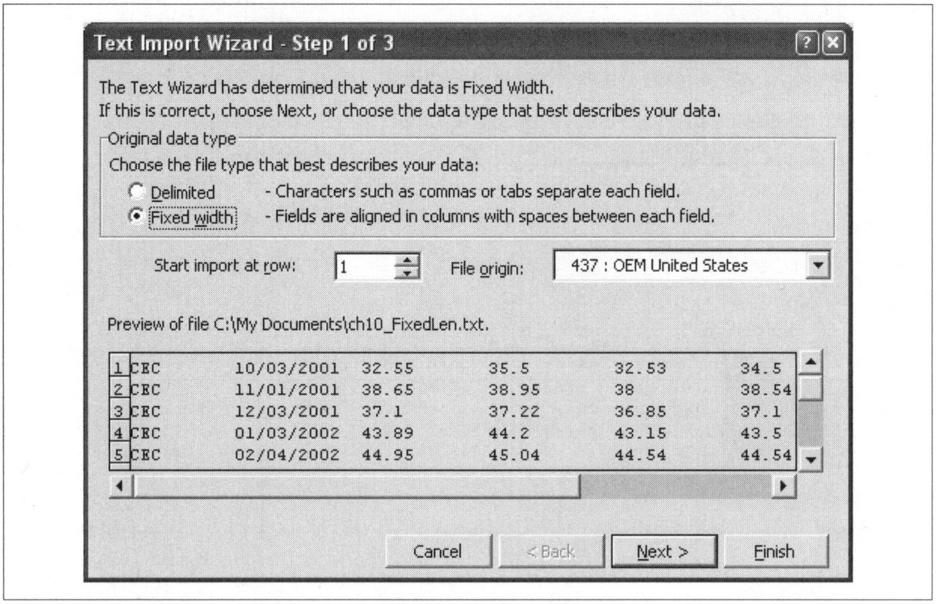

Figure 10-2. Text import – Step 1

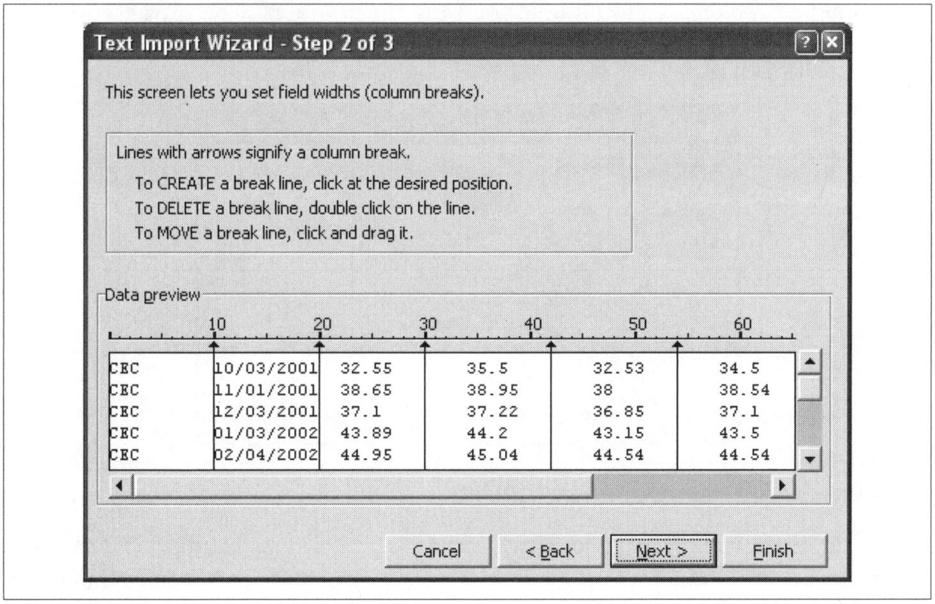

Figure 10-3. Text import – Step 2

Here you can select a data type (general, text, or date) for each data item if necessary. In most cases Excel will get it right and you won't have to do anything. You can also tell Excel not to import some of the data items. Select the data items one by one

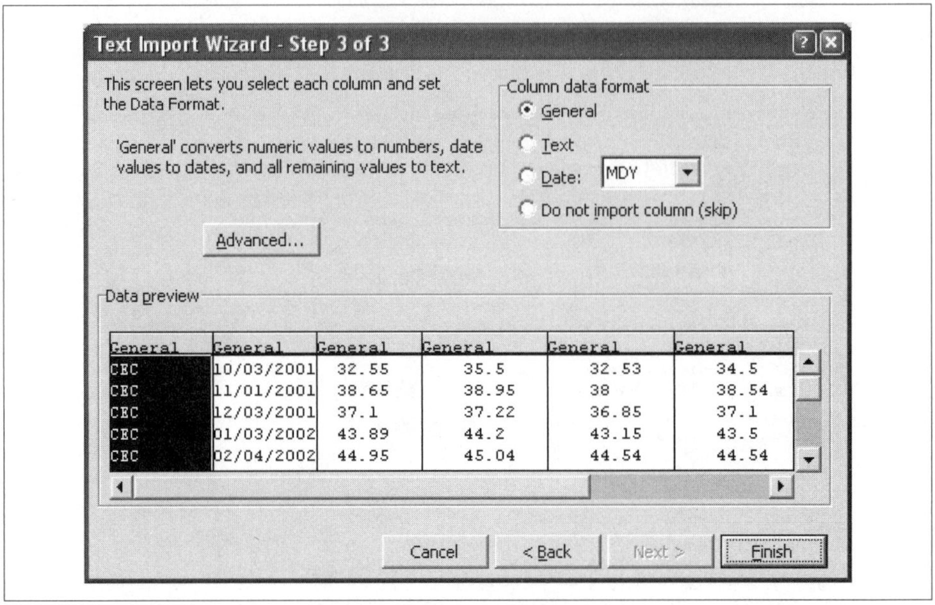

Figure 10-4. Text import – Step 3

by clicking on the data or heading in the Data preview area. The Advanced button displays the dialog shown in Figure 10-5.

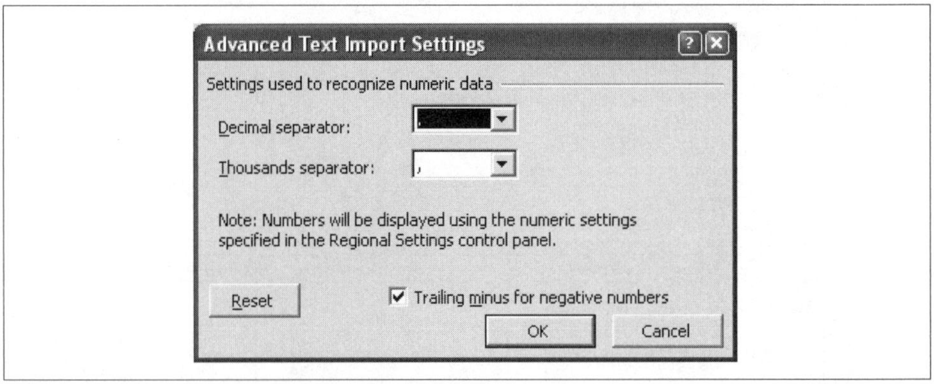

Figure 10-5. Controlling the display of numeric data

This dialog gives you control over how numeric information is handled. It defaults to the normal convention for numbers, but allows you to specify a non-traditional numeric format if needed. When all the settings are right, click on Finish (shown in Figure 10-4), and the dialog in Figure 10-6 is displayed.

Here we set the cell to receive the import. In this case we are putting the data on the active sheet, but there is an option to create a new sheet to hold the data.

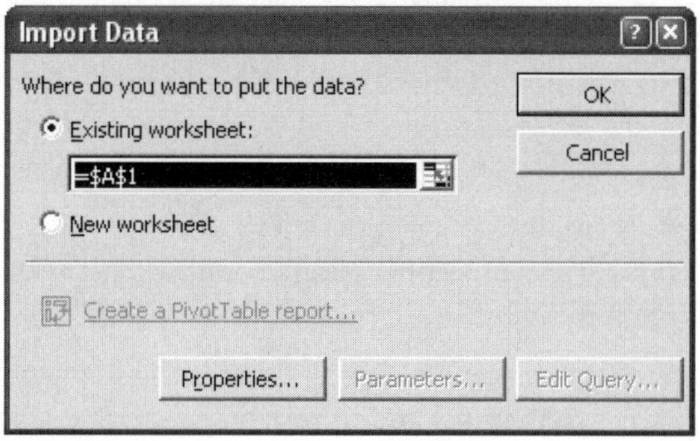

Figure 10-6. Finishing the text import

Excel's data import tool is flexible and makes working with most text files easy. But, its real power is in the Properties option on this dialog. Clicking the Properties button reveals Figure 10-7.

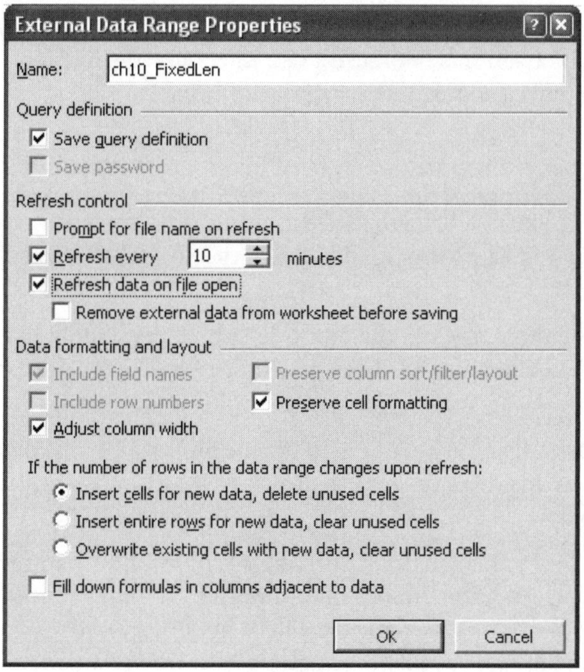

Figure 10-7. The Properties dialog

The options allow you to control how data is put on the sheet and what happens to the older data that is already there. If you are importing data for analysis or a one-time job, these options may not help much. But if you are building an application that needs to be updated periodically, these features can make the job easier. The application in Chapter 8 monitors a queue. Its data is a snapshot taken at a point in time. As work progresses through the day it needs to refresh its data to stay current. Building the logic to do this is complex, and in Chapter 8 we didn't consider that problem.

Suppose the data for the application is exported by another system as a text file every 10 minutes. We would want the application to import new data every time it is started and every 10 minutes while it is open.

The settings in Figure 10-7 let you do exactly that. In the Refresh section I tell Excel to refresh the data every ten minutes and to refresh on file open. The refresh remembers all the settings in the import and handles resetting the sheet automatically. The application is designed with a data sheet that holds all the data and does nothing else. This makes it easy to control the flow of new data into the application using the import properties.

How cool is that? I don't have to write any code; I don't have to change anything in the application. I just set up the import and refresh options on the data sheet and it's done.

All of the applications in this book use a data sheet like the one in Chapter 8, and all of them could be linked to text files using this technique.

Delimited Files

Delimited files are like fixed length files except the data items are separated by a special character. The most common choices for the special character are comma and tab, but any character can be used.

Delimited files are more modern than fixed length, and are more likely to come from a PC or server than a mainframe. They take up less space and are easier to handle in VBA.

Some text files use a text qualifier to mark the beginning of string data. But files coming from older systems often do not use this convention, and for these files the delimiter can be a problem.

It is critical to select a character that absolutely cannot turn up in the data. If it does, the delimiter occurs too many times on a line and the import process loses track of where it is in the data. The rest of the file will be imported out of place. Comma delimited files that contain names and addresses are susceptible to this problem. If there is any doubt, it is best to use a really unusual character as the delimiter, like | or `.

The import process is the same for delimited files except for Step 2, in which instead of mapping the file you specify the delimiter as shown in Figure 10-8.

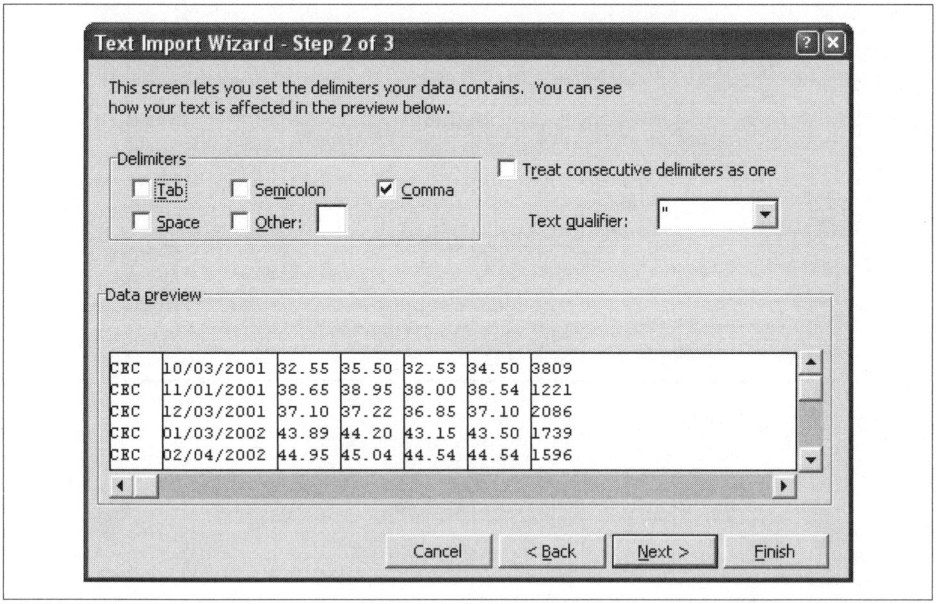

Figure 10-8. Telling Excel what delimiter to use

Here I am importing a delimited version of the same stock file. The delimiter is a comma, but the dialog lets me select any character. The rest of the process is the same, including the ability to control data refresh with the properties dialog.

Databases

The data for an Excel project can come from a database. In newer systems, both client server and web-based, SQL databases are the most common data storage tool. The data for any of the applications in the book could come from such a database. Excel can import data from databases and allows you to filter and sort the data during the import process.

To import data from a database start by selecting Data → Import External Data → New Database Query. This brings up the dialog in Figure 10-9.

This dialog lets me choose a data source to import from. I have an Access database containing the same stock data we have been using. The database is named *ch10.mdb*.

Since it is an Access Database, I could click on the MS Access Database choice. But I can also set it up as a New Data Source. This option allows you to import from other kinds of databases such as Sybase, Oracle, SQL Server, and many others.

Clicking OK with New Data Source selected moves us to Figure 10-10.

I named the new data source *Stocks*. In the future, Stocks will appear as an option in the Choose Data Source dialog (Figure 10-9). In the driver selection box I choose

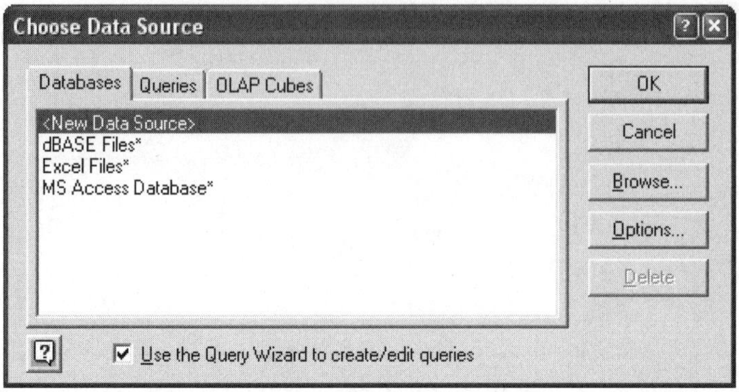

Figure 10-9. Importing from a database

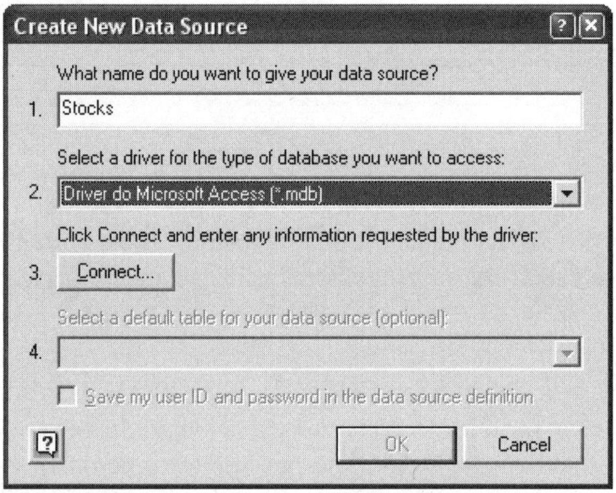

Figure 10-10. Establishing a new data source

Access. If you want to import from a different kind of database you would tell Excel what kind it is here. There is a list of the available drivers. If the PC you are working on has never connected to a database like the one you are going to use, you may need to load the driver.

The next dialog, Figure 10-11, allows you to tell Excel where the database is.

If the database is on a server, you use this dialog to tell Excel what server to look on. In cases where the data is available on a network or local drive, as in this case, you click Select. This brings up a dialog allowing you to navigate to the database, as shown in Figure 10-12.

Once the database is selected, the dialog in Figure 10-13 appears.

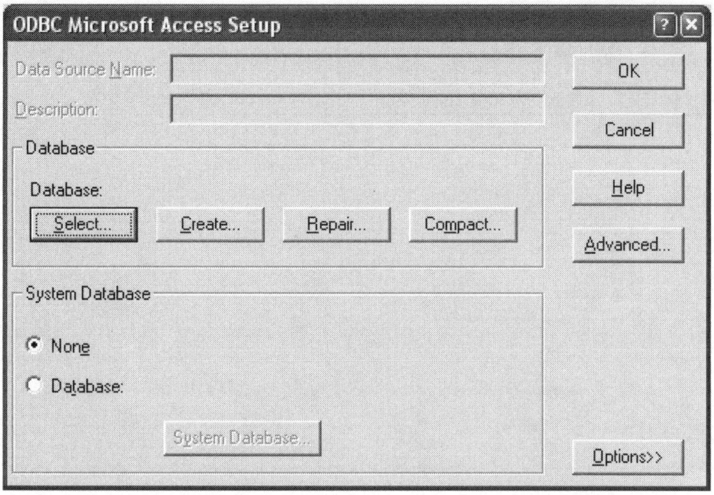

Figure 10-11. Locating the database

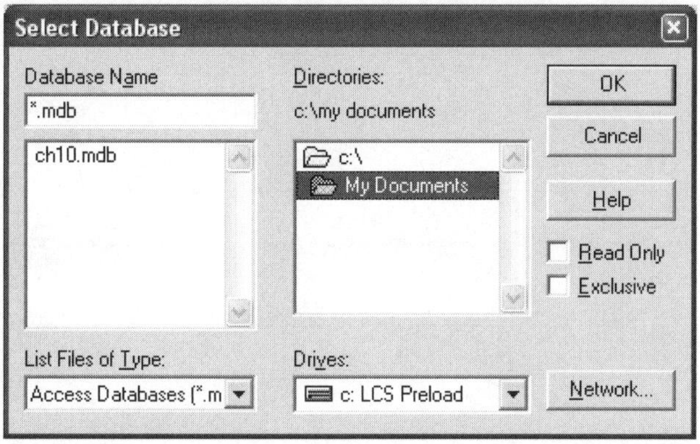

Figure 10-12. Selecting the database

In this step we select the columns to include in the import. I selected all of them, but you can select only the ones you want. This also lets you control the order that they are imported in.

The dialog in Figure 10-14 provides a way to filter the data.

The text file imports did not have a way to filter the stock data, but here it is easy to do. If I want to limit the import to stocks with symbols starting with the letter C, I click on the Symbol in the "Column to filter" listbox. Then I fill the dialog out as shown in Figure 10-15.

You can link conditions with and/or, and you can use any mixture of columns. The next dialog is shown in Figure 10-16.

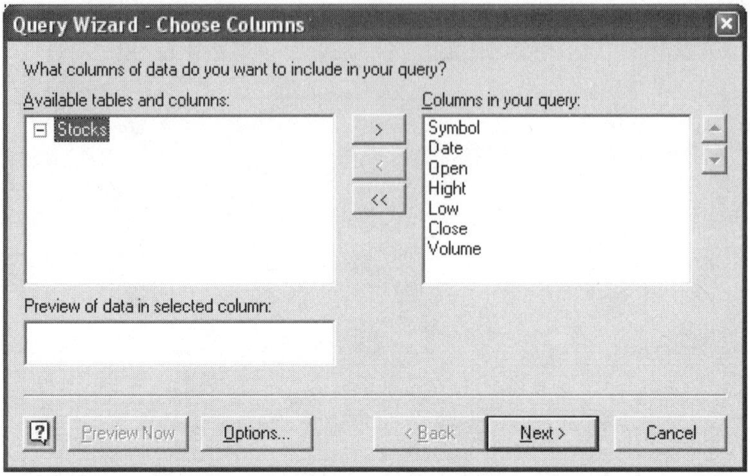

Figure 10-13. Selecting the columns

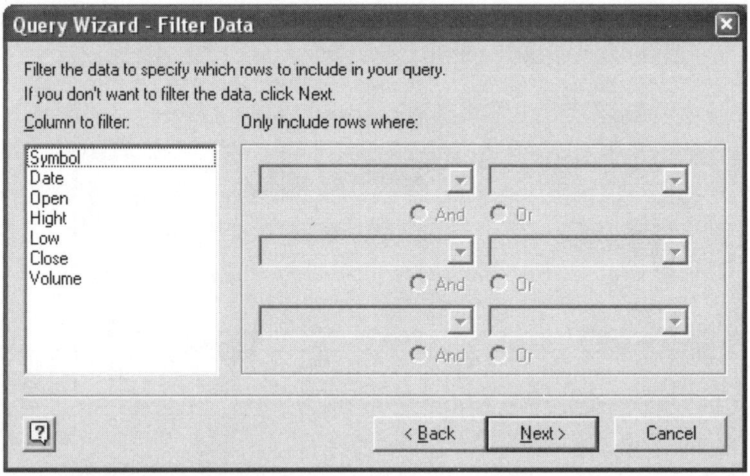

Figure 10-14. The filter data dialog

Here I am telling Excel to sort the data by Date. The Finish page of the dialog comes up next, as in Figure 10-17.

Clicking Finish with the "Return Data to Microsoft Excel" option checked brings us to the final dialog in Figure 10-18.

This is just like Figure 10-6. You specify a location for the data and can modifiy other options by clicking the Properties button. As with importing from a text file, you can control data refresh and other properties. So, if the application in Chapter 8 was getting its data from a database, I could build the import once and set the refresh to run

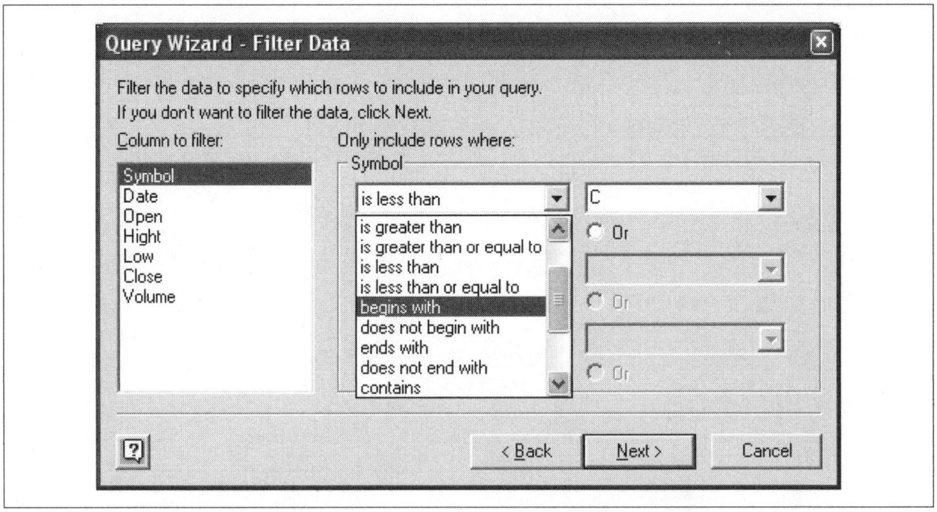

Figure 10-15. Filtering the data

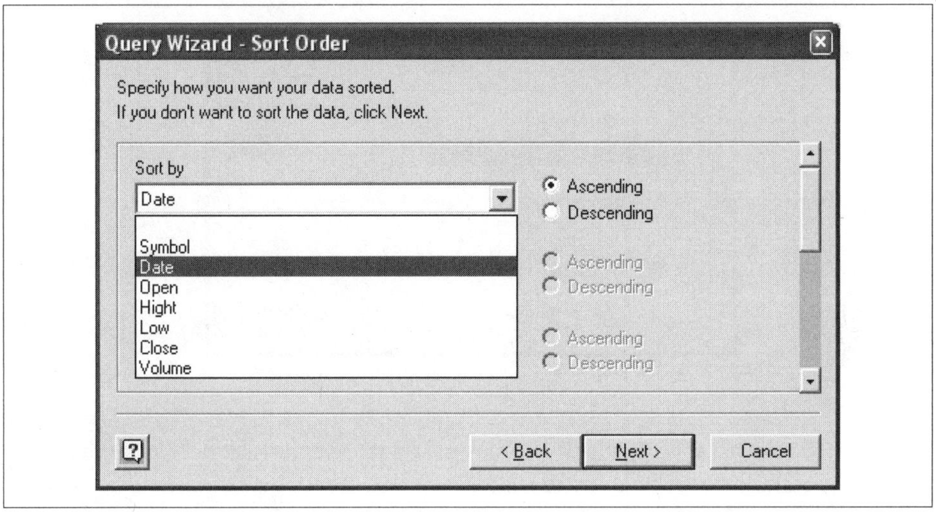

Figure 10-16. The sort dialog

every 10 minutes and at open. I would not need to write a macro or change anything in the application.

Linking Tables

Sometimes databases are more complicated, and the information may be in more than one table. Chapter 7's application had data for items in a queue. Each item's information included an employee number but not an employee name. The names were in a separate list on the Workarea sheet.

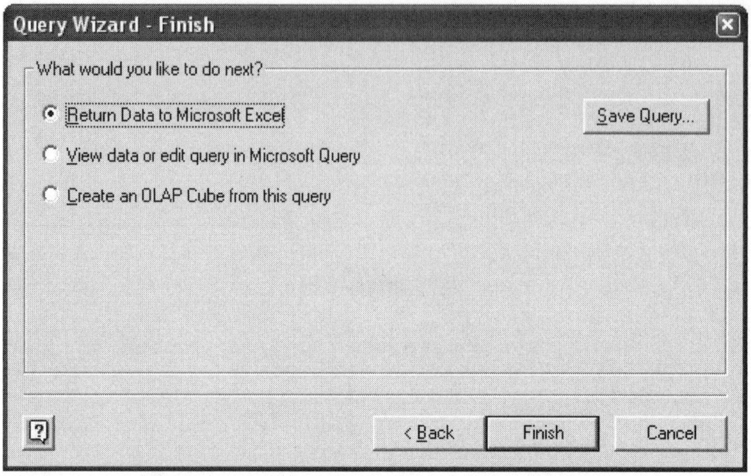

Figure 10-17. Finishing the query

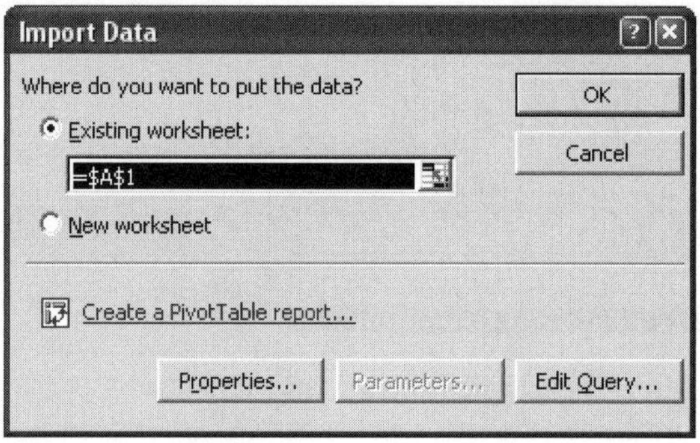

Figure 10-18. Putting the data on the worksheet

I have an Access database with two tables based on the data from that application. One table contains the items in the queue and is called Items. The other table is called Agents and contains the agent employee number and name.

We can get Excel to link the tables during the data import. This eliminates some of the complexity of the application. The data source is set up as before, but when we get to the Choose Columns dialog in Figure 10-19 we have more choices.

I start in the Items table and select all the columns. This can be done quickly by selecting the table name, Items, and clicking the arrow button. Next I click on the Agents table and select the Name column by either double-clicking or using the right arrow button. This is shown in Figure 10-20.

The employee number column is named EmpNum in both tables, and it is the primary key in the Agents table. Therefore, Excel will link the tables automatically. We

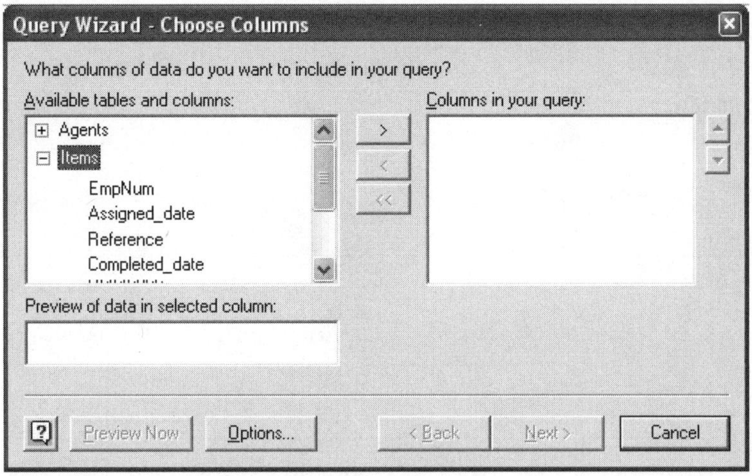

Figure 10-19. Choosing items from two tables

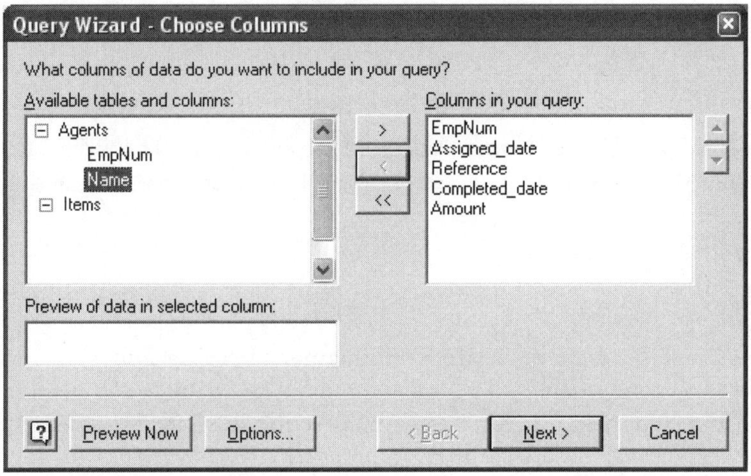

Figure 10-20. Add the Name column

can see the linkage if we go to Microsoft Query. When the finish dialog comes up, select "View data or edit query in Microsoft Query" and Figure 10-21 displays.

The link between the tables is on the column named EmpNum. It is represented by a line between the tables. If the names are different, the link will not happen automatically. In this display you can establish the link manually by clicking on the column name in one table then connecting it by dragging and dropping it on the correct column in the other table.

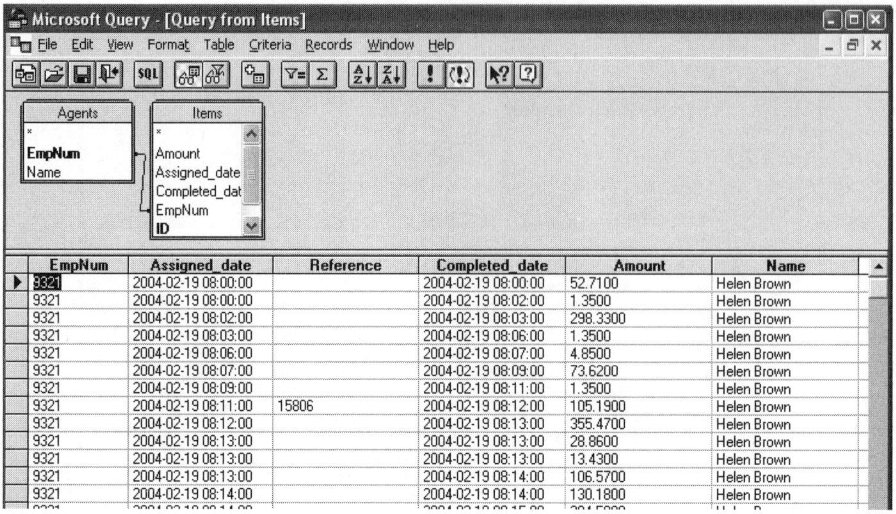

Figure 10-21. Microsoft Query

You can set criteria, which are the same as filters, on this display and even convert the query into its equivalent SQL statement. But the nice thing about this process is that you do not have to deal with SQL directly. Excel and Query take care of that for you.

From the File menu select "Return data to Microsoft Excel". This brings up the dialog in Figure 10-18, where you can select the cell to receive the data and get to the Properties dialog.

XML

Extensible Markup Language (XML) is another potential data source. It is basically a set of rules for storing data and information about the data. It can include formatting or relationship rules, and XML can even describe an entire Excel document. You are more likely to get XML data from Internet-based applications, but it can come from any type of system and is growing in popularity.

XML handling was enhanced in the professional version of Excel 2003. But older versions can import some XML files. Remember, Excel is limited to a two-dimensional view of information. XML is not. If the XML data is too complex to be represented as rows and columns Excel will have trouble with it.

I have created an XML file with the stock data used in the previous examples. The first few lines of the file look like this:

```
<?xml version="1.0"?>
<Stocks>
<Stock>
<Symbol>CEC</Symbol>
```

```
<Date>10/03/2001</Date>
<Open>32.55</Open>
<High>35.5</High>
<Low>32.53</Low>
<Close>34.5</Close>
<Volume>3809</Volume>
</Stock>
<Stock>
<Symbol>CEC</Symbol>
<Date>11/01/2001</Date>
<Open>38.65</Open>
<High>38.95</High>
<Low>38</Low>
<Close>38.54</Close>
<Volume>1221</Volume>
</Stock>
```

An XML file includes descriptive information called tags. This makes XML files larger and a little less efficient to handle. The advantage with XML is that the data is fully described; there are no questions about delimiters or mapping. XML was developed to make information sharing between applications easy.

There are several ways to get XML data into Excel, but the easiest to use is the import found on the Data → XML menu. This allows you to navigate to the XML file you want to import. When you double-click on the file, the dialog in Figure 10-22 appears.

Figure 10-22. Create a schema

XML files can have a data description and handling instructions called a schema. This file doesn't have one and Excel is telling us that it will create one to use with the file. You may want to disable this dialog by checking the "do not show this message" box.

Next you see Figure 10-23.

Unfortunately, the Import dialog doesn't give you a way to schedule a refresh on the data, but there is a refresh XML data function on the XML submenu. A scheduled refresh can be built in VBA using the application object's ontime event. It takes several pieces of code to get this to work. I imported my XML data into cell A1 on a sheet named XML. This code will update the data every five minutes:

```
Public Sub XMLRefresh( )

Dim MySheet as String
```

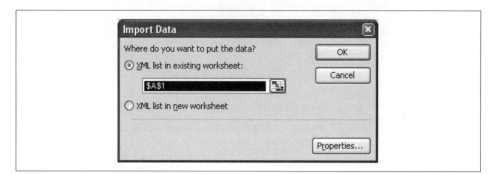

Figure 10-23. Completing the import

```
' Turn off screen updating so the user will not
' see all the jumping around.
Application.ScreenUpdating = False

' Save the name of the active sheet. At the end of
' the update we will go back to this sheet.
MySheet = ActiveSheet.Name

' Go to the XML sheet. This is where
' the XML data is.
Sheets("XML").Select

' Select the cell we imported the data into.
Range("a1").Select

' Refresh the data.
ActiveWorkbook.XmlMaps("Stocks_Map").DataBinding.Refresh

' Establish a time five minutes in the future.
' We need to know this time in the sub that
' ends the process. So, RunTime is setup as a
' Public variable
RunTime = Now + TimeSerial(0, 5, 0)

' Schedule this macro to run in five minutes.
Application.OnTime RunTime, "XMLRefresh"

' Go back to the sheet we started on.
Sheets(MySheet).Select

' Turn screen updating back on.
Application.ScreenUpdating = True
End Sub
```

The variable RunTime needs to be available to another sub so it is declared as public in the declaration sections at the top of the module, as follows:

```
Public RunTime
```

These two small subs are added to the workbook:

```
Private Sub Workbook_Open( )
XMLRefresh
End Sub

Private Sub Workbook_BeforeClose(Cancel As Boolean)
On Error Resume Next
Application.OnTime RunTime, "XMLRefresh", Schedule:=False
End Sub
```

The first one runs when the workbook opens. It runs the refresh which in turn reschedules itself. The ontime event will be there as long as Excel is running. So, if I close the workbook, five minutes later it will reopen and run the refresh. Therefore, I need a way to stop the process when the workbook closes. That is what the second sub does.

The import puts the data on a worksheet, and it can be used to feed data to an application or just populate a sheet for ad hoc analysis.

The result is shown in Figure 10-24.

	A	B	C	D	E	F	G
1	Symbol ▾	Date ▾	Open ▾	High ▾	Low ▾	Close ▾	Volume ▾
2	CEC	10/03/2001	32.55	35.5	32.53	34.5	3809
3	CEC	11/01/2001	38.65	38.95	38	38.54	1221
4	CEC	12/03/2001	37.1	37.22	36.85	37.1	2086
5	CEC	01/03/2002	43.89	44.2	43.15	43.5	1739
6	CEC	02/04/2002	44.95	45.04	44.54	44.54	1596
7	CEC	03/06/2002	49.84	49.85	49.07	49.56	2007
8	CEC	04/05/2002	44.6	44.73	44.6	44.69	1881
1970	DVS	05/20/2002	7.5	7.7	7.3	7.32	58
1971	DVS	06/19/2002	6.95	7.1	6.95	6.95	46
1972	DVS	07/19/2002	7	7.15	7	7.14	35
1973	DVS	08/19/2002	7	7.1	6.9	7	19
1974	DVS	09/18/2002	6.7	6.9	6.7	6.9	142
1975	*						

Figure 10-24. Imported XML data

Excel automatically puts the data in a list. The list feature includes a button by each heading that allows you to sort or filter the data. There are also totaling features available on the Data → List menu. This menu also has a "Convert to Range" option allowing you to turn the list feature off if you don't want to use it.

You can also open an XML document in Excel. The data opens in a separate workbook and the format is less than ideal. But it works, and copying and rearranging the data is not difficult.

To use this approach, start with the File → Open menu. Navigate to the XML file you want and when you double-click on it, the dialog in Figure 10-25 appears.

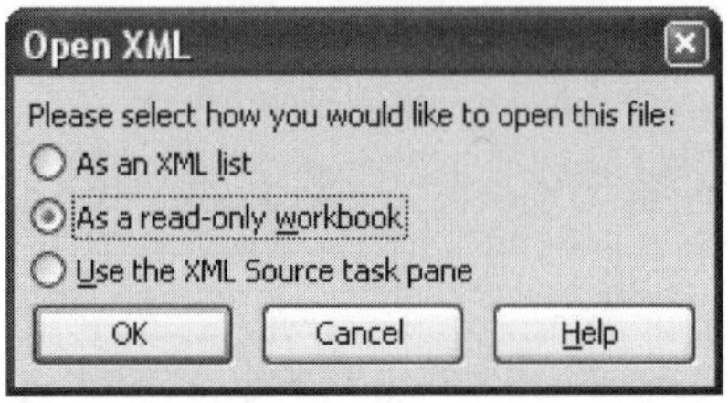

Figure 10-25. Open an XML document

The three choices let you control how the data will be handled. If you open the documents as an XML list, you get the same result as the import except the data will be in a separate workbook. The read-only workbook option returns data that looks like Figure 10-26.

	A	B	C	D	E	F	G	H	I	J	K	L
1	/Stocks											
2	/Stock/Clos	/Stock/Close/#ag	/Stock/Dat	/Stock/Hig	/Stock/High/#ag	/Stock/Lo	/Stock/Low/#ag	/Stock/Ope	/Stock/Open/#ag	/Stock/Symbo	/Stock/Volum	/Stock/Volume/#agg
3	34.5	34.5	10/03/2001	35.5	35.5	32.53	32.53	32.55	32.55	CEC	3809	3809
4	38.54	38.54	11/01/2001	38.95	38.95	38	38	38.65	38.65	CEC	1221	1221
5	37.1	37.1	12/03/2001	37.22	37.22	36.85	36.85	37.1	37.1	CEC	2086	2086
6	43.5	43.5	01/03/2002	44.2	44.2	43.15	43.15	43.89	43.89	CEC	1739	1739
7	44.54	44.54	02/04/2002	45.04	45.04	44.54	44.54	44.95	44.95	CEC	1596	1596
8	49.56	49.56	03/06/2002	49.85	49.85	49.07	49.07	49.84	49.84	CEC	2007	2007
9	44.69	44.69	04/05/2002	44.73	44.73	44.6	44.6	44.6	44.6	CEC	1881	1881
10	46.65	46.65	05/06/2002	48.01	48.01	46.56	46.56	47.4	47.4	CEC	972	972
11	46.63	46.63	06/05/2002	47.36	47.36	46.23	46.23	46.24	46.24	CEC	1837	1837
12	40.3	40.3	07/05/2002	40.49	40.49	39.68	39.68	39.88	39.88	CEC	780	780
13	15.58	15.58	10/03/2001	16.02	16.02	13.68	13.68	13.7	13.7	CECO	24692	24692
14	14.84	14.84	11/01/2001	15.22	15.22	13.35	13.35	13.52	13.52	CECO	40798	40798
15	15.56	15.56	12/03/2001	15.97	15.97	15.41	15.41	15.6	15.6	CECO	7796	7796

Figure 10-26. Read-only XML data

If you are not using Excel 2003 Professional or higher, this is your only option without using VBA. All the data is there, but the headings include some XML tag information, the columns are arranged alphabetically, and there are extra #agg columns added. The #agg columns are intended to make duplicate data in columns easier to understand.

It is less than ideal, but you can build an application using this data, and it can be copied and rearranged without much trouble.

The third option, the XML task pane, brings up the dialog in Figure 10-27.

This allows you to select which columns you want and to control the order. Once you select your columns, you populate the sheet using Data → XML → Refresh XML Data, as shown in Figure 10-28.

The result is a list in a new workbook containing your data.

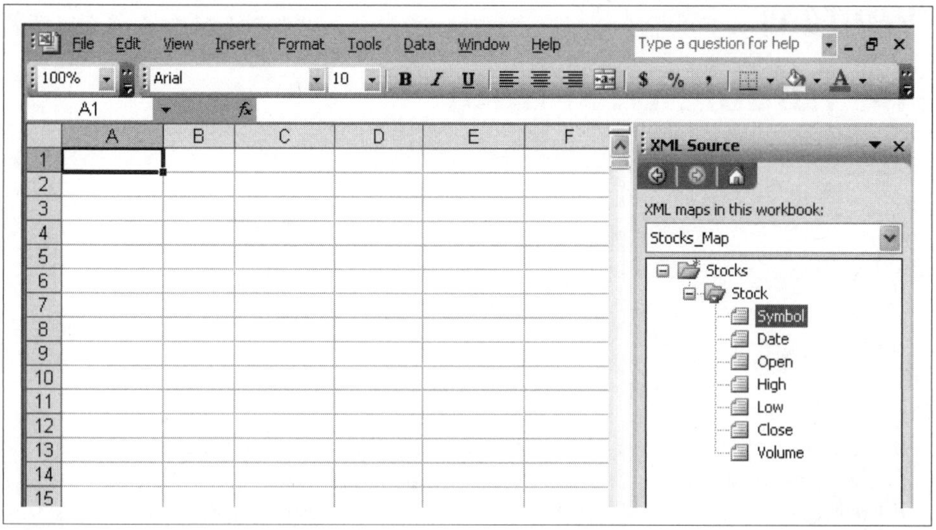

Figure 10-27. The XML task pane

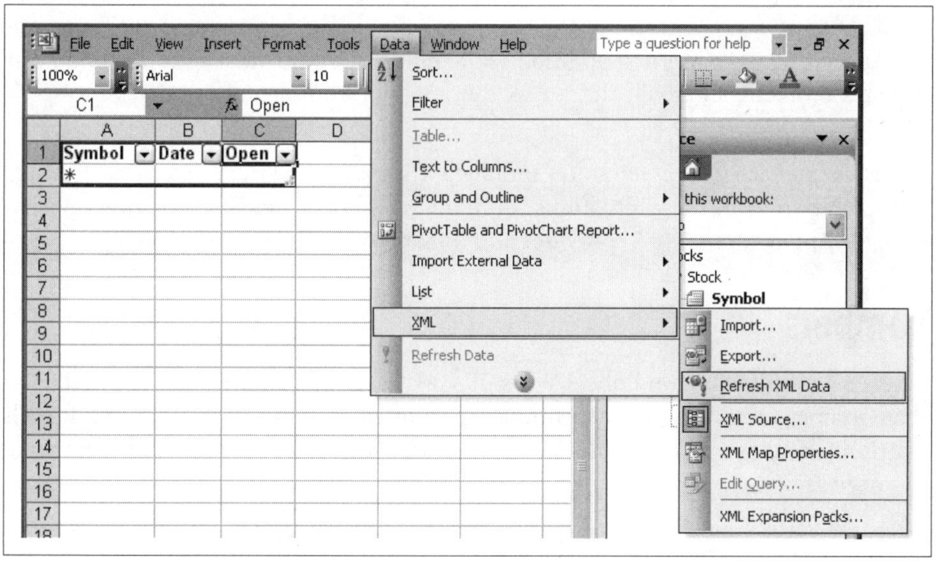

Figure 10-28. Putting data on the sheet.

CHAPTER 11

The Trouble with Data

When data is imported into Excel it brings its history with it. Mainframes store numbers and dates in ways that are awkward for Excel. Text and report files can contain almost anything. Excel uses numbers, dates, and text in the normal Windows format. This is great if you are importing from a Windows data source, but when data comes from other systems there can be problems. Each piece of data coming into Excel must be a number, a date, or text and Excel decides which it is. Too often Excel gets it wrong. Cleaning up imported data is one of the most common and most complex problems in Excel, and a task that must be completed for analysis to work reliably.

In this chapter we look at common problems with imported data. Excel has features that handle some of these situations. In more complex or unusual situations, Visual Basic for Applications (VBA) provides additional power.

Numbers

When is a number not a number? When it's text, of course. Numbers imported from a mainframe, a text file, or lifted from a report often end up as text in Excel. If math functions do not work on a column of imported numbers, some or all of them were imported as text.

Often the VALUE function will fix the problem. The VALUE function attempts to convert the contents of a cell to a number. The value is returned if it is successful, and if not, a #VALUE! error is set.

In the example in Figure 11-1 the data is from a mainframe and the invoice amounts have been imported as text. Cell B2 contains the formula =VALUE(A2). This formula is filled down to B16. Cells A18 and B18 contain =SUM(A2:A16) and =SUM(B2:B16). The formula in A18 does not work because Excel does not know these are numbers. In column B the VALUE function has converted the text to numbers and the SUM function in B18 works properly.

	A	B	C
1	**Invoice Amount**	**VALUE**	
2	0000025666	=VALUE(A2) → 25666	
3	0000066783	66783	
4	0000034538	34538	
5	0000006648	6648	
6	0000035775	35775	
7	0000012563	12563	
8	0000064290	64290	
9	0000069400	69400	
10	0000023821	23821	
11	0000081757	81757	
12	0000425060	425060	
13	0000002142	2142	
14	0000026242	26242	
15	0000202781 =SUM(A2:A16)	202781	
16	0000123781	123781	
17			
18	0 =SUM(B2:B16) → 1201247		
19			
20			

Figure 11-1. Numbers as text

Sometimes the problem is more complicated. In the next example some of the values are negative. Our data source uses CR (Credit) to indicate the number is negative. Excel cannot handle this, so the VALUE function will not help.

A custom function solves the problem. In this case the VALUE function has been replaced with the custom function CleanNumber, which takes two arguments. The first is the text containing the number. The second is the marker that tells when the number is negative. Figure 11-2 shows how it is used.

CleanNumber uses the TextVersion string to build a second string containing only the valid numeric characters. It then converts the second string to a numeric value. In this example the function is entered as =CleanNumber(A11,"CR"). Here is the code for CleanNumber:

```
Function CleanNumber(TextVersion As String, NegMarker As String) As Double
'**************************************************
' This Function will eliminate all non-numeric
' characters from the string TextVersion and
' will return the value of the numeric part of
' the string. If the string NegMarker is
' present in TextVersion the value will be
' returned as negative.
'**************************************************

Dim NegValue, x As Integer
Dim OneByte, cleanText As String

'First we check for the NegMarker
```

```
    If InStr(TextVersion, NegMarker) > 0 Then ' If NegMarker is found in TextVersion
        NegValue = -1                         ' Set NegValue to -1
    Else                                      ' If NegMarker is not found
        NegValue = 1                          ' Set NegValue to 1
    End If

    ' Next we loop through TextVersion and check each character to see
    ' if it is numeric. Only the numbers are kept.


    For x = 1 To Len(TextVersion)               ' Loop for the length of TextVersion
        OneByte = Mid(TextVersion, x, 1)        ' The character in TextVersion we
                                                ' are looking at now
        If IsNumeric(OneByte) Then              ' If it is numeric
            CleanText = CleanText & OneByte     ' put it on the end of CleanText
        End If
    Next x

    ' CleanText now contains the value but still as a string.
    ' It can now be converted to a number. It is multiplied by
    ' NegValue so that negative values will be returned correctly.

    CleanNumber = Val(CleanText) * NegValue
    End Function
```

	A	B	C
1	**Invoice Amount**	**VALUE**	
2	0000025666	=CleanNumber(A2,"CR") → 25666	
3	0000066783	66783	
4	0000034538	34538	
5	0000006648	6648	
6	0000035775CR	-35775	
7	0000012563	12563	
8	0000064290	64290	
9	0000069400	69400	
10	0000023821	23821	
11	0000081757CR	-81757	
12	0000425060	425060	
13	0000002142	2142	
14	0000026242	26242	
15	0000202781	202781	
16	0000123781	123781	
17			
18	0	966183	
19			
20			

Figure 11-2. Numbers as text in non-standard format

You can add this function to your Excel project by selecting Tools → Macro → Visual Basic Editor. You can also launch the editor by pressing Alt-F11. Just type or paste the code into the editor and the CleanNumber function is ready to use.

The first line in the code starts with the word Function. This means the code can be used on the workbook. Once this code in loaded into a project, the CleanNumber function works just like any other workbook function. Not all macros are functions. If the first word was Sub instead of Function it would be necessary to run the macro each time it is needed.

Sometimes even CleanNumber is not enough, though. Consider the example in Figure 11-3.

	Invoice Amount		VALUE
1			
2	0000025	=CleanNumber(RIGHT(A2,LEN(A2)-4),"CR")	25666
3	0000066783		66783
4	0000034538		34538
5	0000006648		6648
6	0000035775CR		-35775
7	0000012563		12563
8	0000064290		64290
9	0000069400		69400
10	0000023821		23821
11	0000081757CR		-81757
12	0000425060		425060
13	0000002142		2142
14	0000026242		26242
15	0000202781		202781
16	0000123781		123781
17			
18		0	966183
19			
20			

Figure 11-3. Complex numeric data as text

Here there is an account code in front of the invoice amount. The account code occupies four characters at the beginning of each number. The CleanNumber function will return the wrong value if used alone. The answer is to combine CleanNumber with the RIGHT workbook function. The formula in B2 is =CleanNumber(RIGHT (A2,LEN(A2)-4),"CR"). We want to skip the first four characters. The RIGHT function returns the right portion of the string starting at any position. In this case RIGHT starts at position LEN(A2)-4. This value is four less than the length of A2, and the function will return all but the first four characters. RIGHT function works inside the CleanNumber function.

If the unwanted characters were at the end of the string, the LEFT function would be used. The MID function would also work and is the best choice if the important information is in the middle of the string.

If you are dealing with this kind of problem, it is worth the effort to learn the LEFT, MID, and RIGHT functions. Using them with VALUE or CleanNumber is a powerful tool for cleaning up dirty data.

Figure 11-4 shows how these functions work. The string in cell A1 is broken up into three parts using LEFT, RIGHT, and MID. In all three, the first parameter is the source string. In the LEFT and RIGHT functions the second parameter specifies the number of characters to be taken. The MID function has three parameters giving the source string, starting position, and number of characters.

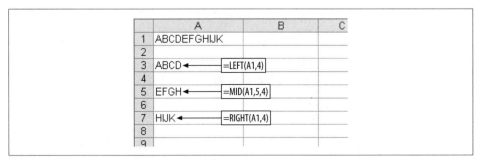

Figure 11-4. LEFT, MID, and RIGHT

Dates

Dates also cause problems. Excel understands dates and has a number of tools for working with and displaying them. But when dates are imported, Excel may not recognize them. When this happens they are stored as text strings. If a date will not format as a date or if functions like DAY or MONTH do not work, the date was imported as text. The DATEVALUE function will solve the problem much of the time. All of the text strings can be converted to a Windows date by DATEVALUE (see Table 11-1).

Table 11-1. Date formats handled by DATEVALUE

7/4/2004

January 24, 2004

Nov 12, 2001

2004-04-15

15 December 1999

07-04-04

15 Dec 1999

At times, however, more logic is needed. If the date is in an unusual order, such as 25-03-2001 (DD-MM-YYYY), DATEVALUE will return a #VALUE! error. The LEFT, RIGHT, and MID functions can correct this kind of problem.

Julian date is a feature of some older systems. The general form is YYYYDDD. The year is in the usual four digit form (e.g., 2004), but the day is a three digit number indicating the day of the year. September 8, 2003 is the 251st day of 2003 and would appear as 2003251. The DATEVALUE function used with RIGHT and LEFT can convert a Julian date to a format that Excel can use.

If cell A1 contains the Julian date 2003251, the formula =DATEVALUE("12/31/" & LEFT(H1,4)-1)+RIGHT(H1,3) will return the Windows date. This works by building a date for the last day of the previous year, then adding the required number of days to it. DATEVALUE converts a date string, such as 12/31/2002, to a Windows date. The formula uses "12/31/" & LEFT(A1,4)-1 to build the string. LEFT(A1,4) is 2003. Then RIGHT(A1,3), which is 251, is added to it.

Reports

Sometimes it is necessary to get data from a report. Data in reports can have any format and can be located anywhere. Some lines on the report will have no useful data and need to be skipped. This problem can often be solved with VBA. No one macro works in every case, but in this section we look at a general purpose macro for extracting data from reports. This macro uses settings that can be changed to handle many report formats.

Consider the sample report in Figure 11-5. It is part of a larger report giving statistics for batters and pitchers from various major league baseball teams. Suppose we need an Excel worksheet with the team name in column A, the batter name in column B, batting average (BA) in C, At bats (AB) in D, and runs batted in (RBI) in E. We are not extracting data about pitchers so we skip those lines.

We need to identify the lines containing information we want. Start by viewing the report in Notepad and inserting lines to make counting positions easy. The inserted lines are marked off in five character sections with a number indicating the tens. In this example two copies of this line have been inserted, as shown in Figure 11-6.

Using these lines as a guide, it is easy to see that the string TEAM starting in position 1 tells us to expect the name of the team starting in position 6 of the same line. Note that lines with batter information have a period in position 14. The data we want from those lines are in the positions shown in Table 11-2.

```
TEAM Anaheim Angels

BATTERS       BA    SLG    OBA   G   AB    R    H   TB  2B 3B HR RBI   BB   SO SB CS  E
Quinlan      .344  .525   .401  56 160   23   55   84 14  0  5  23   14   26  3  1  1
Guerrero     .337  .598   .391 156 612  124  206  366 39  2 39 126   52   74 15  3  9
Anderson     .301  .446   .343 112 442   57  133  197 20  1 14  75   29   75  2  1  2
Galarraga    .300  .600   .364   7  10    1    3    6  0  0  1   2    0    3  0  0  0
Figgins      .296  .419   .350 148 577   83  171  242 22 17  5  60   49   94 34 13 15
Erstad       .295  .400   .346 125 495   79  146  198 29  1  7  69   37   74 16  1  4
Guillen      .294  .497   .352 148 565   88  166  281 28  3 27 104   37   92  5  4  6


PITCHERS      W- L    ERA    BA    G GS CG GF SH SV    IP    H    R  ER HR   BB   SO
Turnbow      0- 0   0.00  .105    4  0  0  4  0  0   6.1    2    0   0  0    7    3
Rodriguez    4- 1   1.82  .172   69  0  0 29  0 12  84.0   51   21  17  2   33  123
Percival     2- 3   2.90  .230   52  0  0 48  0 33  49.2   43   19  16  7   19   33
Donnelly     5- 2   3.00  .224   40  0  0 10  0  0  42.0   34   14  14  5   15   56
Shields      8- 2   3.33  .238   60  0  0 12  0  4 105.1   97   42  39  6   40  109

TEAM Baltimore Orioles|

BATTERS       BA    SLG    OBA   G   AB    R    H   TB  2B 3B HR RBI   BB   SO SB CS  E
Mora         .340  .562   .419 140 550  111  187  309 41  0 27 104   66   95 11  6 21
Segui        .339  .441   .400  18  59    8   20   26  3  0  1   7    5   13  0  1  0
J. Lopez     .316  .503   .370 150 579   83  183  291 33  3 23  86   47   97  0  0  5
Newhan       .311  .453   .361  95 373   66  116  169 15  7  8  54   27   72 11  1  5
Tejada       .311  .534   .360 162 653  107  203  349 40  2 34 150   48   73  4  1 24
Surhoff      .309  .420   .365 100 343   49  106  144 12  1  8  50   30   46  2  0  2


PITCHERS      W- L    ERA    BA    G GS CG GF SH SV    IP    H    R  ER HR   BB   SO
Ryan         4- 6   2.28  .200   76  0  0 19  0  3  87.0   64   24  22  4   35  122
Williams     2- 0   2.87  .232   29  0  0  7  0  0  31.1   26   10  10  2    9   13
Chen         2- 1   3.02  .220    8  7  1  0  0  0  47.2   39   19  16  7   16   32
```

Figure 11-5. Baseball stats report

```
TEAM Anaheim Angels
----*----1----*----2----*----3----*----4----*----5----*----6----*----7----*----8
BATTERS       BA    SLG    OBA   G   AB    R    H   TB  2B 3B HR RBI   BB   SO SB CS  E
Quinlan      .344  .525   .401  56 160   23   55   84 14  0  5  23   14   26  3  1  1
Guerrero     .337  .598   .391 156 612  124  206  366 39  2 39 126   52   74 15  3  9
Anderson     .301  .446   .343 112 442   57  133  197 20  1 14  75   29   75  2  1  2
Galarraga    .300  .600   .364   7  10    1    3    6  0  0  1   2    0    3  0  0  0
Figgins      .296  .419   .350 148 577   83  171  242 22 17  5  60   49   94 34 13 15
Erstad       .295  .400   .346 125 495   79  146  198 29  1  7  69   37   74 16  1  4
Guillen      .294  .497   .352 148 565   88  166  281 28  3 27 104   37   92  5  4  6
----*----1----*----2----*----3----*----4----*----5----*----6----*----7----*----8|
PITCHERS      W- L    ERA    BA    G GS CG GF SH SV    IP    H    R  ER HR   BB   SO
Turnbow      0- 0   0.00  .105    4  0  0  4  0  0   6.1    2    0   0  0    7    3
Rodriguez    4- 1   1.82  .172   69  0  0 29  0 12  84.0   51   21  17  2   33  123
Percival     2- 3   2.90  .230   52  0  0 48  0 33  49.2   43   19  16  7   19   33
```

Figure 11-6. Inserting Position Counting Lines

Table 11-2. The data positions

Data item	Starting column	Length
Batter Name	1	13
Batting Average	14	4
At Bats	35	3
Run Batted In	60	3

We need to save a row when a line with a period on position 14 has been processed. Lines that do not have a period in position 14 or the word TEAM in position 1 have no data we are interested in and are ignored.

The following code will read the report and build a file that can be imported or copied and pasted into Excel. The way it behaves is determined by settings that can be changed for other reports. This macro is not a function and must be explicitly run from the Tools → Macro → Macros menu.

```
Sub ReportExtract( )
'*********************************************
' This is a general purpose macro for extracting
' data from reports.
' *********************************************

' These collections are storage areas for the information
' the macro will use to extract and hold the data.
Dim FindString As New Collection
Dim FindLocation As New Collection
Dim ItemStart As New Collection
Dim ItemLength As New Collection
Dim ItemString As New Collection

Dim InputFile, OutputFile, WriteFlag, ShellFlag, Del As String
Dim InLine, OutLine, MyString, StrItemNum As String
Dim ItemNum, FlagLocation, x As Integer
Dim RetCode As Variant

On Error GoTo Err_Rtn ' If something goes wrong the macro will jump to Err_Rtn.

' InputFile contains the name and full path of the report file
InputFile = "C:\FolderName\ReportFile.txt"

' OutputFile is the name and path of the file that will be
' created with the extracted information. Data from this
' file can be transferred into Excel via copy paste or
' by importing the file.
OutputFile = "C:\FolderName\DataFile.txt"

' The macro needs to know when to write a line to
' the Output file. In this example a line is
' written when the current line in the input file contains
' a period in position 14.
WriteFlag = "."
FlagLocation = 14

' Del is the delimiter that will seperate the data items.
' A comma allows us to create a csv file as the output.
' This kind of file can be opened by Excel. If any of the
' data could contain a comma a different delimiter must be
' used.
Del = ","
```

```
' If you want the macro to automatically open the Output file
' set this value to Y.
ShellFlag = "Y"

' In this section each data item to be extracted is described.
' The FindString entry is the identifying string for the line
' that contains the data.

' FindLocation gives the position in that line that the FindString
' is at. So, the first entry below the line is identified by TEAM
' starting in postion 1.

' ItemStart and ItemLength give the start position and length of the
' data item to be extracted.
' There can be any number of these.

' Data item one
FindString.Add Item:="TEAM ", key:="1"
FindLocation.Add Item:=1, key:="1"
ItemStart.Add Item:=6, key:="1"
ItemLength.Add Item:=50, key:="1"

' Data item two
FindString.Add Item:=".", key:="2"
FindLocation.Add Item:=14, key:="2"
ItemStart.Add Item:=1, key:="2"
ItemLength.Add Item:=13, key:="2"

' Data item three
FindString.Add Item:=".", key:="3"
FindLocation.Add Item:=14, key:="3"
ItemStart.Add Item:=14, key:="3"
ItemLength.Add Item:=4, key:="3"

' Data item four
FindString.Add Item:=".", key:="4"
FindLocation.Add Item:=14, key:="4"
ItemStart.Add Item:=35, key:="4"
ItemLength.Add Item:=3, key:="4"

' Data item five
FindString.Add Item:=".", key:="5"
FindLocation.Add Item:=14, key:="5"
ItemStart.Add Item:=60, key:="5"
ItemLength.Add Item:=3, key:="5"

' After the last item is setup the next item in
' the FindString collection is set to end of job
FindString.Add Item:="end of job", key:="6"
' That ends the setting for the macro

' Open the files
Open InputFile For Input As 1
Open OutputFile For Output As 2
```

```
' Start a reading loop for the input file
While Not EOF(1)
    Line Input #1, InLine  ' Read a line from the input file

    ItemNum = 1  ' Start looking for items with item number one
    StrItemNum = Trim(Str(ItemNum))
    ' This loop checks for each data item and each data item found
    ' on the current line is stored in ItemString( ).
    While FindString(StrItemNum) <> "end of job"
        If Mid(InLine, FindLocation(StrItemNum), Len(FindString(StrItemNum))) = _
        FindString(StrItemNum) Then
            On Error Resume Next
            ItemString.Remove (StrItemNum)
            On Error GoTo Err_Rtn
            ItemString.Add Item:=Trim(Mid(InLine, ItemStart(StrItemNum), _
            ItemLength(StrItemNum))), key:=StrItemNum
        End If
        ItemNum = ItemNum + 1
        StrItemNum = Trim(Str(ItemNum))
    Wend

    ' All of the data on the line has now been extracted
    ' Next we check for the WriteFlag.
    If Mid(InLine, FlagLocation, Len(WriteFlag)) = WriteFlag Then
        ' If the WriteFlag is on the current line
        ' We build the output line by putting all of the data items
        ' together separated by Del (the delimiter).
        For x = 1 To ItemNum - 1
            MyString = ""
            On Error Resume Next
            MyString = ItemString(Trim(Str(x)))
            On Error GoTo Err_Rtn
            OutLine = OutLine & MyString & Del

        Next x
        Print #2, Left(OutLine, Len(OutLine) - 1) ' Print the line skipping the
                                                  ' last delimiter
        OutLine = ""  ' Clear out the Outline so it will be ready for the
                      ' next write.
    End If

Wend
Close  ' Close all files
If ShellFlag = "Y" Then  ' If the ShellFlag is set to "Y"

    If Right(OutputFile, 4) = ".csv" Then   ' If the output file is a CSV file
        Workbooks.Open Filename:=OutputFile  ' Open the workbook
    Else
        RetCode = Shell("notepad.exe " & OutputFile, 1) ' or shell it in notepad
    End If
End If

GoTo TheEnd  ' Jump to the TheEnd
```

```
' If an error has occurred this code will run.
Err_Rtn:
MsgBox (Error)   ' Display the error.
Close            ' If any files are open close them.
Resume TheEnd    ' Continue to TheEnd.

TheEnd:

End Sub
```

This macro uses collections to store the extraction parameters. This could also be done using arrays. Arrays are easier to code, but they have to be dimensioned with a set number of members. Using collections avoids this problem, but there are limited functions with collections and error trapping has to be handled carefully.

Sometimes it is necessary to extract data from the same report periodically; e.g., a monthly sales report. Once the macro is updated with the setting for that report, the macro can be re-saved with a different name. It is important to remember the macro will only be available if the workbook containing it is open. If several versions of this code are required, it might be a good idea to create a workbook just for extracting data from reports.

Equivalence

My name is Gerald Knight. Gerald D Knight is also my name. They are not equal, but since they both mean me, they are equivalent. This happens with the names of people and businesses, with addresses, and with common words like state names or days of the week. When data is entered by hand or comes from more than one computer system, equivalence problems can make it impossible to use.

There is a solution. When you use a spellchecking program, one of the features is word suggestion. If the program does not recognize the word you typed, it suggests similar words. So the spellcheck program knows how to measure the similarity between two strings of characters. It measures equivalence.

We define equivalence as the percentage of characters from one string that occur in another string in the same order. And we can build a custom Function that does the same thing in Excel.

The details of the algorithm are beyond the scope of this book. Basically, it builds a matrix with one string across the top and the other down the left side. The code counts places in the matrix where the letters for both words are the same. It works its way through the strings backwards, and keeps up with the number of matches as it goes. Here is the code:

```
Public Function Str_Comp(st1 As String, st2 As String) As Double

Dim MtchTbl(100, 100)
Dim MyMax, ThisMax As Double
Dim i, j, ii, jj As Integer
```

```
' Remove leading and trailing spaces and
' set to proper case
st1 = Trim(Application.WorksheetFunction.Proper(st1))
st2 = Trim(Application.WorksheetFunction.Proper(st2))

' mymax will be the number of letters in st1 that
' occur in st2 in the same order
MyMax = 0

For i = Len(st1) To 1 Step -1
    For j = Len(st2) To 1 Step -1
        If Mid(st1, i, 1) = Mid(st2, j, 1) Then
            ThisMax = 0
            For ii = i + 1 To Len(st1)
                For jj = j + 1 To Len(st2)
                    If MtchTbl(ii, jj) > ThisMax Then
                        ThisMax = MtchTbl(ii, jj)
                    End If
                Next jj
            Next ii
            MtchTbl(i, j) = ThisMax + 1
            If ThisMax + 1 > MyMax Then
                MyMax = ThisMax + 1
            End If
        End If
    Next j
Next i

' divide mymax by the length of st1
' to get the percentage match
Str_Comp = MyMax / Len(st1)
End Function
```

This is a function so it can be used on the spreadsheet. The arguments are both strings. The function returns the percentage of characters in the first string that occur in the second string in the same order.

The formula =Str_Comp("afce","abcdefghi") returns a value of 0.75. There are four characters in "afce" and three of them (a, c, and e) are in the second string in the same order. The letter f is in both strings but not in the same order. The Str_Comp function processes string in proper case. So it considers the first character of a word to be uppercase and the others to be lowercase.

Figure 11-7 shows how this function is used. The entry in A1 has to be a month, but the data was entered by hand so we cannot be sure what will actually be in the cell. In the range E1:E12 are the correct names of the months. The entry in A1 has to be equivalent to one of these. The formula in F1 is =Str_Comp(A$1,E1). This is filled down to F12. The values in F1:F12 are the equivalence scores between A1 and each of the months.

	A	B	C	D	E	F	
1	Nov	November	=IF(B6=1,INDEX(E1:E12,B5),"Unknown")		January	0	
2					February	0	
3				=Str_comp(A$1,E1)	March	0	
4		1	=MAX(F1:F12)		April	0	
5		11			May	0	
6		1	=MATCH(B4,F1:F12,0)		June	0	
7			=COUNTIF(F1:F12,"="&B4)		July	0	
8					August	0	
9					September	0	
10					October	0.333333	
11					November	1	
12					December	0	
13							

Figure 11-7. Working with the Str_Comp function

In this example the match with November is 100%. This is because all of the characters in A1 occur in November in the same order. The formula in cell B4 is =MAX(F1:F12). This is the value of the best match we got. Cell B5 is =MATCH(B4,F1:F12,0). This tells us which item in the range F1:F12 contains the maximum value. In this case it is 11 because the maximum value (1) is in row 11. Cell B6 checks to be sure the maximum value only occurs once in F1:F12. If the maximum value is in the range more than once, we cannot decide which month is indicated since we have a tie. The formula is =COUNTIF(F1:F12,"=" & B4). We only have a good answer if this value is 1.

Cell B1 has the final answer. It contains =IF(B6=1,INDEX(E1:E12,B5),"Unknown"). If the value in B6 is 1, this formula retrieves the name of the month from the range E1: E12. If B6 is not 1, Unknown is displayed.

This technique can be used to clean up manually keyed data or data coming from an OCR operation. It can help when sets of data from different systems are to be merged, such as two customer files. Variations in addresses and names can be resolved.

Equivalence problems can involve large amounts of data. Merging data from different systems can result in thousands of possible matches. The Str_Comp function can be used inside other macros to read and match large files.

CHAPTER 12

Effective Display Techniques

A computer screen is a small two-dimensional space. The concepts and information displayed in this space are complex and multi-dimensional. It takes planning and careful design to produce a display that represents the information completely and is still easy to understand.

Each application exists for a reason. The display provides information used to manage an operation, identify problems, or plan for improvements. The quality of decisions made by the application's users depends on the quality of the display.

A person can only focus on a small amount of information at one time, and a display can easily overwhelm the viewer. A critical piece of information can vanish in a pile of numbers, or an important conclusion can be overlooked in a disorganized presentation. It is not enough to simply show the user the data; to be useful, an application must answer the user's questions.

Excel is good with numbers. Numeric information doesn't take up much space in the system, is easy to manipulate, and can be formatted any way you like. It is also difficult to understand. An effective display must highlight the important relationships in the data, and explain what those relationships mean.

A good display is easy to use and understand. If it takes a lot of effort to learn to use or understand an application, some users won't bother.

Respect the Information and the Audience

Making information understandable does not mean leaving out complexity. Important issues are complex by nature and it is important to tell the whole story. Users can understand complex relationships and statistical conclusions if the design is clear and focuses on the important points. If you over-simplify or leave out key supporting information, the user is excluded. This reduces the application to an opinion instead of a reasoned argument.

It is not enough for an application to just give an answer. You have to provide enough background and supporting material to justify your conclusions. If your application deals with important matters then both the information and the users are important too.

Large Worksheets

You are reading a book. The information in the book is chopped up and presented one page at a time. Imagine what this book would be like if it were printed on one big sheet of paper—the whole book on a single page. It would not work well for a book, and it doesn't work for spreadsheets either.

It is easier to page then it is to scroll. With paging you go to the right place; with scrolling you look for the right place. Even if the project is large, like a budget or staffing model, it can be broken down into several small easily viewed sheets.

Scrolling and split screens work, but they are inefficient and in most cases it is best to present information in screen-size pieces, like the pages of a book.

Charts

A chart is often the best way to present the meaning in a table of related numbers. Trends and relationships stand out in a chart. Numbers are abstract, but in a well-designed chart conclusions are obvious.

Excel's Chart tool gives you the ability to represent data with up to three dimensions easily. Pivot charts or combining charts with controls can make your display interact with users and allow you to handle more than three dimensions.

There are a lot of chart styles to choose from in Excel, and this can lead to confusion. In general it is best to use the simplest representation that captures the meaning in the data. Just because a feature or chart element is available does not mean you have to use it. In most cases a simple line chart is the best choice. In Figure 12-1 the same information is displayed on two charts.

In the top chart I used several of Excel's charting options to create a complex and messy view of a simple list of numbers. All of the meaning is in the bottom chart. If a feature does not serve a purpose in the chart, it is best to leave it out.

When presenting two-dimensional data, charts with depth or contour can be confusing. This kind of chart can become incomprehensible if printed. A plain surface chart has as much meaning and is easier to understand.

The more complex the data the more important it is to make the visuals simple. For example: I want to show how trading volume and day of the week relate to the probability that a certain stock will go up or down. First, I assemble the data in Figure 12-2.

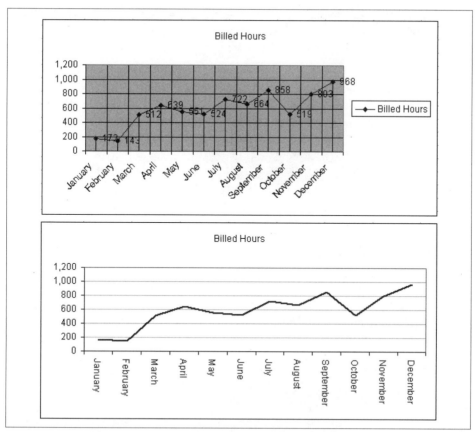

Figure 12-1. Two views of the same information

	Q1	Q2	Q3	Q4
Monday	0.36	0.73	0.41	0.41
Tuesday	0.50	0.59	0.52	0.48
Wednesday	0.48	0.69	0.52	0.58
Thursday	0.42	0.65	0.42	0.54
Friday	0.52	0.48	0.38	0.46

Figure 12-2. Stock performance by day of week and volume

I used Excel's QUARTILE function to assign each trading day to a volume quartile. In the table, the columns tell which quartile the day's trading volume falls in. The volumes in quartile one (Q1) are relatively low, while quartile four's volumes are the highest.

The values in the table are the number of trading days that were up (close was higher than previous day's close) divided by the total number of days for that day of week and quartile. The Wednesday Q1 number is 0.48. This means that 48% of Wednesdays in Q1 were up days.

Just looking at the data you can see that something of interest is going on. But a chart explains it better. Figure 12-3 shows the data on a 3-D column chart.

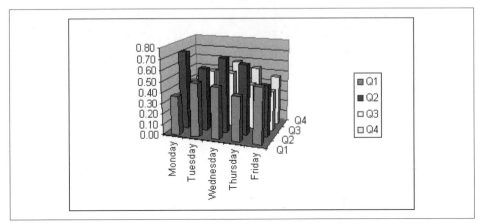

Figure 12-3. 3-D column chart

This is better than looking at the numbers, but is still not clear. The columns for Q3 and Q4 are largely hidden, and it takes a real effort to find the meaning. The plain surface chart in Figure 12-4 does a better job.

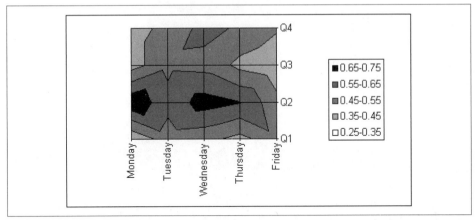

Figure 12-4. Surface chart of the same information

Can you see it now? Q2 has the best performance, especially on Mondays and Wednesdays. This chart is a better way to show the meaning in the data because it is simple and gets right to the point. It respects the limitation of a two-dimensional display and uses shade for the third dimension. The 3-D column chart tries to show all three dimensions using perspective and becomes a work of art instead of a communication tool.

Pictures and Other Objects

Charts are not the only graphic possibilities with Excel. Bitmaps produced with Paint can be added to a worksheet and can even function as buttons if needed. Figure 12-5 is a visual representation of a photo printing process drawn with Paint.

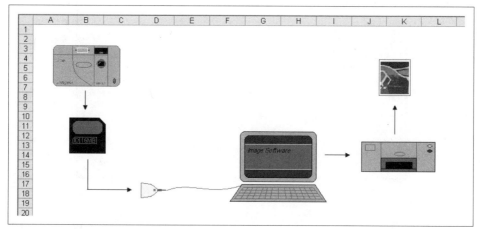

Figure 12-5. Photo printing process

The images were drawn individually in Paint. Figure 12-6 is the camera bitmap.

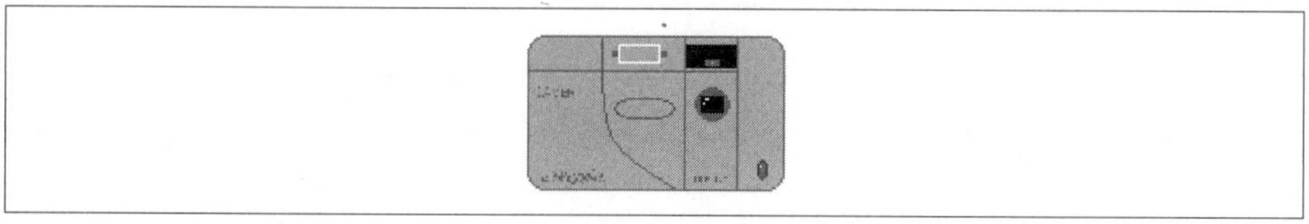

Figure 12-6. Camera bitmap

Images like this can be drawn quickly and it only took a few minutes to draw the whole process. Each picture was cut and pasted onto the worksheet where it was formatted with no line or fill.

Pictures are not the only thing you can paste into Excel. You can insert objects for many kinds of information.

I have a sound file named *test.wav* in my *C:\My Music* folder, and I want to add it to my worksheet. I start by clicking on Insert → Object. The dialog in Figure 12-7 is displayed.

I click the "Create from File" tab, bringing up Figure 12-8.

Here I select Browse and navigate to the *C:\My Music* folder. Then I click on *test. wav*, inserting it onto the sheet. The result is a Sound Recorder Document object named *object 1*, as shown in Figure 12-9.

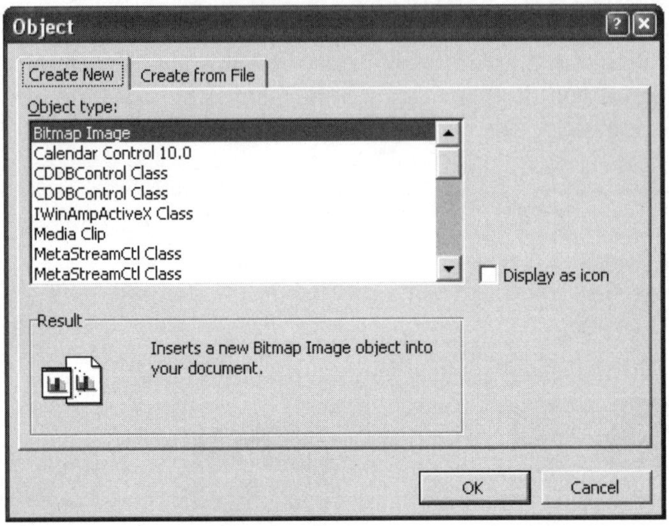

Figure 12-7. Inserting an object

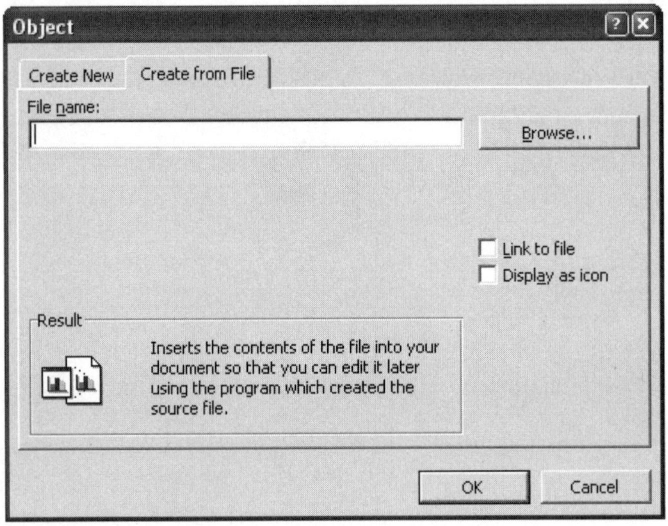

Figure 12-8. Specifying the file

I can play the sound manually by double-clicking on the object, or I could put the following code into a module using the Visual Basic Editor.

```
Sub PlayTheSound( )

    ActiveSheet.Shapes("Object 1").Select
    Selection.Verb Verb:=xlPrimary

End Sub
```

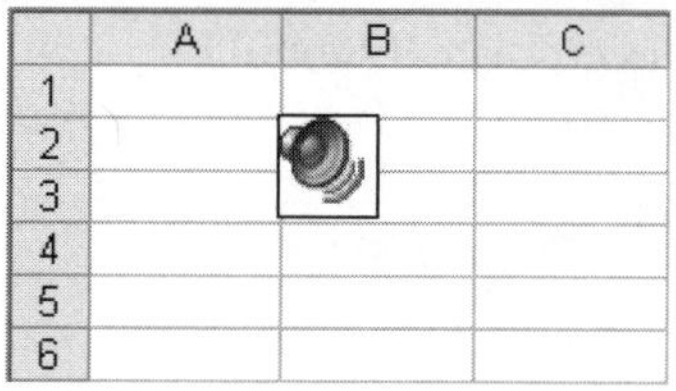

Figure 12-9. A Sound Recorder Object

I can run this code from a button or tie it to an event, such as opening the workbook or selecting the sheet.

This could just as easily be a video clip or even the address of a web page. In most cases, Excel will already know how to handle the file you select based on the file type, and the code to activate the object is the same.

Excel can do far more than just display columns of numbers. You can include almost any kind of resource needed to make your display effective.

Complexity

The relationships in data are often hard to understand. In Figure 12-2 the day of the week and trading volume seem to be related to changes in the stock price. We can see this in the chart, but that does not mean we know what the relationship is. Sometimes statistical tools like regression can explain what is going on but often all you can do is show what is happening.

You can represent anything with Excel as long as you can break it down into understandable pieces. A person can only deal with a limited amount of information at a time, and a display should work with this limitation, not ignore it.

Pivot tables and pivot charts are a good choice when a single view of the data is not sufficient. In some cases, pivot table and charts can be the whole user interface for an application.

You can use controls, like list boxes, to allow users to navigate the options and dimensions. The applications in the book use this approach. It gives you more control than a pivot table over both the final appearance and the user interaction.

Excel makes it easy to change the way information is presented and there is no reason the presentation has to stay the same throughout the life of the project.

In a budgeting application, management might have a specific format for the finished budget. The final format may not be convenient during the budget building process, and you might simplify the process by working on the budget in a different format. You can break information up, build in balancing calculations, and work on the data in any format that makes it easy to handle. Later, after all the changes are in and everything is agreed to, Excel is good at moving information around and refor-matting it to create the required finished product.

Repeated Elements

A small information-rich graphic tells a story better than numbers. Repeating this kind of graphic can handle dimensional complexity.

Figure 12-10 comes from the application in Chapter 8. In it, the same chart is used to represent all of the queues at two points in time. Once the user understands one chart they automatically understand the whole display.

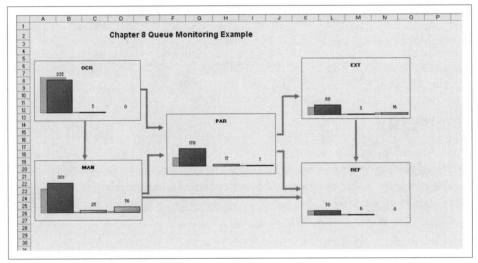

Figure 12-10. Using repeated items

This graphic approach offers a top down way to represent the queue dimension and also serves as a menu for more detailed analysis.

Having all the charts visible at the same time makes comparison easy. In contrast, the summary area from Chapter 8 shown at the top of Figure 12-11 is isolated.

			PAR Queue		8-Jun-2005			
		Type	Count	Oldest	Value		Go Back	
		New	178	5/31/05 12:45	$18,003.64			
		Working	17	5/31/05 11:46	$1,856.46			
		On Hold	7	5/30/05 7:48	$407.29			
Queue	Status	Create Date/Time	Assign Date/Time		Value	Agent	File	
PAR	3	5/29/05 18:28	5/30/05 8:15		$9.46	15988	Figure7-30.TXT	
PAR	3	5/30/05 3:50	5/30/05 7:48		$20.14	74734	Figure7-30.TIF	
PAR	3	5/30/05 4:26	5/30/05 22:21		$1.35	66500	Figure7-30.TIF	

Figure 12-11. Awkward placement of summary information

The user has to return to the main display to change queue and there is no way to see two queues at the same time.

Information Density

Space is limited and it is critical to get as much information per square inch as possible. The charts in Figure 12-10 give a complete picture of each queue in one chart.

We did the same thing in Chapter 7 on the main display shown in Figure 12-12.

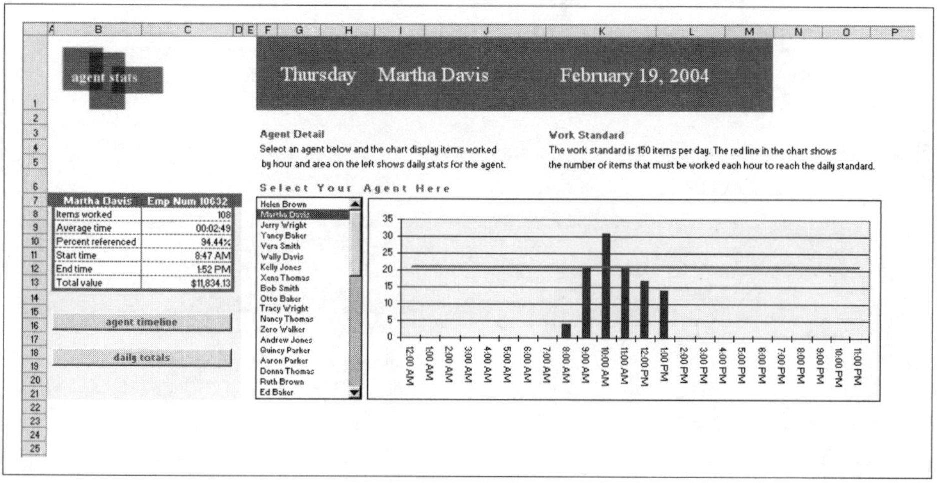

Figure 12-12. A chart can do two things at once

In the chart, two related pieces of information are combined allowing the hourly production to be compared to the standard.

Formatting and white space are important, but they are not content. Chapter 3's hourly sheet, shown again in Figure 12-13, shows some of the danger of over-formatting.

This approach can distract from the message. If the user notices the formatting before noticing the content, something is wrong. In this case it is not a big problem, but it is important to keep style in a supporting role.

Support and Grouping

Position related items in a way that emphasizes their common meaning. This allows them to support each other and saves space. In the display in Figure 12-12, the list box and the chart that it controls are placed next to each other.

They are sized to match and the space between them is very small. This helps the user see how they are related and makes the application easier to use.

The same concept is applied in the display in Figure 12-14.

	Sunday	Monday	Tuesday	Wednesday	Thursday	Friday	Saturday
Hourly Forecasts for the Week Starting Monday 08/24/1998							
7:30		511	660	522	442	440	
8:30		1,191	1,524	1,129	948	900	
9:30		1,545	1,805	1,454	1,281	1,147	
10:30		1,770	2,007	1,700	1,491	1,324	
11:30		1,758	1,879	1,555	1,436	1,221	
12:30		1,739	1,682	1,509	1,366	1,198	
13:30		2,024	1,816	1,679	1,524	1,294	
14:30		2,133	1,730	1,538	1,462	1,178	
15:30		1,782	1,496	1,378	1,233	1,013	
16:30		1,328	1,002	944	857	702	
17:30		708	525	509	463	368	

Return

Figure 12-13. Over-formatting can distract the viewer

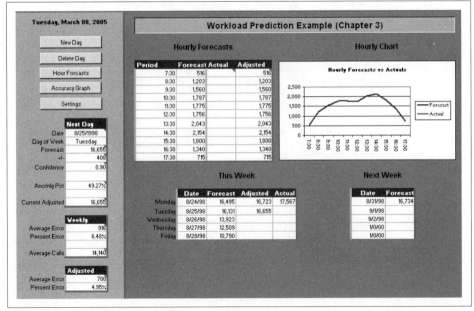

Figure 12-14. The placement of related items

In this display from Chapter 3, the relationship between the hourly forecasts and the chart are obvious. Lower, the day of week labels do double duty because related information is placed on the same row.

Emphasis and Focus

Position, size, and contrast guide the user's attention. The most important items should be toward the middle, larger, and with higher contrast. Supporting items in list form are placed along the left margin. Related information can be at the top or bottom.

These are not hard and fast rules but they make sense. It is a design that people already understand if they use the Web. It evolved as a common design in web pages because it works.

Figure 12-15 shows an application main display.

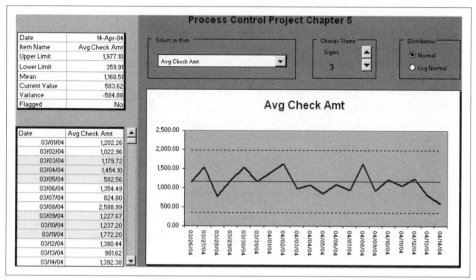

Figure 12-15. Putting the emphasis on the most important item

The real message is the chart and it is the largest item on the display.

If the user only looks at the display for five seconds what will they see? Perhaps all they need to know is if further addition is required. Place the most important answers prominently in the display.

Metaphor

Everyone understands a report, a flow diagram, or a web page. If you stick with an approach that your users already know your application will be easier to use.

It is best to avoid a new and different approach unless you are sure that its meaning is clear.

In Chapter 8's application I put a summary at the top of a report sheet (see Figure 12-11). This is a little unusual. You normally expect to see totals at the bottom, and this placement, while reasonable, has to be explained. In this case it might be better to put the summary on a different sheet.

Fonts

If the user notices the font, you are using the wrong one. Pick one that is easy to read and stick with it. You can create all the separation and emphasis you will ever need without changing font.

We recognize common words by shape as well as letters. In Figure 12-16 there are two buttons with the same caption.

Figure 12-16. Two buttons with the same message

The words and the message are common, and the shape of the words helps make the button on the left easier to read. Using all-caps hides the shape of the words and increases the chance that the user will misunderstand the message or overlook something.

Colors

Color can add interest and make an application more understandable. But it can also confuse, cause eye strain, and distract. When content is based on color alone it can disappear when a screen is printed, and some users will have trouble distinguishing between colors. In most cases a simple black, white, and gray scheme works fine.

The visible spectrum runs from red to violet and the color in the middle is green. Since green is in the middle of the visible range, it is the easiest color to see. This makes green a safe background color. If fine details are displayed using colors far apart in the spectrum it can be impossible for the eye to focus on both at the same time. Placing red and violet details close together is a good way to give users a headache.

You can increase the visibility of your display and reduce the risk of eye strain by using a light green background. The color scheme of old-fashioned green bar reports was based on this, and it still works.

The eye is better at seeing differences in light and dark than in color. So, no matter what color combination you use, keep the contrast between background and content high.

Background Interaction

Sometimes the background can compete with content on a display. In Figure 12-17 the background interacts with the circles, and creates a triangle.

This is just an optical trick, but it shows how the relationship between the content and the background can confuse things.

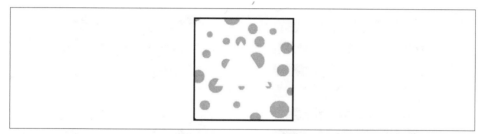

Figure 12-17. An example of background interaction

Contrast between content and background is good, but high contrast between the non-content parts of a display can be a problem. In Figure 12-18 we see two versions of a daily menu.

Monday- Red beans and rice	**Monday- Red beans and rice**
Tuesday- Hamburger steak	**Tuesday- Hamburger steak**
Wednesday- Meatloaf	**Wednesday- Meatloaf**
Thursday- Liver and onions	**Thursday- Liver and onions**
Friday- Catfish	**Friday- Catfish**
Saturday- Spaghetti	**Saturday- Spaghetti**
Sunday- Fried chicken	**Sunday- Fried chicken**

Figure 12-18. Daily menu in two formats

The format on the left is simple and easy to read. The contrast between the white background and the black letters could not be more effective.

On the right things are not so good. Black and white are both used as background colors. The contrast within the background is the same as the contrast between letters and the background. This is confusing to the eye. In this case, contrast reverses direction. It starts by going light to dark then fakes the viewer out by going dark to light.

Even in button design it is better to keep contrast moving in one direction. In Figure 12-19 the menu is reformatted as buttons.

Even though the contrast in the buttons is lower, it is still easier to read.

Another example is the obscuring box shown in Figure 12-20.

Background space can make a big difference. Boxes reverse contrast, but allowing enough background space inside the box eliminates the problem. In the top box the lack of background space inside the box brings the box and the text into conflict. The reverse in contrast confuses the eyes and is difficult to read.

The lower box has enough space to keep the relationships clear.

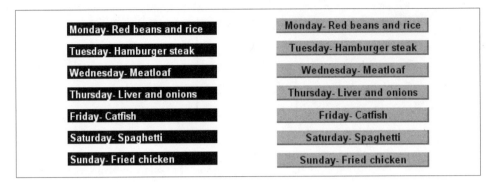

Figure 12-19. Daily menu as buttons

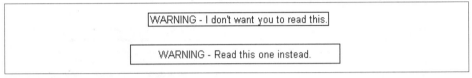

Figure 12-20. Hiding text in a box

Reversing the direction of contrast can be effective in headings or to distinguish between areas in a display. But it does not work with content items being viewed together in small spaces.

Index

Symbols

, (comma), 200

A

ABS function, 47, 49, 125, 182
Access databases, 201, 206
ADDRESS function, 3–6, 59, 103, 153
Address property (range), 178
#agg columns, 212
alignment, X axis, 149
analysis, modeling and, 77–84, 86–89
anomalies, 10, 48
Application Data/Microsoft/AddIns
    folder, 11
applications
    considering data sources, 51
    conventions and names, 53
    customizing, 67, 107–110
    designing example, 50, 51, 97–107
    display techniques, 227, 228, 233,
        237–240
    formatting example, 65
    importing data for, 200
    linking to data, 61, 101–105
    listing requirements, 51
    measuring quality, 96, 97
    monitoring complex systems, 112–114
    named ranges, 54, 55, 58–60
    named values, 54, 55–57
    presentation, 52, 53
    queuing example, 135–137, 155–158,
        168

running example, 65–67
Solver and Goal Seek tools, 194
Visual Basic, 62–65
array formulas
    functionality, 43
    measuring quality, 101, 104, 106, 107
    monitoring complex systems, 119, 124,
        125, 127
    overview, 1–3
    queuing example, 148
    workload forecasting, 49
arrays, extracting report data, 224
Assign Macro dialog box, 191
autocorrelation, 44
average
    changes in, 12–16
    control limits and, 95, 96
    filtered, 10, 46, 47, 49
    finding, 44–46
    moving, 12
    statistical functions, 6–9
    trimmed, 9–11
    X charts and, 94, 95
average error
    regression model, 69, 71, 73, 182, 193
    workload forecasting, 47, 48, 49, 60
AVERAGE function
    depicted, 6
    optimizing example, 192
    queuing example, 139, 141
    workload forecasting, 47, 49
AVERAGEA function, 6, 7

We'd like to hear your suggestions for improving our indexes. Send email to *index@oreilly.com*.

STANDARDIZE function, 49
start command, 167
statistical functions
    averages, 6–16
    correlation, 20
    distributions, 16–20
statistical process control
    application design, 97–107
    customizing applications, 107–110
    measuring quality, 96, 97
    overview, 94–96
statistics
    addressing cells indirectly, 3–6
    array formulas, 1–3
    averages, 6–16
    correlation, 20
    distributions, 16–20
STDEV function, 17, 48, 49, 57
storage, fixed length files, 195
SUM function
    importing numbers and, 214
    modeling, 88
    monitoring complex systems, 125
    queuing example, 139, 148, 162
    workload forecasting, 45, 57
SUMIF function, 9, 163
SUMPRODUCT function, 85, 184

T

tab character, 200
tables
    display techniques, 228
    linking, 205–208
tag sorts, 142–144
tags, XML, 209
testing
    model results, 84
    non-linear relationships, 90–91
text files, importing, 195–201
TEXT function, 58
text import wizard, 196
text strings, 218, 224
time constraints, 193
Tools menu, 179
TREND function, 12–16
trends
    adjusting for, 46–47
    display techniques, 228
    linear, 12
    moving averages and, 12

TRIMMEAN function, 9–11
truth values, 2, 3
.txt file extension, 196

V

VALUE function, 214, 215, 218
#VALUE! error, 214, 219
values
    display techniques, 229
    finding multiple, 179
    future, 13, 42
    named, 54–57
    Solver tool and, 192
    truth, 2, 3
VAR function, 16–18
variables, independent, 115, 119, 121
variance, 16, 17
VBA (Visual Basic for Applications)
    building applications, 62–65
    delimited files and, 200
    functionality, 43
    queuing example, 163–168
    reports and, 219
vectors, 175, 176
Visual Basic Editor
    adding code via, 178, 190
    starting, 11, 217
    viewing code, 62
Visual Basic for Applications (see VBA)
VLOOKUP function, 38

W

WEEKDAY function, 56, 57, 58
weights, 182
word suggestion, 224
Workarea sheet
    links on, 61, 101–105
    measuring quality, 98, 99
    named ranges on, 58–60
    named values on, 55–57
    regression model example, 118–128
workbooks
    macro availability and, 224
    opening XML data in, 211–212
worksheets
    display techniques, 228
    drilling down and, 35
    exposing events, 178
    look-and-feel of web pages, 136

About the Author

Gerald Knight has nearly 30 years of experience in the computer industry as a developer, teacher, and consultant. For more than 20 years, he was a project leader and system architect working on imaging and revenue control systems at FedEx. He has specialized in Excel development for the last 10 years. Now retired, he consults and occasionally writes in Memphis, Tennessee.

Colophon

The animal on the cover of *Analyzing Business Data with Excel* is the endangered *Cynogale bennettii*, more commonly known as the otter civet. These animals live in peninsular Malaysia, southern Thailand, Indonesia, and Vietnam. Despite the fact that they can be found across a vast geographic range, otter civets are scarce. They are nocturnal and are rarely found in the wild. Scientists believe their population has declined recently by at least 50 percent for a number of reasons, including the loss of their natural habitat to human development and water pollution.

Otter civets live on land, but are never too far from the water. They spend much of their time on the outskirts of streams and rivers and near swampy wetlands. Their feet are wide and webbed, and while they swim, flaps cover their ears and nostrils. However, their short tails lack special muscular power, and the webbing between their toes is only partially developed, so they are slow swimmers and cannot turn very quickly in the water. Surprisingly, they are very skilled climbers.

Their diet consists mostly of fish, frogs, mollusks, and crayfish. Birds and small mammals are other favored targets because they stop often at the edges of rivers and streams for a drink of water. Much like crocodiles and alligators, otter civets skim the surface of the water, with only their eyes and nostrils exposed, hunting for prey.

Otter civets resemble sea otters. Their fur is agouti—in other words, pale at the roots and much darker toward the tips—and the long gray hairs scattered throughout their coats give their fur a frosted look. Their appearance is also distinguished by their several long, white whiskers.

The cover image is from *Lydekker's Royal History*. The cover font is Adobe ITC Garamond. The text font is Linotype Birka; the heading font is Adobe Myriad Condensed; and the code font is LucasFont's TheSans Mono Condensed.

Better than e-books

Buy *Analyzing Business Data with Excel* and access
the digital edition FREE on Safari for 45 days.

Go to www.oreilly.com/go/safarienabled
and type in coupon code A9LB-AJAM-7M7D-EUMP-LMPY

Search
thousands of
top tech books

Download
whole chapters

Cut and Paste
code examples

Find
answers fast

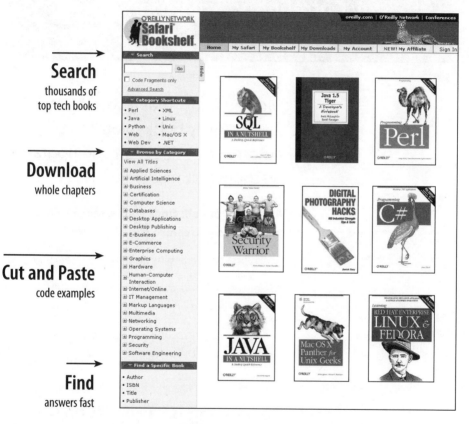

Search Safari! The premier electronic reference
library for programmers and IT professionals.

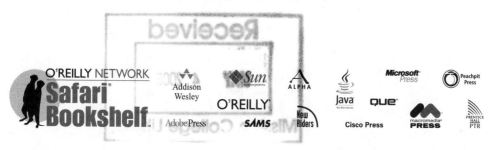

39.99

The O'Reilly Advantage

Stay Current and Save Money

Did you know that if you register
your O'Reilly books, you'll get
automatic notification and upgrade
discounts on new editions?

**And that's not all! Once you've registered
your books you can:**

» Win free books, T-shirts and O'Reilly Gear

» Get special offers available only to registered
O'Reilly customers

» Get free catalogs announcing all our new
titles (US and UK Only)

**Registering is easy! Just go to
www.oreilly.com/go/register**